ROMAN CÓRDOBA

Roman Córdoba

by Robert C. Knapp

UNIVERSITY OF CALIFORNIA PRESS
Berkeley · Los Angeles · London

UNIVERSITY OF CALIFORNIA PUBLICATIONS: CLASSICAL STUDIES

Volume 30

UNIVERSITY OF CALIFORNIA PRESS
BERKELEY AND LOS ANGELES
CALIFORNIA

UNIVERSITY OF CALIFORNIA PRESS, LTD.
LONDON, ENGLAND

ISBN 0-520-09676-2
LIBRARY OF CONGRESS CATALOG CARD NUMBER: 83-1195

Library of Congress Cataloging in Publication Data
Knapp, Robert C.
    Roman Córdoba.
    (University of California publications, classical
studies; v. 30)
    Bibliography: p.
    Includes index.
    1. Córdoba (Spain)--History. 2. Córdoba (Spain)--
Antiquities, Roman. 3. Romans--Spain--Córdoba.
4. Spain--Antiquities, Roman. I. Title. II. Series.
University of Caoifornia publications in classical
studies; v. 30.
DP402.C7K58 1983   936.6'03   83-1195
ISBN 0-520-09676-2

For Carolyn

Contents

List of Illustrations

Preface

There is at present no adequate account of Roman Córdoba, although it
was one of the main cities of the Western Roman Empire. My hope is that
the current study will fill this gap in Roman provincial studies.

The monograph is designed as a synthesis of Córdoba's ancient history
and also as a compilation of the sources for the study of that city in the
Roman period. This dual function of the work explains why the appendices,
notes and bibliography are almost as long as the history itself: I intend
that other students of Roman municipal history and archaeology benefit from
the collection of research materials as well as (I hope) from some of my
conclusions. Of course new archaeological discoveries, publication of old
ones, and new interpretations of existing material will continue to increase our knowledge of the city; a history such as this one can never be
"finished". But I expect to have established a firm foundation upon which
other treatments of the city can be based.

Research on this project was made possible primarily through the gen-
erosity of a Humanities Research Fellowship granted me during 1978 and 1979
by the University of California. It is also a pleasure to thank E. Buchner
(Munich) and J. M. Blázquez (Madrid) for the hospitality of their respective
research institutes. A large number of scholars in Europe and America aided
me at various stages of my work. I should like to thank especially M. Koch
(formerly of Konstanz), G. Alföldy (Heidelberg), A. Stylow (Madrid), L.
Villaronga (Barcelona), and R. Rowland (Missouri). In Córdoba, the University faculty (especially J. F. Rodríguez Neila and A. Ibáñez Castro)
were most kind and helpful.

Abbreviations

AE	Année Epigraphique
AEA	Archivo Español de Arqueología
AJPh	American Journal of Philology
Anales ... Córdoba	Comisión de Monumentos de Córdoba, Anales de la Comisión
ANRW	Aufstieg und Niedergang der Römische Welt
BH	Bulletin Hispanique
BJ	Bonner Jahrbücher
BRAC	Boletín de la Real Academia de Ciéncias, Bellas Letras, Nobles Artes de Córdoba
BRAH	Boletín de la Real Academia de la Historia
BSAA	Boletín del Seminario de Arte y Arqueología de Valladolid
Bull. Epig.	Bulletin Epigraphique
CAN	Congreso Nacional de Arqueología
CIL	Corpus Inscriptionum Latinarum
CP	Classical Philology
CQ	Classical Quarterly
DE	Dizionario Epigrafico di Antichità Romana
EE	Ephemeris Epigraphica
Epig. Stud.	Epigraphische Studien
FHA	Fontes Hispaniae Antiquae
GRBS	Greek, Roman, and Byzantine Studies
HAE	Hispania Antiqua Epigraphica
HSCP	Harvard Studies in Classical Philology
ILG	Inscriptions Latines de Gaule
JRS	Journal of Roman Studies
JS	Journal des Savants
MM	Madrider Mitteilungen

MMAP	Memorias de los Museos Arqueológicos Provinciales
NAH	Noticiario Arqueológico Hispánico
NC	Numismatic Chronicle
Nott. Med. Stud.	Nottingham Mediaeval Studies
Num. Hisp.	Numario Hispánico
PIR	Prosopographia Imperii Romani
RE	Real-Encyclopädie der Classischen Altertumswissenschaft
REA	Revue des Etudes Anciennes
RIL	Rendiconti del r. Istituto Lombardo di Science e Lettere
SEG	Supplementum Epigraphicum Graecum
ZPE	Zeitschrift für Papyrologie und Epigraphik

1

PRE-ROMAN CÓRDOBA

PHYSICAL SETTING

Córdoba, like most cities, must be understood in its geographical setting. Three features of physical geography have influenced Cordoban history: the mineral-rich Sierra Morena to the north, the Guadalquivir River,
upon whose banks the town is situated, and the relatively flat, rich land
that stretches away to the south of the river (see Map 1).

These physical features emerged aeons ago. First the Sierra Morena
was formed--not actually a mountain range, but the eroding edge of the
ancient central Iberian plateau called the Meseta. More recently, in the
Tertiary period, the Sierra Nevada--a range of mountains contemporary with
the Pyrenees to the north--was formed in southern Andalucía. Between
these two land masses an arm of the Atlantic Ocean reached the Mediterranean Sea in Miocene times. As this arm was gradually cut off, a river
formed in the remaining depression, draining water from the mountains into
the ever-receding ocean. By historical times, only the swamps and lakes
at the mouth of the river (near the Strait of Gibraltar) remained of the
original salt-water estuary; the valley was gradually filled in and was
drained by the Guadalquivir River.[1] Thus, Córdoba was favored with the
mineral, fluvial, and agricultural resources that, combined with a climate
favorable to farming, virtually assured prosperity once an urban stage of
development was reached.

PREHISTORY

Many thousands of years passed before human beings appeared in the
area later occupied by Córdoba, and more millennia elapsed before full
urban development was achieved, under the Romans. The prehistoric archaeology of Andalucía in general, and of Córdoba in particular, is lamentably

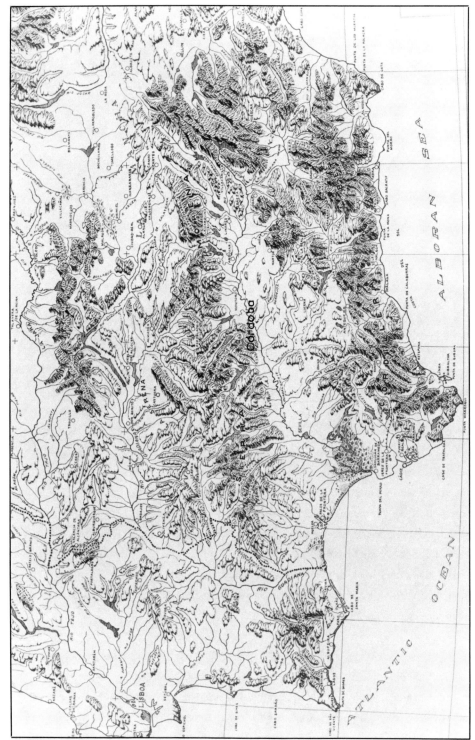

Map 1. Physical Setting (Terrain Map of Spain and Portugal, copyright 1967 by Robert Frank Collins)

underdeveloped; nevertheless, a sketch can be made of the prehistory
of the area.[2]

The oldest artifacts found, rough quartzite tools, come from the left
bank of the Guadalquivir.[3] These date from the Lower Paleolithic period,
perhaps 250,000 to 300,000 years ago. A gap in the archaeological record
follows, for no remains of the Upper Paleolithic period have been discovered. However, for the Mesolithic period, about 8000 B.C., there is once
again some evidence--not from Córdoba itself but from the Dolmen de las
Sileras, ten kilometers from the city, where cave art exists. Similar art
has been discovered at Espejo, which is not far from Córdoba.[4]

In the Neolithic period (5000-3000 B.C.), when farming was first introduced to Andalucía, the rich Guadalquivir valley was doubtless well settled,
although the archaeological record is incomplete.[5] Skeletal remains of
Neolithic men have been found five kilometers from Córdoba, at Alcolea del
Río and Palma del Río, and dolmens exist within twenty kilometers of the
city, though none have, as yet, been discovered any nearer. In addition,
cave dwellings and a few flint implements have been found in and around
the city.[6] Typically Neolithic ware has been found in central Andalucía
as well.[7]

The developments in the Cordoban area after the Neolithic period continue to be obscure. Any general discussion runs afoul of the current
controversies regarding the origins of metallurgy in the Peninsula,[8] the
nature of the "Bell-beaker complex" that appears in Andalucía at this
time,[9] and the development of the peninsular megaliths.[10] Conclusions are
difficult because of the lack of data from Córdoba and its environs.

Of central importance is the continuity that the prehistoric archaeology of Córdoba shows from the Neolithic to the Bronze Age cultures.
Renfrew notes a "major regional group" of burial artifacts centered in
Córdoba: "passage graves,[11] simple undecorated pottery, stone axes, flat-
based triangular arrowheads with fine flat-flaked working, and schematic
anthropomorphic figuration".[12] Into this cultural assemblage intrudes the
beaker ware, of which a few samples have been found in or near Córdoba.
However, there is no archaeological break with the past; an "invasion" of
"Beaker folk" is out of the question.[13] According to recent investigations,
the copper metallurgy that developed at this time was indigenous. Theories
that colonists from the Aegean area imported metallurgical expertise to
peninsular peoples do not stand close scrutiny.[14] Extensive communication
with outside areas did occur--for example, through an ivory trade that made

the Guadalquivir River a link in commerce between the Tagus estuary and
Africa.[15]

Interpretations of the data on all of these developments are still
very conjectural. Recent progress in establishment of "calibrated" Carbon-
14 dates for western Mediterranean sites has pushed back the Chalcolithic
Los Millares culture to c.3000 B.C.; further alterations in long-held
chronologies can be expected.[16] It is best to state simply that the period
from the end of the "pure" Neolithic culture, through the Chalcolithic
culture (with the development of metallurgy), to the early Bronze Age El
Argar culture, occupied about three millennia, from c.4400 B.C. to 1400
B.C. During this time, the prehistory of the Cordoban area seems to have
reflected the prehistory of the Guadalquivir River in general; indigenous
peoples, heirs of the Neolithic cultures, continued to develop and were
affected but not determined by outside influences.

The successors to the Chalcolithic cultures of "Los Millares" type in
Andalucía are the Bronze Age peoples of the Argaric culture (named after
the type-site of El Argar, in Almería). The cultural complex reflects the
ceramic types of the Los Millares culture and life in fortified settlements; the metallurgy is at first arsenical, then true bronze.[17] In Andalucía no Argaric settlements have been found, although finds from graves
provide examples of pottery and work in metal.[18] The continuity of the
central Andalusian cultures from the Neolithic on is shown by the absence
of early Bronze Age material in the area. The first major change comes
toward the end of the first millennium B.C. and is reflected by the foundation of the first known settlement at Córdoba. Before that time, the same
culture continues to evolve, along with its beakers and other accoutrements.
Sometimes it is influenced by the Argaric culture. There are beaker cups
from Carmona that may show Argaric influence, while closer to Córdoba
Argaric ceramics have been found at Alcolea del Río and at Montilla, as
well as in the valley of the Genil River and in the mountains north of
Córdoba. (See Map 2).[19] In Córdoba itself only one piece of Argaric
ceramic is reported.[20] Argaric influences in the area begin c.1400 B.C.[21]
Knowledge of the extent of this influence must await further archaeological
investigation.

It is from the Bronze Age, however, that for the first time there is
adequate archaeological evidence upon which to base generalizations concerning Córdoba in prehistory. J. M. Lúzon and D. Ruiz Mata, excavating

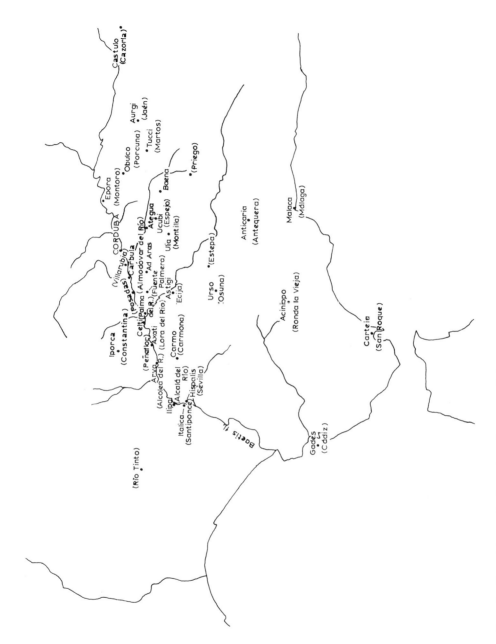

Map 2. Locations in Baetica (Andalucía). Modern names are in parentheses.

at the Colina de los Quemados, have provided the best material to date.
They discovered an indigenous settlement at this site, which is situated
in the outlying area of the modern city.[22] The oldest remains are of a
rough pottery dating from late in the second millennium B.C.[23] In suc-
ceeding strata a burnished ware appears and gradually increases in fre-
quency, crowding out the older, rougher ceramics. There is no evidence of
violent change; that is, there are no destruction layers. Blanco compares
this situation to that at Ategua, twenty kilometers to the south. There,
as well, an "infiltration" of a new culture or cultural group is documented and dated (as is the Cordoban material) to between the ninth and
eighth/seventh centuries B.C.[24] This "burnished-ware cultural complex"
was uniform and widespread in Andalucía at that time. Thus, Córdoba was
in the mainstream of regional prehistoric developments.

From the strata dating from the eighth to the sixth centuries further
change takes place; an incised ware replaces the burnished ware.[25] At the
same time the round dwellings of the previous period are replaced by
square structures. There are other changes as well. The scoriae that
have been found indicate that metal smelting was now taking place; ceramic
types, decorations, and imports prove an ever-increasing influence from
Phoenician contact with the coastal areas. By the sixth century, imported
and imitation ware completely dominate the finds. Then the exotic influence wanes, and by the fourth century Luzón characterizes the finds as
"totalmente ibérico".[26] This situation continues until the end of the
native remains in the stratum dating from the first half of the second
century B.C.[27]

The people who lived on the Colina must remain something of a mystery.
Settled (if, as Blanco maintains, the Río Tinto settlement is an analog)[28]
in randomly placed huts upon the hill, the inhabitants probably represented
an intrusive element in the area. The scoriae indicate that metals may
have drawn them to Córdoba; a new smelting technique was introduced, ori-
ginating either to the north or in the Middle East.[29] Blázquez thinks that
this was probably a warrior folk from the Meseta and Estremadura, who
brought with them not only their distinctive incised ware but also their
chariots and advanced bronze swords.[30]

Besides the well-attested native site at the Colina de los Quemados,
there is another location that has been designated as an indigenous settle-
ment--a rise, now crowned by the Colegio de Santa Victoria and other

buildings, on the eastern side of the city. Santos Jener gives a very
circumstantial account of this supposed settlement; he follows without
much conviction the guesses of José de la Torre. The only archaeological
evidence presented is the remains of the Iberian wall reported to be in
the street Maese Luís, and only a single native artifact--a figurine of
terracotta--has been found within the supposed town.[31] With a thriving
native town a few kilometers away at the Colina, it is inherently unlikely
that another native town existed at this site. However, the question must
remain open; new archaeological discoveries may someday clarify the
situation.[32]

The name of the town--Corduba in its Latinized form--is certainly
native. The elements of the name have, rather fancifully, been given exotic origins such as "Chaldeo-Aramean" or Punic.[33] However, the -uba suffix occurs in various native town names of Andalucía, and the element
Cord- probably is cognate with the native name for the Guadalquivir River;[34]
the name might mean something like "town by the Guadalquivir." Alterna-
tively, the element Cord- could be an old form of Tord- = Turd- as in
Turdetanti, the native people of the area. This explanation would make
Corduba mean "the town of the Turdetani." Some plausibility for this latter explanation comes from Strabo 3.2.2; a town, probably Córdoba, is
called the metropolis of the area.[35]

The language of the region as reflected in the script used locally and
in the name of the town seems to be Tartessian--that is, that of the southwestern part of the Peninsula, as opposed to Iberian, which begins a little
to the east of Córdoba and appears in southeastern and eastern areas.[36]
But Córdoba was on the edge of these linguistic areas, and only additional
native inscriptions might help positively determine to which linguistic
group its people belonged.[37]

Attention may now be paid to the nonlocal elements that influenced
Córdoba in prehistory. Clearly the Phoenicians played an important, if
indirect, role in the development of the Colina settlement.[38] The influence of their ceramic types on local wares is patent, and fragments of
their pots and plates have also been found.[39] It is certain that the pottery wheel was introduced following their example, and the new smelting
techniques may also owe something to them.[40] However, Santos Jener is almost certainly incorrect when he says that a Punic factory existed in the
area. The archaeological evidence points to contact and some assimilation

but not to a factory such as those that existed at sites along the southern Iberian coast.[41] The Phoenicians and, later, the Carthaginians must
have passed the site regularly on land and river journeys to the rich mineral deposits of the upper Guadalquivir areas, but the direct archaeological evidence for such contact remains slight.

The Celts must also have come into contact with the early native
settlement. There is clear linguistic and archaeological evidence for the
presence of Celtic peoples in Andalucía in general, although the area of
most frequent Celtic placenames touches the region only slightly, to the
north and west.[42] What Celtic infiltration there was, it seems, was ab-
sorbed by the prevalent local culture; at the Colina and at Ategua, the
strata of c.500 B.C. onwards, when Celts are known to have been in the
south, show no signs of Celtic presence.[43] For the history of Córdoba,
Celts have much less significance than Punic peoples.

Finally there are the Greeks.[44] Their impact in the southern part of
the Iberian Peninsula during the period from 650 B.C. onwards is still
being assessed. Their influence on native art may prove more pervasive
than now seems to be the case. However, it is certain that there never
were any Greek outposts in the interior of Andalucía. Greek objects, especially ceramics, have been found all over Andalucía, including the upper[45]
and lower Guadalquivir valley.[46] These artifacts are the result of trade,
not colonization. No item of Greek provenance has been reported in the city
or at the Colina.[47] So far as the local archaeology is concerned, the
Greeks did not exist.

At the close of the prehistoric period, then, the area of Córdoba was
inhabited by a people in the mainstream of Andalusian development. It was
a local culture that had been influenced by Celtic and Punic contacts but,
judging by the excavations at the Colina, had become quite free of foreign
traits by the fourth to third centuries B.C. Whether the settlement attested at the Colina or the other that possibly existed on the heights of
Santa Victoria was called "Corduba" is not known; one of the two surely
was. It is probably no accident that the site is unmentioned in ancient
sources before the middle of the second century B.C. A small native village,
bypassed by recent foreign influence, Córdoba became important only when the
Romans sought a bulwark against the marauding Lusitanian tribes of the area
between the Guadiana and the Guadalquivir rivers. It emerges from prehistory only when the Romans found a colony at the site.[48]

2

EARLY ROMAN CÓRDOBA

FOUNDATION

One of the most interesting results of the excavations at the Colina
de los Quemados is the evidence for the end of that community. Luzón has
concluded that the town was abandoned by the beginning of the first century B.C. Evidence for a Roman foundation during the second century B.C.,
composed of natives and Italians, is discussed below. It appears that the
native town was either voluntarily or forcefully evacuated when the new
town was created. Indeed it seems likely that the natives who were included in the new town were the aristocracy of the Colina settlement. Continuity of population, if not of location, obtained.[49]

While the situation of the native, pre-Roman town (or towns) at Córdoba
is relatively clear, evidence for Roman occupation before the foundation
is nonexistent. Others have pointed out that there is no basis for the
idea that there was a legionary camp at the site as early as 206 B.C.[50]
There is no evidence for a Roman base in the area, although the possibility
cannot be ruled out. Italica, a town founded in 206 B.C. on the Guadalquivir opposite the site of modern Seville, certainly had strategic value,
and at least one citizen of that town served in the Roman forces of the
midsecond century (Appian Ib. 66). Nevertheless, permanent legionary
bases were not normal at this period; arrangements varied from year to year
according to the theaters and fortunes of war. Troops were billeted in
various towns, not in a single camp, for the winter months.[51] At best, the
prefoundation Roman presence at Córdoba was limited to some resident Roman
businessmen and, perhaps, a garrison such as that attested at Ilipa, a
little downstream from the town.[52]

The fuzzy picture of prefoundation Córdoba is sharpened when Strabo
3.2.1 reports on the circumstances surrounding the foundation of the town.
He notes that the town is Μαρκέλλου κτίσμα.[53] This Marcellus can be

none other than M. Claudius Marcellus, who was consul at Rome three times
(166, 155, 152 B.C.). No other Marcellus served in Iberia until late in
the Republic, and M. Claudius Marcellus was there twice, once in 169/68
and again in 152/51 B.C.[54] In 169/68 he had charge of both Iberian provinces in order to free more magistrates for the third Macedonian war,
then in progress (Livy 43.15.3). The only evidence of his activities is
the notice that he captured Marcolica, an urbs nobilis of unknown location
(Livy 45.4.1).[55] In 152/51, however, Marcellus' activities as consul are
more fully recorded.[56] He was chosen as consul for the third time and
sent to Iberia with a large force (Appian Ib. 48). He warred with the
Celtiberians and opened negotiations with his primary enemies, the Belli,
Titti, and Arevaci.[57] He then campaigned in Lusitania, taking Nertobriga
in the process, and retired to Córdoba for the winter.[58] The following
spring Marcellus returned to Rome after exacting peace and a tribute of
six hundred talents from the Celtiberians (Strabo 3.4.12; Appian Ib. 50).

The dates of both periods of Marcellus' service have been proposed as
dates for the foundation of Córdoba.[59] In favor of the year 169/68 is the
fact that Polybius, in mentioning Marcellus' wintering in 152, gives no indication that the town is a new foundation. In fact the wintering in
152/51 might imply that Marcellus chose this location because he had earlier founded a colony there. In addition, there are other towns founded
in the 170s B.C.--for example, Gracchuris, by Ti. Sempronius Gracchus, in
178 B.C., and Carteia, by L. Canuleius, in 171 B.C. Córdoba's foundation
in 169/68 would fit well into this established activity.[60] However, 152/51
has been favored by most scholars,[61] mainly because Marcellus was consul
and Polybius' mention of the town falls at this time.[62] Neither year is
demonstrably the foundation year. Unfortunately the archaeology of Córdoba
itself cannot help at all in solving this problem. Probabilities must be
weighed. The foundation seems to fit better at 169/68 than at 152/51 B.C.,
especially when the archaeology of the Colina settlement and the close historical similarities to the foundation of Carteia in 171 are considered.

The meaning of κτίσμα , "foundation," must now be examined. Various
suggestions have been made about what Marcellus founded. The old view,
still supported by a few, that Córdoba was ab initio a colonia civium Romanorum must be rejected; a citizen colony outside Italy and including natives is impossible in the middle of the second century B.C.[63] Other pos-
sibilities include the foundation of a colonia Latina, a vicus, a

conciliabulum, a forum, or a conventus civium Romanorum.[64] Three facts
are relevant to the investigation of this problem: means, at
the very least, the beginning of a specific entity; Strabo speaks of this
entity as the "first colony in the area"; Caesar (Bell. Civ. 2.19.3, Bell.
Alex. 57-59) speaks of a conventus civium Romanorum in Córdoba in 49-48
B.C. These facts can best be explained by the assumption that Córdoba
was founded as a colonia Latina and remained one until the late Republic.

As noted above, a citizen colony is simply impossible at this early
date. Velleius Paterculus 2.6 is specific in citing Narbo Martius, founded
c.118 B.C., as the first extra-Italian citizen colony. In addition, the
political climate of the day was very much against overseas citizen colonies, and against the extension of citizens' rights to non-Romans who
might join such a colony. A hundred years later, Córdoba was involved in
the civil war between Caesar and Pompey. But it is never referred to as
a colony, even though it is mentioned frequently in the ancient accounts.
It is true that Seneca the Elder refers, in the Controversiae, to colonia
mea in the context of the 40s B.C., but this reference may only apply to
Córdoba's status when the Controversiae were written down, between A.D.
37 and 41. A source contemporary with events in the 40s B.C. (Bell. Civ.
2.19.3) does refer to cohortes colonicae in connection with Córdoba, a reference which Vittinghoff took to show Córdoba's colonial status in 49
B.C.[65] This interpretation is unconvincing, however; the account makes it
clear that the cohortes colonicae were brought into Córdoba, which suggests
that they were a general provincial levy.[66]

Strabo's reference to Córdoba as the first colony in the area eliminates
the possibility that the settlement was "founded" as a mere vicus. The
manner of Strabo's account indicates that this "first colony" was the entity established by Marcellus, so the statement cannot refer to a later
elevation to colonial status in, for example, the first century B.C. "First
colony" therefore cannot mean "the first of the Julian colonies."[67]

In the face of these various considerations, the best solution to the
problem of Córdoba's original status is to posit that the town was founded
as a Latin colony by Marcellus.[68] Carteia, founded in 171 B.C., provided
a prototype for such a κτίσμα . Neither Carteia, which was far to the
south of Córdoba, nor Italica, which was not a colony, would contradict
Strabo's statement that Córdoba was the first ἀποικία in the area. Subsequently similar colonies were founded at Valentia on the eastern coast of

Iberia and at Palma and Pollentia on the Balearic island of Majorca.[69]
That Córdoba is never mentioned in the literary sources as a colonia
Latina (or, indeed, as any sort of colony) during the Republic is no obstacle to this solution; Carteia, definitely a Latin colony (Livy 43.3),
is never called a colonia either. As a technically peregrine town, a conventus civium Romanorum could exist. It is true that there are no Latin
colonies with an attested conventus c.R. In addition, the status of other
towns in Iberia with an attested conventus is unclear.[70] Certainty is not
possible, but in principle, at least, a conventus in a Latin colony is
conceivable. The conventus would not control the entire town, but would
exist side by side with the local government. Lissus, in Dalmatia, seems
exceptional, since the town was handed over to the conventus (Bell. Civ.
3.29.1; 40.5). Perhaps the Romans of the conventus did not, as they did
in the east, hold themselves apart but intermarried and generally joined
the life of the community.[71] By the time of the civil war, the conventus
of Roman citizens apparently dominated the town.[72]

   Every Roman town was enrolled in one of the thirty-one rural tribes
as a necessary part of being Roman. One further indication of Latin status
for Córdoba is that there are two tribes, not one, well attested in Córdoban epigraphy; these are the Sergia and the Galeria.[73] The Galeria
seems to be the tribe of the Augustan colony, while the Sergia is the tribe
that dates back to the Latin colony. The Sergia is known from other Iberian
towns, including some, such as Hispalis and Carthago Nova, that were thriving in the pre-Caesarian period. But, most significantly, a recently published inscription from the excavations at Carteia solves the question of
Carteia's early tribe--it too was the Sergia. Thus the only positively
identifiable Latin colony in the south has the same tribe as Córdoba had
in its early period.[74]

   The original settlers in the colony were a mixture of "Romans" and
natives. Strabo 3.2.1 is explicit: ᾤκησαν τε ἐξ ἀρχῆς ῾Ρωμαίων τε
καὶ τῶν ἐπιχωρίων ἄνδρες ἐπίλεκτοι   ("from the beginning chosen men
of the Romans and natives settled here"). Who these "Romans" were is not
very clear. They could have been Roman citizens (including veterans),
Italians, hybridae ("half-breeds"), or any combination of these. If
Carteia provided any sort of model, even freedmen may have been included.[75]
The problem of the "select" nature of these ῾Ρωμαίοι is perhaps insolu-
ble. Romans, Italians, and hybridae might all have had sufficient claim

to such a vague term. It may simply mean the men "chosen out," "enrolled" in the colony, without any specific "excellence" in mind. However, it probably implies better than average financial and social standing among the first Roman colonists.

The natives who were included at the foundation are easier to identify. Probably they came from the indigenous community near the new town. Possibly some veteran native auxiliary troops were settled as well.[76] In principle there was nothing unusual about the inclusion of natives in the foundation. In Spain the example of Carteia was at hand, while in general, although natives were not necessarily included in a foundation, they certainly could be.[77] The notion of the "select" nature of the natives may carry more force here than in the case of the "Romans" who were settled. It would be logical to assume that only the native aristocracy were enrolled,[78] but again the example of Carteia, where any natives who wanted to do so could join the colony, is instructive. Not too much weight need be placed on the "aristocratic" nature of the native participation; the desertion of the Colina settlement indicates that the entire native population moved to, or near to, the new town.

The final question about the foundation of the town concerns its configuration. Was there a double town, a <u>dipolis</u>, from the beginning? Three pieces of evidence--archaeological, epigraphic, and historical--point to an affirmative answer to this question. Archaeological evidence is provided by the remains of a wall that ran approximately from east to west through the center of Córdoba (as it was during the Empire). The identification of this wall as Roman rests on the opinion of Santos Jener, but, taken with the other evidence, the identification should stand.[79]

Epigraphic evidence is provided by two recently discovered inscriptions that throw light on the problem. They are stone statue bases, virtually identical except that one was set up by the <u>vicus forensis</u> while the other was dedicated by the <u>vicus Hispanus</u>. Both honor L. Axius Naso, a senator and provincial quaestor c. A.D. 20.[80] The interest in the stones is not due to the dedication itself--for local <u>vici</u> and their dedications are well documented in the Roman world--but to the mention of the two Cordoban <u>vici</u>, the <u>vicus forensis</u> and the <u>vicus Hispanus</u>.[81] These <u>vici</u> may reflect a division of the town into one area around the forum and another area occupied at the time or formerly by natives (<u>Hispani</u>). It would be easy to associate the forum area with the <u>conventus</u> <u>c.R.</u>'s

business activities and, perhaps, residential area. The <u>vicus</u> <u>Hispanus</u>
would then be that part of the old native area incorporated into the settlement.[82] That these are natural, not artificial, names for <u>vici</u> is in-
dicated by a look at the list in <u>ILS</u>; few vici listed there reflect local
geographical or ethnical conditions; most are artificial borrowings from
the names of persons or gods. The <u>vicus</u> <u>forensis</u> and <u>vicus</u> <u>Hispanus</u> are
therefore more than just conventional names. They may reflect a real distinction in the composition of the settlement.

There is also historical evidence for the double-town theory. Castejón,
in his study of Arabic Córdoba, indicates that the part of the Arab city
that corresponded to the old walled Roman city (Al-Medina) was divided, in
Arabic times, by a wall.[83] This is merely, it appears, a carry-over from
the divided Roman city.

These archaeological, epigraphical, and historical considerations suggest that a double community of some sort existed at Córdoba.[84] Double
communities were not unusual. Sometimes a wall even separated the elements of the town, as at Minturnae in Italy and Salonae in Dalmatia.[85]
The original settlement pattern in all probability reflected the mixed
origin of the inhabitants. The mark of this settlement pattern remained
long after its ethnic origins were erased, much as today the old Jewish
quarter in Córdoba is still called the Judería, although no Jews live
there now.

The evidence, then, points to the conclusion that M. Claudius Marcellus
founded a <u>colonia</u> <u>Latina</u> of mixed "Roman" and native peoples, possibly in
152/51, but more likely in 169/68 B.C.

EARLY HISTORY

Scattered references make reconstruction of the main outline of Cordoban history possible down to the civil wars; then more detail is available. Almost from its beginning the town was threatened by hostile forces
from the areas known as Baeturia, between the Guadalquivir and Guadiana
rivers, and Lusitania, beyond both rivers. The life of the settlers was
dominated by native unrest in the early years, at least until Viriathus,
the Lusitanian chieftain, was assassinated in 139 B.C. after more than a
decade of struggle against Roman forces.[86] An epigram called <u>de se ad</u>
<u>patriam</u>, preserved in the <u>Anthologia</u> <u>Latina</u> under the name of the younger
Seneca, indicates that Viriathus actually attacked the city's walls.

Lusitanus quateret cum moenia latro,[87]
Figeret et portas lancea torta tuas.

Lusitanians also attacked Hispalis (Seville) during Caesar's campaigns
in Spain in 45 B.C. (Bell. Hisp. 36.1), and some scholars have attributed
this reference to that time.[88] However, the reverse chronological order
of events in the poem tells against reference to such a late time. The
position of emphasis at the beginning of the line that is given to Lusitanus conjures up the great Lusitanian chieftain Viriathus. During the
Viriathic war there was much military activity in the area of Córdoba.
The attack may have come in 145 B.C.; in that year the consul Fabius Ae-
milianus used Urso as a base, and this use indicates that the towns along
the Baetis (Guadalquivir) were not secure.[89]

By the winter of 144 B.C. Córdoba was safe enough to be used as a winter headquarters. It was also used as winter headquarters by the commander
Quinctius in 143 B.C.[90] One may suppose that Córdoba had already become a
major town in Ulterior and was frequently used as the Hauptstadt by the
Roman commanders.[91]

For the next half century virtually no specific references to Córdoba
exist. Numismatic evidence can help fill the gap. The only local Cordoban
coinage of the Republic can be assigned to this period. The evidence from
finds, particularly the coins from Castra Caecilia dated to about 90 B.C.
and before, shows that this local coin dates to c.120-100 B.C. The type,
which seems to be a goddess obverse and a local genius reverse, throws no
light on Cordoban history. However, on the obverse the coin is signed by
Cn. Iulius L.f. q(uaestor)--possibly evidence for the presence of a Roman
quaestor at the town.[92] The quaestor may not be a local official; later
in the town's history no local quaestor is attested, and on other issues
of coins the quaestor is clearly a Roman official who is minting in conjunction with a native town.[93] However, the praenomen Cnaeus is unheard-of
in the Julian gens in Italy and it is almost nonexistent in conjunction
with Julii of any date or provenance.[94] Certainly this Cn. Iulius has no
direct relationship with the family of C. Julius Caesar, although the pa-
tronymic 'L.f.' may point to the family of Caesar's distant relatives represented by the consul of 64 B.C. and others; this family had men with
the praenomen Lucius. But this Cn. Iulius seems rather to be a local man.
It is possible that he was a quaestor of the conventus civium Romanorum,
although minting by such an official is unattested. Perhaps the best supposition is that Cn. Iulius, an obscure local quaestor, minted or began to

mint these coins in response to a need for small change produced by the
lack of new Roman official bronze coinage in this period. The issue may
have been a response to the commerical activity of the local conventus or
to the needs of a garrison stationed there or nearby.

Although the local bronze issue points to some prosperity for Córdoba,
the series of coin hoards found in the area indicates unrest and disorder
during the period (see Maps 3 and 4). Of the twenty hoards buried in
Iberia between c.124 and 92 B.C., twelve are located in and near that part
of Ulterior across the Guadalquivir to the north.[95] Other sources cor-
roborate this picture of unrest. Appian (Ib. 99) indicates that war was
raging in Spain during this period. Q. Servilius Caepio celebrated a tri-
umph in 107 B.C. because of military success in Ulterior.[96] The adven-
tures of Sertorius at Castulo in 99-98 B.C. also indicate disorder (Plutarch Sert. 3.3-5), and Castulo is in the middle of the hoard area in the
mining region of the upper Guadalquivir. The presence of a garrison at
Castulo may also point to unrest. H. Mattingly relates these hoards to
the Germanic incursions of 105-104 B.C.,[97] which could have added to the
general insecurity of the times. The hoard from Córdoba shows that fear
reached the town itself.[98]

During this time Córdoba was almost certainly the main seat of the commander in Ulterior. Cicero (Verr. 2.4.56) shows that the praetor L. Calpurnius Piso Frugi held court in the forum at Córdoba in 113 or 112 B.C.[99]

The next mention of Córdoba comes in the period of Q. Caecilius Met-
tellus' command in Ulterior during the Sertorian war, 80-71 B.C. Probably
the city itself was never in much danger; the military action was almost
entirely in Lusitania, Celtiberia, and near the Levantine coast.[100] However, Metellus evidently made Córdoba his headquarters or at least wintered
there. After his successes against Hirtuleius and at the river Turia in
75 B.C., Metellus retired to Ulterior for the winter. He was fawned over
by the inhabitants of the towns and lived extravagantly.[101] Here the important notice of Cicero Arch. 10.26 should be considered:

> qui [Q. Metellus Pius] praesertim usque eo de suis rebus scribi
> cuperet, ut etiam Cordubae natis poetis, pingue quiddam sonantibus
> atque peregrinum, tamen aures suas dederat.

Here is valuable evidence of the cultural level of natives of Córdoba.
The additional conclusion sometimes drawn--that the event shows Córdoba's
political partisanship for Metellus--is untenable. Likewise Etienne's
supposition that the adulation was a result of the "milieu tartesso-ibere"

that encouraged the "culte du chef" is hardly necessary. The poets themselves need not have been in Metellus' clientage.[102] Cicero's point is
merely that Metellus loved flattery and would stoop even to having his
praises sung by heavily accented Cordoban bards. However much Cicero dis-
dained provincial performances, it is most interesting that less than a
hundred years after its foundation Córdoba had sufficient cultural life to
produce its own poets.

   During this same period a natural disaster struck. Lines 9-10 of the
epigram _ad patriam_ run:

   Tempore non illo, quo ter tibi funera centum
   Heu nox una dedit, quae tibi summa fuit.

Blanco correctly relates this to Sallust _Hist._ 2.28 (M):[103]

   Sed Metello Cordubae hiemante cum duabus legionibus alione casu
   an, sapientibus ut placet, venti per cava terrae citatu rupti
   aliquot montes tumulique sedere.

The date is between 79 and 72 B.C., when Metellus was a general in Ulterior.[104] The damage to property must have been extensive; three hundred
lives were lost.

   Not many years later, the man who would influence Córdoba both directly
and indirectly as much as almost any other, C. Julius Caesar, appeared.
Suetonius (_Div. Iul._ 7.1) does not mention Córdoba by name, but Caesar,
under command of the praetor Antistius Vetus, was sent around the assize
circuit of the _conventus_ (plural) of his province of Hispania Ulterior
in 69 B.C. Gades (Cádiz) is specifically mentioned, and Córdoba was also
probably a _conventus_ center by this time. Thus Caesar came to Córdoba
while performing his official duties. Further evidence of his familiarity
with Córdoba exists: the elder Seneca tells us (_Contr._ 10, _praef._ 16)
that the grandfather of Clodius Turrinus had been a _hospes_ (guest-friend)
of Caesar. Since Turrinus was a contemporary of the elder Seneca, it is
probable that the grandfather formed his _hospitium_ in 69 B.C. or during
Caesar's propraetorship in 61/60 B.C. Velleius Paterculus 2.43.4 assures
us that Caesar carried out his quaestorship _mirabili virtute atque in-
dustria_; how his stay affected Córdoba, if at all, is unknown.

   Caesar was in Ulterior again, this time as propraetor, in 61/60 B.C.
In all likelihood his headquarters were at Córdoba.[105] His only known administrative action was a measure to relieve problems of debt (Plutarch
Caes. 12): creditors were entitled to two-thirds of a debtor's income
until the debt was paid. Sutherland argues that the extensive debt was

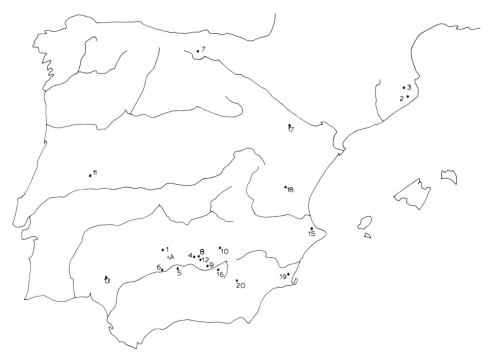

Map 3. Coin hoards: c.124-92 B.C. (See legend)

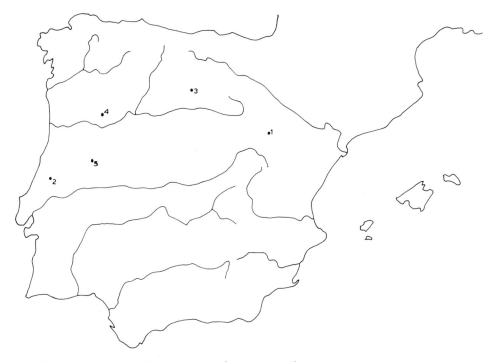

Map 4. Coin hoards: 79-71 B.C. (See legend)

LEGEND: MAP 3

Coin hoards c.124-92 B.C.

Source: Crawford 1969

 1. Pozoblanco (Crawford #174)   11. Penhagarcia (#191)
 2. La Barroca (#178)   12. Santa Elena (#193)
 3. Segaró (#180)   13. Río Tinto (#194)
 4. El Centenillo (#181)   14. Sierra Morena (#196)
 5. Montoro (#182)   15. Oliva (#197)
 6. Córdoba (#184)   16. Mogón (#200)
 7. Soto Iruz (#185)   17. Azuara (#204)
 8. Sierra Morena (near El   18. Salvacañete (#205)
    Centenillo) (#186)   19. Crevillente (#206)
 9. Cazlona (#188)   20. Orce (#211)
10. Torre de Juan Abad (#189)

Note: Number 3, Segaró, may not be correctly placed. Number 13,
Sierra Morena, is only a general location; no specific data
are provided.

LEGEND: MAP 4

Coin hoards 79-71 B.C.

Source: Crawford 1969

1. Maluenda (Crawford #282)   4. Poio (#305)
2. Cabeça de Corte (#300)   5. Moita (#326)
3. Palenzuela (#314)

Note: The location for Poio is general; I can find no town of
that name. A number of physical features called "Poio" appear
near the location given.

"the outcome of a period of economic development and rising exports."[106]
It could also have been the result of damage from the Sertorian war to ag-
riculture and commerce and, at Córdoba, the result of damage from the
earthquake. Caesar's measure suggests severe economic dislocation, and
Córdoba probably had its share of the troubles.

During the decade before the civil wars there is no mention of Córdoba.
M. Terentius Varro presumably had his headquarters here as *legatus* of
Pompey, probably from 55 B.C. on (cf. Bell. Civ. 1.38.1-2), but no activity
is recorded.

In the period just before the civil wars, the picture of life in Córdoba is sketchy. For example, there is no evidence, such as that provided
by Carteia's coins, for a local senate and magistrates.[107] There is also
no evidence for the organization of the conventus, although perhaps there
were the normal two magistri and quaestors.[108] Few names of this genera-
tion of Cordobans are known. The father of Clodius Turrinus, himself the
wealthiest man of his day in Spain, was alive. Turrinus' name may indicate
that he either was or was the descendant of an enfranchised native, since
his nomen could derive from a Roman Claudius, and the obvious candidate is
someone of the family of the Claudii Marcelli.[109] The family of Annaeus
Seneca pater was already in the town; the elder Seneca was born at Córdoba
about 50 B.C. The nomen Annaeus points to Etrurian or Illyrian roots.[110]
Perhaps Vibius Paciaecus, friend of M. Crassus, was connected to Córdoba;
his son was sent from Córdoba to aid Ulia in 45 B.C. (Bell. Hisp. 3.3-9).
It is more likely, however, that these Vibii were from southern Andalucía.[111]
From the few names that are known it appears that both Hispani and Romans
were in the highest social class of the town.

There is no archaeological or epigraphic material to broaden our view.
Some level of culture has been suggested, and indications of economic conditions both good and bad. The town certainly had a busy forum, and many
Romans on military and administrative duty were present. Terms such as
"capital" should be avoided,[112] but, for a provincial town, Córdoba was
prosperous, cultured, and politically important on the eve of the civil war.

CIVIL WARS

Terentius Varro was the legate of Pompey stationed at Córdoba when the
civil war broke out in 49 B.C.[113] His task was to support M. Petreius and
L. Afranius in the struggle against Caesar in northern Spain. He levied

two legions[114] and thirty cavalry cohorts in Ulterior, sent grain to Petreius and Afranius and to the besieged Pompeians at Massilia (Marseille),
and in other ways prepared for war. He secured Cádiz (confiscating weapons
and temple money) and ordered that ships be built there and at Seville
(Bell. Civ. 2.18.1-3). At Córdoba (ex tribunali) he spoke harshly (and
falsely, Caesar implies) of Caesar and made further monetary exactions
from the province. The demands in cash, bullion, and grain amounted to
nearly two million denarii, a staggering amount.[115] He then attempted to
secure the loyalty of the province by punishing towns and individuals who
favored Caesar and by exacting an oath of allegiance to himself and to
Pompey (Bell. Civ. 2.18.5). However, Varro clearly lacked confidence in
all of these measures; he planned to retreat to Cádiz with his legions,
ships, and supplies (Bell. Civ. 2.18.6).

Caesar, after defeating Petreius and Afranius at Ilerda, headed for
the southern province in the late spring of 49 B.C. He sent in advance
Q. Cassius Longinus, a tribune of the people, with six hundred horsemen.
Longinus proceeded toward Córdoba, which Varro now evacuated. Caesar
meanwhile summoned all the magistratus principesque omnium civitatum to
Córdoba for a meeting (Bell. Civ. 2.19.1). There was a massive response;
all sent their senators, and all Roman citizens were present. The conventus
of Córdoba took matters into its own hands, closing the town gates to Varro,
manning the walls, and taking over the provincial troops (cohortes colonicae) that happened to be there.[116]

Varro was also discomfited on other fronts. Carmona (Carmo) ejected
his garrison. A provincial legion, Cádiz, Seville, and Italica deserted
him. Finally he surrendered his forces to Sex. Caesar and presented himself to Caesar at Córdoba, handing over his account books and forces as to
a successor in command (Bell. Civ. 2.19.4-20.8). The Pompeian forces in
Ulterior were neutralized without a blow.

Thus Caesar was able to hold his meeting at Córdoba, and he stayed
there two days. In his speech to the assembled principes he thanked them
for their support, returned all money that Varro had taken, remitted all
money that had been promised, and passed out rewards. This account may be
one-sided. Dio 41.24, using another source, notes that Caesar exacted
money from Cádiz, which, like Córdoba, had resisted Varro and indeed may
have suffered more than Córdoba at Varro's hands. But it is clear that
Caesar left Córdoba on good terms. After marching from Córdoba, he went

on to Cádiz and, after leaving Cassius in the south with four legions, he
continued to Narbo and Marseille, stopping at Tarraco (Tarragona) on the
way (Bell. Civ. 2.21-22).

This episode shows Córdoba to have been the major town in Ulterior.
Bell. Hisp. 3.1 makes its position explicit: eius provinciae (i.e.,
Ulterioris) caput esse existimabatur. Other towns are important, especi-
ally Cádiz, but Córdoba stands out as the leading community in southern
Iberia.

One of the sorriest episodes in the history of Roman Spain follows.
After Caesar left, he gave the command of southern Iberia to Cassius Longinus (Bell. Alex. 48). He could not have made a worse choice. Longinus
turned savage almost immediately. Either he harbored a grudge because of
a wound he had received at the hands of treacherous Spaniards while quaestor
in Spain in 52 B.C.,[117] or, as it was said, he was simply cruel by nature.
He hated the inhabitants of the province, and they hated him. Cassius
kept the loyalty of the army by donatives and loose discipline (Bell. Alex.
48). After a campaign in the area of Medobriga,[118] he put his troops into
winter quarters and returned to Córdoba ad ius dicendum (Bell. Alex. 49.1).
Although previously Córdoba has seemed only one of many places ad ius dicendum, here it is clearly the main court town of the province. Perhaps,
when Caesar was sent around to the other conventus on an assize circuit in
69 B.C., the commander Antistius Vetus remained in Córdoba.

During the winter of 49/48 B.C. Cassius continued his depredations.
He demanded money from the rich and punished any opposition or complaint.
He needed the money to pay for his generous treatment of his soldiers.
Rich and poor were united in a desire to rid themselves of the commander,
and he exacerbated matters by levying a new legion--the fifth--and sump-
tuously fitting out three thousand more cavalrymen at the expense of the
provincials (Bell. Alex. 49-50).

Meanwhile Caesar was concerned about aid that Juba, king of Mauritania,
was giving to Pompey. He therefore commanded Longinus to bring his army
to Africa. Longinus was overjoyed at the thought of new areas to plunder
and left Córdoba to pick up the legions that were wintering in Lusitania.
He left orders behind that grain be provided and one hundred ships prepared by the Spanish towns. In his zeal for the new adventure he hurried
back to Córdoba, arriving sooner than expected, established a camp near

the city for the legions. Again he promised extra cash to the soldiers, once the crossing had been made to Mauritania (Bell. Alex. 51-52.1).

By this time hatred for Cassius had resulted in a plot against his life. The assassins, led by Minucius Silo, Minucius Flaccus, T. Vasius, and L. Mercello, all of Italica, attacked the commander in Córdoba's courthouse (basilica).[119] He was wounded but lived (Bell. Alex. 52.2-4). In the subsequent uproar more plotters were identified, including Calpurnius Salvianus (Bell. Alex. 53.2) and Annius Scapula (Bell. Alex. 55.2). Possibly Calpurnius was a Cordoban; the Calpurnius Salvianus mentioned by Tacitus (Ann. 4.36) as the prosecutor of Sex. Marius was very probably from the city.[120] The plotter Calpurnius Salvianus was probably the prosecutor's father and also a Cordoban. Annius Scapula was from Córdoba; according to Bell. Hisp. 33.3,4 he committed suicide in Córdoba, which was where his familia was.[121] None of the other plotters can be related to Córdoba or to any other Spanish town.[122] Perhaps a few were even Romans on Cassius' staff (cf. Bell. Alex. 50.2).

One of the plotters, L. Iuventius Laterensis, hurried to the legionary camp after the attack and was proclaimed praetor by the troops. Cassius' largess had not prevented the troops from hating him. At the news that Cassius lived, however, most of the troops except the vernacula, a local levy, deserted Laterensis and went to Córdoba to give aid to their commander. The plot collapsed and the plotters were punished--except for those who could afford bribes.

As Cassius carried out plans for the African expedition his legio vernacula joined the second legion, also a provincial legion, in mutiny. Cassius, a slow learner, had exasperated the provincials even further by announcing a levy among Roman equites (Bell. Alex. 56.4) and by demanding that those who owed him money come to him personally at Seville. About half of Cassius' troops had now mutinied--not only the vernacula and the second but also most of the newly raised fifth legion. Cassius, on the road to Seville, sent his quaestor, M. Claudius Marcellus Aeserninus, to hold Córdoba; but Marcellus and the garrison joined the mutineers there, and Marcellus was proclaimed praetor.[123]

Marcellus Aeserninus was not directly related to M. Claudius Marcellus the founder of Córdoba, but the name itself would have been enough to establish a connection with the town.[124] Caesar had chosen Cassius Longinus because of his previous experience in Ulterior. Had he chosen Marcellus

because of his family's real or imagined link to the founder of the most
important city in the province? That Marcellus was immediately proclaimed
praetor by the mutineers is no proof that he had special ties with the soldiers; as mentioned above, Laterensis, an Italian without obvious connections to Spain, had been chosen as praetor shortly before. However, at
the very least, Marcellus' name must have aided him in his dealings with
the Cordobans and, therefore, with other Spaniards of the area.

Marcellus was in charge only of Córdoba's garrison and the rebellious
elements of the provincial fifth legion (Bell. Alex. 57.4-5). T. Torius
of Italica, dux of the vernacula and second legions, soon arrived in Córdoba as well. At first Torius claimed to support Pompey, as did his soldiers, who had fought with Varro (Bell. Alex. 58.1-4). But Torius changed
his tune when he saw that Córdoba stood united, led by Marcellus and pro-
Caesarian. Torius had Marcellus named praetor of his own troops and set
up his camp near Córdoba (Bell. Alex. 58.4-59.1). Meanwhile, Cassius
marched to Córdoba, camped on the south side of the Guadalquivir across the
river from the town, and pillaged Cordoban land. Marcellus crossed the
river but avoided battle because Cassius held an advantageous position.
When Marcellus retreated toward Córdoba, Cassius attacked him at the river
crossing; in response Marcellus moved his camp to the south side of the
Guadalquivir. Cassius, lacking confidence in the outcome of a pitched
battle, then retreated to Ulia and was besieged there by Marcellus
(Bell. Alex. 59-62).

At this point the commander in Citerior, Aemilius Lepidus, arrived with
thirty-five cohorts and many auxiliaries. As a result of his mediation,
he and Marcellus retreated to Córdoba and Cassius went to Carmo. The matter was finally settled when C. Trebonius, the new commander of the province, arrived, and Cassius put his troops into winter quarters. He met
an ignominious end, drowning on the way back to Rome during the winter of
48/47 B.C. (Bell. Alex. 63-64).[125]

Córdoba was important throughout this affair. It was Cassius' headquarters. He made efforts to hold it against the insurgents through his
second in command, Marcellus the quaestor. The town showed its intense
loyalty to Caesar in the face of instigation to join forces sympathetic to
Pompey and, as a result, suffered the devastation of its territory on the
far side of the Guadalquivir. However, this loyalty was not beyond
question. The town had joined the mutineers against Caesar's appointed

commander Longinus. Caesar could interpret this Cordoban action negative-
ly--much to the disadvantage of the town.

   As might have been predicted, there was unrest in Ulterior in 47 B.C.,
for the towns and legions that had mutinied feared reprisals from Trebonius.
Apparently the Caesarian commander was able to maintain quiet during this
year, but in 46 B.C. the situation deteriorated (Dio 43.29.1-2). The
Spaniards from Ulterior sent a legation to ask for aid from Cornelius
Scipio, one of the Pompeian generals who had survived the defeat of Pompey
the Great at Pharsalus in 48 B.C. and who had formed a new line of resistance to Caesar with other Pompeians in Africa. Scipio sent Cn. Pompey,
Pompey the Great's son, and other Pompeians to their aid. This mission to
Scipio was before Scipio's death in the summer of 46 B.C. and must have
been after the sailing season began in mid-March. Cn. Pompey sailed to
the Balearic Islands and took them, including Ebusus, after a struggle.
He stayed there for a time because he was ill. The Spaniards were wor-
ried by this delay because a new commander, C. Didius, had been sent
against them by Caesar. They launched another full-scale revolt, led by
T. "Quintius" Scapula and Q. Aponius, both Roman _equites_. Trebonius was
driven out, and all Baetica rose in revolt (Dio 43.29.3).[126]

   This T. "Quintius" Scapula seems to be the same man as the Annius
Scapula who was involved in the earlier revolt (Bell. Alex. 55.2). Both
men were wealthy. Annius is a common name for important persons in
Baetica; Quin(c)tius is not. Scapula is not at all a common cognomen. Dio
or his source has apparently mistaken Aponius' praenomen for Scapula's
nomen. Dio should perhaps read "T. Scapula, Q. Aponius."[127] Scapula was
a native of Córdoba, as his suicide there shows (Bell. Hisp. 33.3-4).
Aponius' origin is impossible to trace definitely. Aponius is an important name in Andalusian epigraphy; Aponii are scattered throughout the
region. To judge from the evidence of the Dillii, a senatorial family who
lived in Córdoba during the Empire, Aponius may also be from Córdoba.[128]

   Meanwhile Cn. Pompey reached and laid siege to Carthago Nova. He was
joined there by Scapula's forces (Dio 43.30.2) and, after Scipio was defeated in Africa, by Sex. Pompey, Varus, and Labienus. Eventually eleven
legions were assembled, and various towns went over to the Pompeians.[129]
But, concluding that Caesar would march to Spain and diffident about holding all the Peninsula, Cnaeus withdrew to Ulterior. A plot to capture

Cnaeus and hand him over to Caesar failed, and the stage was set for the
final confrontation between Caesar and the Pompeians at Munda.[130]

In Ulterior Cnaeus managed to take over some towns, either by force or
persuasion, and he gathered a large force. However, not all towns were
pro-Pompeian, and some shut their gates against him.[131] As Cnaeus consoli-
dated his position some communities sent urgent requests to Rome for aid.
Caesar responded by marching to Obulco, a town fairly close to Córdoba, in
record time--perhaps as little as twenty-four or twenty-seven days.[132]
Ambassadors from Córdoba met him and asked that he surprise the town and
take it at night. The enemy was unaware of his approach; Sex. Pompey,
brother of Cnaeus, was holding the town with a garrison while Cnaeus himself besieged Ulia, a pro-Caesarian town in the area. Caesar sent a re-
lieving force to Ulia and apparently attempted to take Córdoba by ruse.
He sent legionaries on horses; when a force emerged from Córdoba to attack
the "cavalry" squadron, the men dismounted and slaughtered the Cordoban
force. The city was not taken (if that was Caesar's intent), but Sextus
was so frightened that he summoned his brother to return to Córdoba from
Ulia. Thus Caesar effectively relieved the siege of the loyal town, which
had been on the point of surrendering.[133]

Caesar now built a bridge across the Guadalquivir and set up camp opposite Córdoba so as to cut off Cnaeus' return from Ulia. When Cnaeus
arrived there was a struggle for the bridge, but Caesar was unable to ob-
tain what he most desired, a pitched battle with Cnaeus' forces. In the
hope of drawing Cnaeus into battle, Caesar decided to leave the area of
Córdoba and to attack Ategua; after a struggle, the town finally surrendered to Caesar. There followed a series of skirmishes at different
towns, and many towns deserted Cnaeus. Cnaeus finally took a stand in the
campus Mundensis, near Munda (the modern Montilla).[134] After a bitter
struggle, Caesar routed the Pompeians.[135]

M. Valerius Messala brought the news to Sex. Pompey at Córdoba. Sextus
immediately fled the city, leaving the Cordobans to fend for themselves
when Caesar arrived on the scene. Scapula, leader in the revolt, committed
suicide in a most flamboyant manner; he gathered his household and children
around him, dressed in sumptuous clothing, ate a gourmet meal, anointed
himself, and had himself strangled by a slave. He was then cremated. As
Caesar threw up a circumvallation the Cordobans began to quarrel among
themselves. Those of the legions that were composed of freed slaves and

deserters tried to surrender, but the thirteenth legion managed to seize part of the wall and the towers and to attack the Caesarians in the garrison. As soon as Caesar heard of these developments he sent in his troops, and resistance was no longer possible. The author of the Bellum Hispaniense records that 22,000 of the enemy died, not counting casualties outside the walls. He adds that the fleeing enemy began to set fire to the city. Dio says that Caesar killed all resisters and sold the rest of the population into slavery.[136]

This was a black day for Córdoba. The town was partially destroyed, citizens dead or enslaved. Some escaped, either by showing Caesarian sympathies or by avoiding involvement; the Annaei Senecae, for example, do not seem to have suffered.[137] Total damage is impossible to assess. However, Caesar could give as well as take away. Although loyal towns might be the first to receive favors (cf. Dio 43.38,39), Caesar was not necessarily one to hold a grudge.[138] Notices (scant as they are) from the following years indicate that the town remained what it had been before the civil wars, the chief town of the southern province.

Caesar stayed at Córdoba long enough to receive the heads of his enemies Varus and Labienus (Appian BC 2.104) and then moved on to regain control of other towns.[139] He finally returned to Italy, leaving C. Carrinas in charge of Ulterior. For the following years the sources give little definite information on Córdoba. Letters written from the city by Asinius Pollio to Cicero when Pollio was commander in Ulterior, after Carrinas, in 44-43 B.C. contain little about Córdoba, except that apparently the thirteenth legion was there as a garrison in the aftermath of the renewed rampaging in the area by Sex. Pompey in 44 B.C.[140] During his years in Ulterior Pollio must have formed many friendships, including a lasting one with the elder Seneca,[141] but details are lacking. For the remainder of the Republic and the whole of the Empire, full information on Córdoba such as that available for the 40s B.C. is lacking. But Córdoba prospered, and much can be deduced about its history.

CITIZEN COLONY

Sometime between the civil wars and the end of Augustus' reign, Córdoba underwent fundamental changes. It gained a new name, "Patricia," a new status as a citizen colony, and an addition to its population, a settlement of legionary veterans.

As previously noted, Córdoba's status before the civil wars has been
the subject of much debate. Likewise the occasion of the change in status--
the granting of citizen colonial rights--has been variously explained. The
major distinction has been made on the basis of an argument ex cognomine.
Many have supposed that the lack of a Iulia or an Augusta in Córdoba's official name (Colonia Patricia) means that the colonial grant must be pre-
Caesarian.[142] The favored candidate as the founder of the colony is a
Pompey, either Pompey the Great or a son.[143] However, the presupposition
that all Julio-Augustan towns bear Julio-Augustan cognomens is false; the
Iberian-Latin communities of Obulco Pontificense and Ugia Martia are cases
in point, and many other examples could be adduced. There are no other
indications of Pompeian or pre-Caesarian citizen colonial status in the
numismatics, prosopography, or history of the area.[144] In addition,
"Patricia" is a curious cognomen to come from a plebeian, Pompey.[145] All
in all, it is very unlikely that a Pompey was involved in a colonial
foundation at Córdoba.[146]

The probable sequence of events can be guessed. Córdoba's Latin status
lasted until the civil wars, and it was in this context that ex-magistrates
of the city were enrolled in the Sergian tribe. The city's fate after Sex.
Pompey fled in 45 B.C. is unknown, but the analogy of Hispalis (Seville)
can be cited; Seville, although it had showed anti-Caesarian tendencies
and, like Córdoba, had suffered at Caesar's hands, was granted citizen
status by the dictator.[147] Therefore there is no a priori reason to doubt
that Caesar could have advanced other Spanish towns that had opposed him
in the civil war to citizen status. In fact a list of anti-Caesarian
towns mentioned in the Bellum Hispaniense includes four Caesarian foundations: Hispalis Iulia Romula, Ucubi Claritas Iulia, Urso Genetiva Iulia,
and Hasta Regia.[148] Córdoba would fit into this series very well. All
(except perhaps Ucubi) were important towns in the south; all, to judge
from the Sergian tribe each carried at the time, were previous Latin
towns.[149] Córdoba's cognomen, Patricia, also fits this pattern. These
towns' cognomens celebrate the Julian gens and, in the case of Ucubi Claritas Iulia and Iptucci Virtus Iulia (a town whose tribe and attitude toward
Caesar is unknown), Julius Caesar himself. Romula (Hispalis) and Genetiva
(Urso) recall divine progenitors; Patricia (Córdoba) and Regia (Hasta)
recall high birth.[150] It seems probable that Córdoba was granted citizen
colonial status by Caesar and that it retained its Sergian tribe.[151]

Before going into other problems, a pause to consider more closely the cognomen <u>Patricia</u> is necessary, for it has caused great puzzlement. It is unparalleled in cognomens of other towns.[152] Its origin has been sought in the most far-flung and far-fetched places, beginning with the foundation of the town by Marcellus.[153] As mentioned before, the Pompeii have often been credited with the name, but their plebeian origins, coupled with the supposition that Caesar would not have let a Pompeian cognomen stand, militate against this thesis.[154] Augustus has recently come into vogue as the originator of the name; Griffin has offered an ingenious connection between the epithet and the young Marcellus, husband of Augustus' daughter Julia.[155] Patricia may be a divine epithet related to the god Liber Pater, on whose festival day, the Liberalia, Caesar defeated Cn. Pompey at Munda.[156] But all of these suggestions are much less plausible than the explanation suggested above--that Caesar recalled his own patrician nobility in the name he gave to the newly advanced town.

In Cordoban epigraphy the Galeria tribe is attested as much as the Sergia. The next major event in Córdoba's history is the settling of veterans of Augustus' legions. As Henderson argued in the case of Hispalis, the best explanation of the two tribes in the town's epigraphy is that one was the tribe of the Caesarian civil colony and the other was that of an Augustan military colony.[157] In Córdoba the Augustan soldiers were given land in the outlying <u>territorium</u> of the town and also plots in the newly annexed area between the original town wall and the Guadalquivir River. They were enrolled in the Galerian tribe. A similar explanation may apply to the two-tribe towns Carthago Nova and Urso.[158]

The origin of the veterans who settled at Córdoba is uncertain. The only direct evidence of their presence is in a coin type of the town that shows, on the reverse, two standards with a legionary eagle in between.[159] The coin dates from the period 18 B.C. to 2 B.C.; if the veterans were settled then, the new <u>deductio</u> would have come after the end of the major wars in the northern part of the Peninsula in 19 B.C. Augustus was in Spain during the years 15 and 14 B.C. and founded colonies at that time (Dio 54.23.7; 54.25). This period would have been appropriate as an opportunity for the new <u>deductio</u> at Córdoba.[160] The coinage probably dates from about this time and commenorates the refoundation.[161]

However, it remains impossible to tell which veterans were involved. The "standards" coin cited by Cohen, with the numbers X and V interpreted

as meaning the settlement of veterans from legiones V and X or from legio
XV, is fictional: Cohen only records earlier reports of the coin, and no
actual exemplar has been verified.[162] The misreading is due to the interpretation of letters A and R in the legend COLONIA PATRICIA as V and X
(the A and the R appear upside-down because of the location of the legend
on the coin). Given the absence of any numismatic, epigraphical, or archaeological indication, the military identity of the legionaries at Córdoba must remain a mystery.

AUGUSTAN AGE

Apart from the foundation of Córdoba as a citizen colony and the settlement of legionary veterans there, there is scant information about the city
in the time of Augustus. Its coinage reflects a visit by Augustus in 15-
14 B.C.[164] If the inscriptions reported by Masdeu are genuine they show
that M. Agrippa was a patron of the city.[165] Certainly Augustus caused a
good deal of work to be done on the via Augusta in the vicinity, as the
many milestones from this period indicate.[166] But historical sources are
silent. The Augustan Age is a watershed in Córdoba's history. Before this
period some sort of continuous narrative is possible, afterwards only a
description of local life and topography.

At this period Córdoba was all that it was to become: the major city
in the new senatorial province of Baetica, the capital of the province and
seat of a juridical conventus, the home or origo of literary and political
figures, a prosperous provincial city. Its political importance at this
time dated from its very beginnings. Its intellectual tradition rested on
the rude local poets of seventy years before and on the family of the elder
Seneca. Despite the ravages of civil war, the city boasted a massive wall,
a stone bridge across the Guadalquivir, a courthouse (basilica) in the
forum, and good road connections with other Baetican towns. However the
local language may have been tainted by the admixture of natives in the
population,[167] Cordobans of any status surely sought to be as Roman as the
Romans themselves, or more so. There is no evidence of a "national con-
sciousness" in the likes of the elder Seneca, although there was presumably
a certain sympathy among native sons who found themselves in Rome together.[168]

As Córdoba enters the imperial age it is an important city, but one
whose history becomes increasingly difficult to reconstruct, even in outline.

3

CÓRDOBA DURING THE EMPIRE

Early in the Empire Córdoba probably suffered, as much as any other
city, from the depredations of the governor Vibius Severus. His effect
on the city is not mentioned specifically, nor are any effects from the
excesses of Umbonius Silo, Baebius Massa, Marius Crispus, and Caecilius
Classicus that occurred later in the first century.[169] Cordobans play
both major and minor roles in Rome. Seneca the Younger gained influence,
wealth, and finally death under Nero; Sex. Marius was murdered by Tiberius
for his wealth (Tacitus Ann. 6.19, cf. 4.36); Aemilius Regulus lost
his life in an abortive attempt against Caligula.[170] Closer to home
the effects of the struggles of A.D. 69–70 go unrecorded, as do any results
of Vespasian's grant of Latinity to Spain and subsequent municipal
reorganization.[171] Frustrating blanks in the historical record, and a
few tantalizing snippets of information such as those just mentioned and
those noted below are all that is left of Córdoba's history during the
Empire.

In the period following the Flavian rule at Rome Córdoba, it is said,
was restored by the Emperor Nerva. This contention comes from an inscription reported to have been found in the seventeenth century at Cuesta del
Espino, twenty kilometers from Córdoba on the road to Seville.[172]

    IMP. NERVA. CAES.
    AVG. PONT. MAXIM.
    TRIB. POTEST. II. COS. II[I]
    PROC. PAT. PATRIAE
    CORD. RESTITVIT.

Santos Jener, following a long line of local Cordoban historians, related this stone to the work supposedly done by Nerva in rebuilding the
city after the destruction suffered during the Caesarian civil wars.
García y Bellido likewise thought that the restorative work mentioned was
to Córdoba itself.[173] Given the scarcity of historical references to

31

Córdoba in this period, it would be tempting indeed to adduce this inscription as evidence of imperial activity, but this stone is certainly a milestone and has nothing whatsoever to do with the restoration of Córdoba by
Nerva. Hübner saw that the CORDUBA of the transcription must be an inter-
polation for VIAM VETUSTATE COR[R](VPTAM) or something similar.[174] The
inscription should thus be resolved as follows:

    Imp(erator) Nerva Caes(ar)
    Aug(ustus) Pont(ifex) Maxim(us)
    Trib(unicia) Potest(ate) Co(n)s(ul) II[I]
    Proc(onsul) Pat(er) Patriae
    [viam vetustate] cor[r](uptam)
    restituit.

Some activity might be expected in Córdoba under the Spanish emperors
Trajan and Hadrian; none is evidenced. Perhaps Hadrian visited Córdoba on
his tour of the West in A.D. 122. During his reign an army levy may have
been held in the Peninsula; such a levy would have affected the city (cf.
SHA Hadr. 12.4). Local inhabitants who had made good in Rome contributed
to the city, and prosperity continued,[175] interrupted only by the unrest
that attended the Moorish invasions of Baetica in the 170s. During these
incursions some cities in the area built or rebuilt their walls; Córdoba
probably withstood the raids with a minimum of difficulty.

Through the period of the Severi and on into the middle of the third
century Córdoba prospered unnoticed. However, the period of approximately
A.D. 260-280 brought upheaval to Baetica in general, and, therefore, to
Córdoba as well. There is no evidence of the city's reaction to the usur-
per Postumus and his Imperium Galliarum, but with the breakdown of central
Roman authority in Baetica came Germanic invasions. In A.D. 264 the Germans made raids across the Pyrenees into Cataluña, then down the Levantine
coast and into Baetica. Italica, downstream from Córdoba, was threatened,
and coin hoards indicate general unrest. A plague followed the raids, and
times were bad. Symptomatic of these troubles is the end, in material
from about A.D. 260, of fragments of amphorae attributable to Baetican manufacture that have been found at Monte Testaccio in Rome.

Recovery was slow. Although Córdoba probably regained some prosperity
under Diocletian, the effects of so many troubles must still have lingered.
Prosperity returns, but Hispalis displaces Córdoba as the pre-eminent city
of the province.

LOCAL GOVERNMENT

In Latin historiography little attention is paid to a city uninvolved in the wars of the times. Fortunately it is possible by utilizing nonliterary sources to reconstruct something of the life of Córdoba, even though its vicissitudes through the centuries are elusive. Administrative machiery was essential to any Roman town. In no case is the constitution of a Roman city preserved whole but, as M.I. Henderson well remarked, there was less variety in local government throughout the Roman Empire than there was among the towns of a single medieval English county. A combination of explicit evidence and comparative deduction produces an accurate picture of the local administration of Córdoba.[176]

At the head of the administration, as was usual for colonies, were the duoviri.[177] Their full title (which does not appear in Cordoban examples) was duovir iure dicundo, as befitted their chief function, that of primary judicial officers. Of course two men were elected. The year was reckoned by their names (CIL 2.2216, 2242). They presided at council and assembly meetings, supervised the local religious life, and commanded the local militia. At Córdoba there are fifteen examples of duovirs recorded over a period of perhaps three hundred years.[178]

1. M. Iunius [L.f.] L.n. Gal. Terenti[anus] Servilius Sabinus (CIL 2.1347 add.)
2. [...] f. Pyramus (CIL 2.2133)
3. M. Lucretius Marianus (CIL 2.2216)
4. Q. Vibius Laetus (CIL 2.2216)
5. [...] Iunius Bassus Milonianus (CIL 2.2222)
6. L. Iulius M.f.Q.n. Gal. Gallus Mummianus (CIL 2.2224)
7. L. Manlius A.f.A.n. Gal. Bocchus (CIL 2.2225)
8. T. Mercello Persinus Marius (CIL 2.2226)
9. L. Valerius Poenus (CIL 2.2242)
10. L. Antistius Rusticus (CIL 2.2242)
11. A. At(ilius) (CIL 2.4963.9)
12. L. Ai(milius) (CIL 2.4963.9)
13. L. Iunius P.f. Serg. Paulinus (CIL 2.5523)
14. L. Aelius L.f. Gal. Faustinus (CIL 2.5524)
15. [L. Ful]cinius Pacatus (AE 1971.185)

Details of their activities are scant. Servilius and Pyramus were honored in other towns of Baetica (Acinippo, Obulco), so their influence extended beyond Córdoba itself. Paulinus gave games to celebrate his selection as flamen provinciae Baeticae; Mummianus had also been such a priest, and the wife of Pacatus has been the female equivalent. There is little evidence of the supervision of religious life, although two, Servilius and Paulinus, were local pontifices and flamines. No testimory is

left of military and judicial roles. As mentioned above, the year is dated
by duoviri, and this case is the only example of such dating, apart from
Italica, in Baetica.[179]

In many towns a special executive college was selected each five years
to conduct the local census and to arrange the public contracts for lands,
buildings, and works.[180] These were the duoviri quinquennales. However,
none is evidenced at Córdoba; few are recorded in all of Iberia, and only
two in Baetica. The tasks must have been performed when needed, without
special title, by duovirs and other officials.[181]

From time to time a duovir would be out of town or otherwise temporarily
unavailable. In this situation he appointed a substitute, a praefectus
iure dicundo.[182] L. Manlius Bocchus was such a prefect at an unknown date
(CIL 2.2225). [Cn. Corne]lius Cinna (CIL 2.5525) may have been a [praef]-
ectus IIviro [(?)aedilicia pot]estate, but the restoration of the inscription is far from certain; it is hard to see why a duovir (as opposed to
one-half of a college of quattuorviri) would have "aedilician power" and
why he would have a prefect.[183] Special prefects were elected to hold
local elections and to carry on until new chief magistrates were elected,
but none is attested at Córdoba. A prefect could be named by the emperor
or any other Roman authority who declined to hold personally a magistracy
to which he had been elected in a provincial town. There is a coin, sometimes attributed to Córdoba, which shows Cn. Statius Libo as a prefect
(presumably for M. Agrippa). This coin has been used to show Agrippa's
involvement with Córdoba, but correct attribution puts the coin in Carthago
Nova, not Córdoba.[184] Thus this special prefect is lacking from Córdoba's
extant records.

Of the regularly elected local magistrates, the aedile ranked immediately below the duovir.[185] He was in charge of the general supervision of
public areas and activities, for example of the baths, grain distribution,
public markets, and games. At Córdoba only one aedile is attested, T.
Mercello Persinus (CIL 2.2226).[186] As discussed above, if CIL 2.5525 is
[aedilicia pot]estate then [Cn. Corne]lius Cinna performed the duties of
an aedile as well.

Quaestors, like quinquennales, pose a problem; although in theory they
should be prominent in local administration, supervising financial matters
of the town, in fact they are rare in Spanish cities.[187] Sometimes their
job must have been done by a duovir, or as a munus. Rodríguez Neila

suggests plausibly that, since quaestors seldom appear in the inscriptions, the office was early subsumed under IIviri.[188] None appears at Córdoba, nor in all of Baetica.[189]

These magistrates, representative of what can be termed the viri principales of the town,[190] were important and prestigious men locally, but in imperial terms they were small fry indeed. Seneca (Contr. 3.12) puts it well:

> Cum in foro dico, aliquid ago; cum declamo, id quod bellissime Censorinus aiebat de his qui honores in municipiis ambitiose peterent, videor mihi in somniis laborare.

The cursus of the viri principales from Córdoba show that few advanced from local to imperial posts. This lack of advancement was normal. At best, a local man could hope to advance to the lowest ranks of an equestrian career, for example, praefectus fabrum or praefectus cohortis. Rarely was the second rank, the military tribunate, achieved.[191] In Córdoba, Junius Bassus Milonianus,[192] a duovir, became a praefectus fabrum (CIL 2.2222). L. Manlius Bocchus[193] had probably been tribunus militum of the fifteenth legion before he was duovir--that is, he does not represent a local inhabitant who worked his way through the local cursus and then went on to imperial office. Usually Cordoban magistrates did not advance beyond their local posts; we do not know if they had any desire to.[194]

Of course the magistrates did not govern alone. There was a local council, called an ordo at Córdoba but termed a senatus in other towns.[195] The members were usually selected from the holders of minor local offices and were styled senatores, decuriones (as at Córdoba), conscripti, and, rarely, patres. There were usually one hundred members, although fifty and thirty are attested in the West.[196] Their names were set down in an album, which was revised every five years. These men virtually controlled the town; all public business passed through their hands. At Córdoba only the title of the body is given, and this only in relation to decrees authorizing specific acts. In one case it decreed a bronze statue (CIL 2.2216), in another a statue for a flamen provinciae Baeticae (CIL 2.2224), in others dedications to various important local men (CIL 2.2225, to a duovir; 5522, to a young senator; HAE 1856, to a youth of distinguished family). The meeting place of the ordo, presumably a curia, has not been located with certainty, but logically it would have been in the area of the forum.

While little is known of Córdoba's ordo, nothing is known of the

popular assembly. As at other sites, the assumption must be that any such
assembly lost to the ordo whatever power it had had during the early
Empire.[197]

At Córdoba one of the major preoccupations of local government was
probably the supervision of its territorium. Strabo 3.2.1 remarks on the
town's large territory as a source of wealth: Κόρδυβα ηὔξηται ... διὰ
... χώρας ἀρετῆ καὶ μεγέθει. Can the extent of this territory be
determined?

In recent literature, the problem of assessment of the territorium
of towns has been discussed, with some relevance to Córdoba's situation.
The list of data sources that Chevallier provides gives an adequate frame-
work for determination, in very general terms, of the limits of Córdoba's
territory.[198]

Ancient evidence from written sources provides a starting point.
Córdoba was situated on the north side of the Guadalquivir. The Bell.
Alex. 59.2 shows that there was also Cordoban territory on the near (south)
side as well. As mentioned above, Strabo 3.2.1 indicates a large territory. The Antonine itinerary and a Vicarello vase add a location that may
be on the southern Cordoban border: a station (mansio) called Ad Aras is
situation twelve or twenty-three miles from Córdoba and fifteen or twelve
miles from Astigi.[199] This site appears to take its name from the altars
set up at the municipal fines.[200]

The ancient towns that may border Cordoban territory add a further
dimension. These are:

1. Astigi, colonia Augusta Firma, which borders Córdoba at Ad Aras
2. Ulia Fidentia, a municipium civium Romanorum
3. Ucubi, colonia Claritas Julia
4. Sacili Martialium, a municipium
5. Epora, a municipium civium Romanorum
6. Onuba
7. Sisapo
8. Mirobriga
9. Mellaria, municipium Flavium
10. Municipium Iulium V[...]
11. Regina
12. Iporca
13. Celti
14. Detumo/Detunda.[201]

An arbitrary line drawn midway between Córdoba and each of these towns
would give a fair, if very generalized, idea of the minimum territorium
of Córdoba.

On the western <u>fines</u>, the <u>conventus</u> boundary was likely also the city
boundary. Enclaves could exist in other provinces and so, <u>a fortiori</u>, in
other <u>conventus</u>, but logic dictates that the general city territory would
be in Córdoba's own <u>conventus iuridicus</u>.[202] The <u>conventus</u> boundary was
probably the Retortillo River, and this river probably also formed the
frontier with Iporca, Celti and Detumo.[203] However, such considerations
do not help in determination of the southwestern frontier because the <u>con-
ventus</u> boundary with Astigi is uncertain, although it probably ran along
the Genil River a short way and then to Ad Aras.

To the north the territory stretched away from the Guadalquivir in a
broad ribbon. The location of the towns along the river confirms that
each, spaced along the north shore of the middle Guadalquivir, had a slice
of the hinterland to complement the river frontage; no towns impinged on
these hinterland areas. How far inland from the river did Córdoba's territory go? Nierhaus has skillfully attacked this problem in his analysis
of a relief found in the Sierra Morena along the road from Córdoba to
Augusta Emerita, at the watershed between the Guadiana and the Guadalquivir
rivers. He identified this relief as part of an arch that stood at the
frontier between Cordoban territory and the next town to the north.[204]
A plausible conclusion is that the northern boundary of Córdoba's territory
extended to this watershed.

Archaeology can tell nothing so neat about the southern <u>fines</u>. Blanco
notes that excavations at Ategua reveal that the town decayed during the
Empire; he suggests that Ategua was incorporated into Córdoba's territory
and so atrophied. If so, perhaps the frontier ran along the Guadajoz
River in this area.

No other natural boundaries are obvious. If Onuba was located at modern Villafranca de Córdoba (far from certain) perhaps the Guadamellato
River formed the northeastern border; the Arroyo de Guadalín could have
formed the southeastern border, at least up to the edge of the Guadalquivir.
Anything more than a very general description of the frontier to the east
is guesswork.[205]

The boundaries suggested on Map 5 are a solution to the question of
the extent of Córdoba's <u>territorium</u>.

This territory was divided into rural districts, <u>pagi</u>. A <u>Pagus Augusti</u>
is mentioned in <u>CIL</u> 2.2194; its location is unknown, but probably it was
near the city itself. <u>CIL</u> 2.2322 notes another, more interesting, <u>pagus</u>,

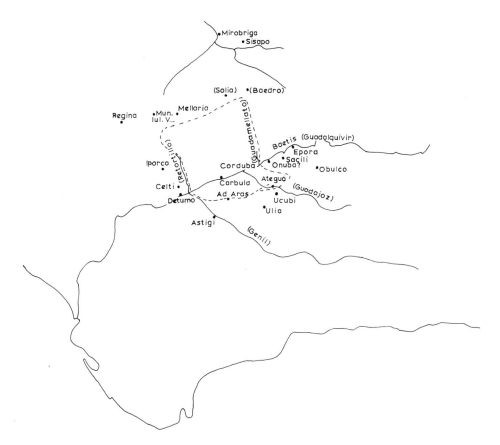

Map 5. Córdoba's <u>territorium</u>.   Modern names are in parentheses.

<u>Carbulensis</u>, situated downstream from Córdoba. Carbula was an independent town when Pliny's source was written (<u>HN</u> 3.3.10), and coins from the first century B.C. are extant. It looks as if the town lost its independent status and was attached to Córdoba as a <u>pagus</u>; certainly Córdoba is the nearest town of any size, and a <u>pagus</u> could not be independent. Perhaps a similar fate befell Ategua. No pagus Ateguensis is attested, but, as discussed above, its decay during the Empire suggests annexation to Córdoba and extinction as an independent town. In these two instances at least, Córdoba may have had large outlying areas to administer. The usual method was with <u>praefecti</u>; for example the huge territory of Augusta Emerita was divided into <u>praefecturae</u> served by <u>praefecti</u>. But no such <u>praefecti</u> are recorded in the sources for Córdoba.[206]

The entire city territory was centuriated in antiquity; it was divided up for settlers and, later, for Augustan veterans. Perhaps it was surveyed in part on the same axes as the city; perhaps, as with at least part of the territory of Astigi, the axis was the <u>Via</u> <u>Augusta</u>. A patchwork of different orientations at different times, like that around Orange, is to be expected.[207] López Ontiveros states that he has found no remains of Roman centuriation around Córdoba.[208] However, Ponsich's investigations have turned up so many new indications of Roman activity along the Guadalquivir that it is certain that when his investigations extend to Córdoba's territory, evidence of centuriation will be found.[209]

ECONOMIC LIFE

Córdoba's wealth was based upon nearby mineral riches, the extent and fertility of its territory, and the Guadalquivir, which provided a trade link with the sea.[210] The most spectacular wealth came from the mines of the Sierra Morena. A succession of the wealthiest men in Spain came from Córdoba (for example, Clodius Turrinus and Annius Scapula). The last of these (unless Seneca, who at the height of his power was surely wealthier than any other Spaniard, is included) was one Sex. Marius who, according to Tacitus (<u>Ann.</u> 6.19), was forced to commit suicide on a trumped-up charge of incest with his daughter so that Tiberius could confiscate his vast holdings.[211] Marius' wealth came from mining, as that of Turrinus and Scapula may have. Marius owned all the mines of the Sierra Morena. The very name of the mountains may be derived from the ancient <u>mons Marianus</u>.[212]

The bronze produced from the copper of these mines was called aes <u>Marianum</u>, or aes <u>Cordubense</u> (Pliny <u>HN</u> 34.4). Its exact nature is unknown.[213]

Silver was of course a great source of wealth in ancient Iberia, especially in the northeastern portion of the Sierra Morena near Castulo. There does not seem to have been much, if any, silver in the hills near Córdoba, although men such as Sex. Marius could have owned mines near Castulo while maintaining residence at Córdoba.[214] Gold, however, was found in the vicinity of Córdoba, or so Silius Italicus (<u>Pun</u>. 3.401) attests.

Cordobans not only benefited from direct involvement in mining operations but also from commerce in metals. Córdoba was probably the major transhipment point for the copper of the central Sierra Morena, and mercury ore from the Sisapo (Almadén) mines may have passed through Córdoba as well.[215] Although much metal was exported, local industry utilized some of it. A Marcus Aerarius is mentioned as a freedman of the <u>socii aerariorum</u>, which indicates that there was a <u>collegium</u> of metal workers in the city.[216] C. Octavius Augusti libertus Felix and C. Octavius Primus, his freedman, are also <u>aerarii</u> at Córdoba (<u>CIL</u> 2.2238); here a whole <u>familia</u> is dedicated to metal smithing.[217] Artisans were on hand to fashion the metal in artistic ways; <u>CIL</u> 2.2242 records a <u>caelator anaglyptarius</u> named C. Valerius Diophanes and his apprentice C. Valerius Zephyrus. <u>Vasa anaglypta</u> are mentioned by Martial <u>Epig</u>. 4.39, and <u>caelatores</u> are known from Rome; they are metal sculptors.[218]

The good agricultural land around Córdoba, today called the <u>campiña</u>, was a second source of prosperity for the city.[219] The devastation of the Lusitanian wars and Caesarian civil wars (cf. <u>Bell</u>. <u>Alex</u>. 59.2) produced setbacks, but during the Empire peace brought good crops and return on investment. There is no ancient mention of wheat farming or viticulture, but it would be surprising if these staple crops of the Mediterranean area were not produced. Some of the amphorae shipped to Rome and attested in the sherds of the Monte Testaccio could have been filled with such products. There is evidence of irrigation in the area.[220] As Martial notes, the olive was cultivated. The poet also points out that Córdoba was famous for its wool (<u>Epig</u>. 12.63.1-5), so sheep raising was an important industry as well.[221] The wealth of many Cordobans was probably in agricultural estates, although no serious survey of the area has been made to determine the existence and distribution of villas, rural settlement patterns, and so on.

A <u>dispensator</u> is attested at <u>CIL</u> 2.2234, and he may have been a supervisor of a country estate.[222]

Commerce in general added to Córdoba's well-being. The town was located at the last point on the Guadalquivir that could be reached by small freight ships; transhipment was presumably necessary at Hispalis or some other down-stream town for goods being transported by sea to and from distant ports. The Senecan epigram <u>ad patriam suam</u> mentions the importance of Córdoba's sea link. The large number of Cordoban amphorae discovered at Monte Testaccio bear witness to export.[223] Remains of a dock complex, apparently built to facilitate the transport of goods on the Baetis, have been discovered along the river. At such docks the imperial tax men cleared goods and, when appropriate, assessed duties, for Córdoba was an official export point for the area.[224] <u>Mercatores</u> not only organized the export of local produce but also supplied many goods. However, only one kind of imported item, a-part from ceramics, is attested: the magnificent sarcophagi found in the city were imported from Rome in the fourth century A.D., although workers in marble lived in Córdoba itself.[225]

Numerous professional groups and individuals were active in the economic life of the city. The <u>aerarii</u> have already been mentioned. The only other <u>collegium</u> is that of the <u>fabri</u> <u>subitani</u>, who appear to be a construction fraternity.[226] We also hear of a broker (<u>coactor</u>), a <u>grammaticus</u> <u>Graecus</u>, an <u>aurifex</u>, a dyer (<u>purpurarius</u>), three doctors (one of whom was an offi-cial town physician), a seamstress, a clothing dealer (<u>vestiarius</u>), and on a less prestigious level, a doorman (<u>ostiarius</u>), and a <u>musicarius</u>.[227]

Little mention is made of industry in the city. The metal workers and the contractors plied their trades as noted above, and to judge from local imitations of Arretine ware found in the Almodóvar cemetery to the west of the city, the cheap wares, and the amphorae exported in such great numbers, there must have been a local pottery industry as well.[228] Beyond this the evidence does not go.

SOCIAL LIFE

As in every ancient city, life in Córdoba was divided along class lines. At the top were the men who had achieved imperial positions--the senators and equestrians who generally lived in Rome or Italy, although of course some remained in their <u>patria</u>. Locally the decurions, the local senators, formed an elite led by men who had achieved the post of <u>duovir</u> or <u>duovir</u>

quinquennalis. Most of these men must have possessed the equestrian census, and many possessed the equus publicus, a sign of membership in the official equestrian class, as well. Freeborn artisans and merchants, freedmen, poor ingenui, and slaves made up the rest of the population, along with an admixture of foreigners visiting or working in the city. Most of these men (and even more of the women) remain anonymous, but in some instances the sources allow a glimpse of the members of the various segments of Cordoban society.

At the highest level, Córdoba provided a number of senators during the first and early second centuries A.D. The first family to reach the consulate was that of the Senecae. The elder Annaeus Seneca, who died in A.D. 39 or 40, had been an equestrian (Tacitus Ann. 14.53). Two of his sons advanced to the senatorial order and reached the consulship, although only as suffecti. The eldest son, L. Annaeus Novatus, later known by his adoptive name L. Junius Annaeus Gallio, was suffect consul in the mid-50s A.D., perhaps in 54.[229] The middle son, the philosopher-politician-author L. Annaeus Seneca, began public life as an equestrian like his father (Tacitus Ann. 14.53) but then followed a senatorial cursus culminating in a suffect consulship in A.D. 56. A son of the third son, Annaeus Mela (i.e., Seneca the Elder's grandson), was the poet Lucan who, along with his uncles, died in the aftermath of the Pisonian conspiracy of A.D. 65; he had advanced only to the quaestorship.[230]

The Aponii may have been another senatorial family from Córdoba. C. Dillius Aponianus, honored at Córdoba (AE 1932.78), was consul between A.D. 71 and 73; he was related to C. Dillius Vocula, praetor before A.D. 69, who was murdered in A.D. 70. Syme has suggested that M. Aponius Saturninus, proconsul of Asia in A.D. 73/74, was also related to Aponianus. A suffect consul of A.D. 119 also bears Aponianus as a cognomen. Perhaps A. Platorius A.f. Nepos Aponianus Italicus Mamilianus C. Licinius Pollio was from Córdoba, although Italica is also likely; he may have had ancestors from both towns. Q. Aponius was an equestrian Pompeian during the revolt in 46 B.C. (Dio 43.29.3). His name is linked to that of Annius Scapula as a leader in the action. Scapula was a Cordoban; perhaps Aponius was as well and, like the elder Seneca, was the equestrian founder of a senatorial family.[231]

Other senators possibly from Córdoba are attested. Castillo relates Marius Priscus, a suffect consul in the mid-80s, to the family of mining mogul Sex. Marius, killed by Tiberius.[232] L. Antistius Rusticus, consul

suffectus in A.D. 90, may be the son of a duovir L. Antistius Rusticus,
attested at Córdoba (CIL 2.2242); his family would then be Cordoban.[233]
L. Dasumius Hadrianus, if he is the testator of the famous testamentum
Dasumii, was a Cordoban; his suffect consulship fell in A.D. 93.[234] Another inscription (CIL 2.5522) records a IIIvir capitalis, and so a senator, who was honored by Córdoba and was presumably a native son--C. Annius
C.f. Lepidus Marcellus. Nothing more is known of his career, but he may
be related to Annius Verus, the grandfather of Marcus Aurelius, and to Annius Scapula, the equestrian Pompeian of 46 B.C.[235] Finally, Wiegels argues plausibly for identification of [Ca]ssius Agrippa, proconsul in Baetica and suffect consul in A.D. 130, as a Cordoban.[236]

The equestrians attested from Córdoba are fewer even than the senators.
In the late Republic, Annius Scapula, Q. Aponius (if he is from Córdoba)
(Dio 43.29.3), and perhaps Clodius Turrinus[237] might qualify as equestrians.
The family of the Senecae was of that order; the father, L. (?)Annaeus
Seneca was certainly an equestrian. Annaeus Mela (who managed imperial
estates) remained in that station, unlike his brothers; he married Acilia,
daughter of Acilius Lucanus, a local orator, lawyer, and probably an equestrian too.[238] P. Postumius Acilianus, who rose to the rank of procurator
Syriae under Trajan, may be a descendant of Acilius.[239] Perhaps Sex. Marius
was equestrian as well.[240] There must have been others, but they go
unrecorded.

Three other Cordobans make brief entrances into history during the
early years of the Empire. Aemilius Aelianus, a friend of the emperor Augustus, provided Suetonius (Div. Aug. 51.2) with an anecdote. Calpurnius
Salvianus was the accuser of Sex. Marius before Tiberius (Tacitus Ann.
4.36). Aemilius Regulus headed an abortive plot against Caligula (Josephus
AJ 19.17.19). The status of these men is unknown. Presumably they were
at least equestrians and possibly senators.[241]

The careers of senators and important equestrians, in Spain at least,
never included local offices. The cursus were entirely distinct, although
in some cases a local magistrate might subsequently advance to minor equestrian posts. So the sort of men noted above never deigned to hold local
office. Local positions were filled by the viri principales. Very occasionally a man might take up a local career after service in the lowest
equestrian offices (such a man is L. Manlius Bocchus, CIL 2.2225), but generally the viri principales did not leave home. The names of such men have

been preserved in a fair number of inscriptions. The duoviri and aediles
are mentioned above; the provincial priests are given below. The complete
lack of data on their general activities should not cloud the fact that
these men were the powers in Córdoba. The senators and equestrians were
likely to be in Rome and Italy, but these men remained behind, holding office, attending senate meetings, and basking in the prestige their pre-
eminence gave them among their fellow Cordobans. Such a career could be
sneered at from Italy, but it must have had many satisfactions until the
impoverishment of city life in general made the burdens of office holding
outweigh the rewards.[242]

The freemen of lesser social standing are present in Cordoban epigraphy, but they tell little of their lives. Some men, such as M. Fabius
and the two Valerii, were merchants. The livelihood of most escapes us.
It is mostly the freedmen, to judge by their names, who record themselves
as artisans and "service" people. It is doubtful that the city did much
for the free middle and lower classes. Thouvenot's suggestion that the
town employed a medicus to look after the poor is unlikely to be
correct.[243]

There were both private and public slaves in the city.[244] The public
slaves are attested in Republican times (Bell. Hisp. 34.2), and during the
Empire they formed a burial club (CIL 2.2229). These slaves performed the
daily clerking and administrative tasks in the city, as well as other,
dirtier chores. The private slaves performed the same sort of tasks for
their masters, but their lives are generally unrecorded.

In Córdoba a fair number of foreigners either passed through or resided permanently (see Map 6). Semites are represented by a Thaddeus who
was a Jew--one of only two attested in Baetica.[245] Syrians are in evidence
as well, especially attested by a dedication to Elagabalus.[246] Greeks were
there, but as slaves, freedmen, and temporary residents for the most part;
the efforts of Del Río Oliete, Santos Yanguas, and others to see a significant Greek substratum in the population of Baetica are methodologically
unsound.[247] Men from elsewhere in Spain and from the Roman West appear--
for example, L. Manlius Bocchus (CIL 2.2225), who served in an army post
and then settled in the city, C. Valerius Avitus, the caelator anaglyp-
tarius (CIL 2.2243), and C. Olynthius from Uxama (underline{AE} 1915.12). Gladiatorial shows brought in Germans and Gauls. Official duties as flamen
provinciae Baeticae brought men from nearby towns such as Iporca and

Ilurco. Some men came from the imperial capital--for example, an L.
Salvi[...] Sedatus and a marmorarius, P. Publicius, who was a devotee of
the Great Mother.[248]

Conversely, Cordobans often settled or sojourned away from home.
Twenty-four persons who either certainly or at least probably did so are
attested epigraphically. Over half (thirteen) never got far from the city,
but of the others some ended up in Rome, one as a merchant in Narbo, and
others on army service in some distant land (Albulae in Mauritania Caesari-
ensis, Moguntiacum, Deva, Volubilis, Colonia Agrippinensis) (see Map 7).
Most dedications are epitaphs, and these persons generally did not return
to their native town. From these inscriptions one thing is clear: average
Cordobans did not go far from their town unless compelled to do so by army
service.

Little can be said concerning the entertainment of the people of Córdoba. The gladiatorial school, apparently situated in the west of the
town, is the best attested outside Italy. In recent years a whole series
of sepulchral inscriptions have been found in the cemetery that existed
just outside the ancient city, along the modern road to Almodóvar del Río,
downstream from Córdoba. Marcos has collected and discussed these inscriptions. The results of his studies and those of others show how extensive
the ludus must have been. Thirteen gladiators are so far attested, and
the concentration of their graves may indicate a special area for burial
of gladiators, although other types of graves occur there as well. It is
not clear whether the fighters were permanent residents of a ludus in Córdoba or were members of a traveling troupe; Marcos opts for the latter.
The inscriptions give a rare glimpse of the world of provincial gladiatorial
activity.[249]

Other entertainments are not attested. Even the location of the theater
and amphitheater is uncertain. The Cordobans must have had their public
feasts and festivals, but nothing specific can be said.

Similarly, little can be said about daily life and manners. A solitary
notice has survived about the customs of the Cordobans, assuredly in most
aspects much like the customs all over the western Empire. Griffin sees
evidence in the Senecan fragment 88 of an antiquus rigor characteristic of
provincial life in Spain in general, but especially in Córdoba.[250] This
fragment speaks of marriage customs.

Map 6. Non-Cordobans attested at Córdoba. (See legend)

Map 7. Cordobans
attested away from
Córdoba. (See legend)

LEGEND: MAP 6

Non-Cordobans attested at Córdoba

Modern names of towns are in parentheses.

Celti (Peñaflor)	M. Fabius Basileus	CIL 2.2221
Ucubi (Espejo)	T. Iulius T.f. ...	CIL 2.2223
Arva (Alcolea del Río)	L. Iulius M.f. Qui. Saxio	CIL 2.2245
Tucci (Martos)	Valeria C.f. Paetina	CIL 2.3278
Lacimurga	Norbana Q.f. Quintilla	CIL 2.5068
Uxama (Burgo de Osma)	C. Olynthius Acconis f.	AE 1915.12
Iporca (Constantina)	C. Antonius -.f. Gal. Seranus	AE 1971.183
Ilurco	L. Cominius L.f. Gal. Iulianus	HAE 2091
Rome	L. Salvi[...] Sedatus	HAE 1861
	P. Publicius Fortunatus	MMAP 1958-61 p. 29

Gladiators (not shown on map) are attested from:

Germania	Ingenuus	HAE 323
	Probus	AE 1971.179
Greece	Cerinius	HAE 1406
	Aristobulus	Corduba 1 (1976) p. 15
Gaul	Alipus	HAE 1408
Spain	[...]	HAE 1833
Syria	Ampliatus	Corduba 1 (1976) p. 15
Alexandria	Faustus	HAE 324
Placentia	Amandus	HAE 325

LEGEND: MAP 7

Cordobans attested away from Córdoba

Modern names of towns are in parentheses.

1.	Moguntiacum (Mainz)	M. Lutatius M.f. Ser. Albanus	CIL 13.6869
2.	Colonia Agrippinensis	Q. Licinius Q.f. Ser. Rusticus	AE 1974.452
3.	Hispalis (Seville)	L. Licinius L.l. Cogitans	CIL 2.1201
		Q. Fabius Q.f. Qui. Fabianus	CIL 2.1200
4.	Roma (Rome)	L. Dasumius Hadrianus (?)	CIL 6.10229
		C. Iunius Celadus	CIL 6.20768
		Baebia Venusta	CIL 6.34664
		L. Manlius A.f. Cor. Canus	CIL 6.3895
5.	Narbo (Narbonne)	M. Fabius M.M.M.l. Gi[...]	AE 1916.41
6.	Deva (Chester)	L. Antestius L.f. Ser. Sabinus	EE 9.1075
7.	Obulco (Porcuna)	-f. Pyramus	CIL 2.2133
8.	Castulo (Cazlona)	[...] L.f. Optata	CIL 2.3272
9.	Aurgi (Jaén)	Q. Annius Gallus	CIL 2.3358
10.	Singilia (near Antequera)	C. Sempronius C.l. Nigellio	CIL 2.2026
11.	Tucci (Martos)	Aurelia Leucothoe	CIL 2.1619
12.	Priego	L. Messius Rufinus	CIL 2.1637
13.	Acinippo (Ronda la Vieja)	M. Iunius L.f.L.n. Gal. Terentianus Servilius Sabinus	CIL 2.1347 add.
14.	Axati (Lora del Río)	L. Lucretius Severus	CIL 2.1055
15.	Ostippo (Estepa)	Elia Memmesis	Est. Gien. 1976 p. 85
16.	Iponuba	Vibia Crocale	CIL 2.1600
17.	Torremilano	P. Frontinius Sciscola	CIL 2.2348
18.	Albulae	[...]	CIL 8.21666
19.	Volubilis	Valeria Bastula	AE 1951.46

> Cordubenses nostri, ut maxime laudarunt nuptias, ita et qui sine
> his convenissent, excluserunt cretione hereditatum, et iam pactam
> ne osculo quidem nisi Cereri fecissent et hymnos cecinissent, at-
> tingi voluerunt. Si quis osculo solo parentibus aut vicinis non
> adhibitis attigisset, huic abducendae quidem sponsae ius erat,
> ita tamen, ut tertia parte bonorum sobolem suam parens, si vel-
> let, multaret.

It is impossible to say whether this notice has more than antiquarian interest; at least it preserves for us a glimpse of Cordoban everyday life.

Finally, mention must be made of life-span statistics for Córdoba.
Such figures have been assembled for samples of many populations. The
results of a complilation of the ninety-seven attested ages in Cordoban
epigraphy are shown (see Graph). However, these figures are presented
more for possible use by others than as valid reflection of Cordoban
longevity. It is probably impossible to draw valid conclusions from the
sort of sample that Cordoban epigraphy provides.[251]

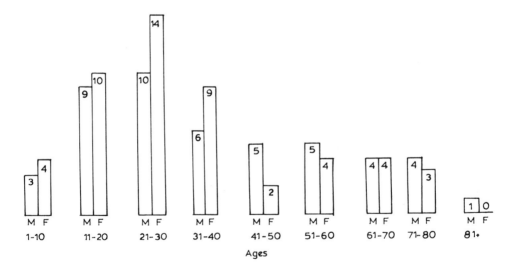

Graph: Life spans recorded on Cordoban inscriptions.

     (M = Male; F = Female)

RELIGIOUS LIFE

A wide spectrum of religious activity occurred at Córdoba. The old
Roman gods are represented by dedications to Silvanus and to Minerva;
genii of various sorts are also noted. Blanco relates these "old-time"
deities to the archaic period of Córdoba's foundation; too little is known
of religious habits to affirm or deny this theory.[252] A Greek deity is
honored, as are two commonly worshiped powers, Fortuna and Nemesis.[253]
The eastern religions that became popular in the Empire are also at Córdoba. The Greek inscription honoring Elagabalus and other Syrian gods is
a case in point, and sculptural and epigraphic evidence indicates that
Mithra was worshiped in the city. Two declarations that taurobolia
had been performed, once at the order of the Mother of the Gods and once
for the health of the Emperor Severus Alexander, were set up by Publicius
Fortunatus in A.D. 234 and 238. This Fortunatus was a freedman of the
province, a marble sculptor, and a native of Rome.[254]

Both folk religion--worship of local gods, belief in spirits of the
underworld, use of magic--and the exotic cults have left their mark in
Cordoban epigraphy. The dedication to Volturnus is exemplary of the worship of the local deities (CIL 2.2196); Volturnus was the name of the
sweltering, dust-bringing southeast wind that blew up from the Sahara and
scorched everything in its path. Columella 5.5.15 mentions this August
wind and notes that his uncle in Baetica used to shelter his vines with
palm mats to protect them. Someone in Córdoba wanted to placate this
power, or perhaps, since the inscription is in the nominative, a statue
was erected to the wind god. Could it have been a directional sign of a
monumental "compass"? In other dedications a fons sacer is mentioned, and
the powers of the underworld are alluded to twice. Recently an interesting
magic text has also come to light.[255]

On the official level, there is more evidence of religious activity.
Besides a bland notice of a dedication by the colony (CIL 2.2218), there
are many inscriptions naming local priests. In towns of the Empire some
combination of augures, pontifices, sacerdotes, and flamines appears. At
Córdoba no augurs appear, a fairly common situation; for although the lex
Ursonensis 67 would lead us to suppose that every colony had augurs, relatively few are attested. Only three appear in Spain.[256] Pontifices,
priests not for a particular cult but for religious observances in general,
do occur, but the inscriptions shed no light on their activities at

Córdoba.[257] The title _sacerdos_ is by its nature vague; frequently it was
held by a woman, the female equivalent of a _pontifex_.[258] Two _sacerdotes_
appear at Córdoba, one apparently for the cult of Roma (_CIL_ 2.2228), the
other mentioned only in general terms (_CIL_ 2.3278); both are women. The
flamens left the most evidence at Córdoba; four men and a woman are attested. The flamens were usually associated with the local imperial cult.
One at Córdoba (_CIL_ 2.2233), an L. Bruttius Barga Firmus, made a dedication
to Mercurius Augustus. They seem to have been elected and could serve
annual (as most other priests) or lifelong tenures (_flamen perpetuus_);
lifelong tenure seems to have been more normal. Although the imperial cult
languished somewhat on the provincial level in Baetica, it remained popular
on the local level, at least among the oligarchs who gained prestige from
holding its priesthood. Two men, perhaps duovirs, set up a dedication to
Nemesis as vowed, after they successfully held a flaminate.[259]

A _cursus_ as such does not seem to have existed for the priesthoods.
The inscriptions show every possible sequence of office, and often the
priesthoods are grouped apart at the beginning or end of a _cursus_, which
prevents speculation on their relationship to various other local offices.
The priesthoods were seen as concomitants of "civil" office, but without a
pecking order; even the flaminate, which has often been held to be more
prestigious than the other priesthoods, was not necessarily so.[260]

These priesthoods were, of course, reserved for the ruling oligarchy.
For the freedman class a special priesthood existed--the _VIviri Augustales_,
a board of six men in charge of rites for the Emperor. Only one _sevir_
is attested at Córdoba, a man who subsequently moved to Anticaria (_CIL_
2.2026). _CIL_ 2.2233 records what seems to be a _magister Larum_. The sevirs
were also _magistri Larum Augusti_, but whether this man himself was a sevir
cannot be determined.[261] Perhaps the puzzling inscription with PA AUGUSTALIS
also has something to do with the college.[262] Still lower down the social
scale, a _sacerdos familiae publicae_ appears at _CIL_ 2.2229. As mentioned
previously, the public slaves of the city were organized into a burial club,
complete with _magistri_ and priests. A similar religious function of an
association may be reflected in the dedication to a genius which is recorded on an unpublished inscription.[263]

Córdoba, as the provincial capital, was the site of the activities of
the provincial imperial cult. Of the provincial flamens recorded, only
three are from Córdoba itself: L. Junius Gallus Mummianus (_ILS_ 6905 =

CIL 2.2224), L. Junius Paulinus (ILS 5079 = CIL 2.5523), and M. Helvius Rufus.[264] The first two men had previously been duovirs in Córdoba. Paulinus had been pontifex and flamen perpetuus as well. No other offices are recorded for Rufus. The other flamens recorded at Córdoba are from inconsequential towns in the outlying areas, evidence that, although important locals may have held the position from time to time, the flaminate may not have been as intrinsically prestigious as some have thought.[265]

The inscriptions at Córdoba are not as extensive as those at other provincial capitals such as Tarraco, but even with its more limited sample, the religious activities of various segments of Cordoban society, from the servi publici to the provincial flamens, are fairly well represented.

INTELLECTUAL LIFE

Córdoba, more than any other Latin city of the West, outside Italy, had a long and flourishing intellectual and artistic tradition. It produced literati in abundance--from the poets who performed for Metellus Pius to the Augustans of the time of the elder Seneca and the masters of the Silver Age, Seneca the Younger and Lucan. By the first century B.C. Suetonius (Gramm. 3) says that the study of literature was widespread in the provinces. When Seneca the Elder was at school in Córdoba there were about two hundred other students.[266] One of these was M. Porcius Latro, an orator admired by Ovid (Seneca Contr. 2.2.8) who made a good career in Rome; Statorius Victor, a fellow Cordoban and contemporary fabulist, may have been another.[267] After the first century A.D. the famous Cordobans were quite removed from their provincial origins, but the Cordoban origins of Seneca, Lucan, and Mela deserve mention. Another Cordoban, unnamed, was a poet contemporary with Martial, that Spanish poet from Bilbilis who possibly visited Córdoba himself. What passed for culture certainly continued alive and well at Córdoba in the first centuries of the Empire. That only one grammaticus Graecus is attested, merely indicates that more extensive training must have been available locally, although Rome of course was the only goal of a really serious intellectual.[268] The sculptural and architectural remains of the city also indicate that the artictic sense of the leading citizens was well developed. More than most provincial cities, Córdoba must have provided a good intellectual environment for those unable or unwilling to go to Rome.

CORDOBA AS A PROVINCIAL CAPITAL

Although "capital" is too strong a term to use, Córdoba was from the
very earliest days of its existence an administrative center of the further Spanish province. In Augustan times, perhaps after the creation of
the citizen colony, it is legitimate to speak of Córdoba as the official
capital of the province of Baetica. The reorganization of the Spanish provinces and the transfer of Baetica to the control of the Senate occurred
at this same time, about 16-13 B.C.[269] The province was divided into judicial districts called conventus. Córdoba was the assize seat of one of
these four districts.[270] The proconsular governor, a man of praetorian
rank, resided in Córdoba, and perhaps a lieutenant was stationed at Hispalis (Seville).[271] A fair number of provincial proconsuls are known, but
only one is epigraphically attested from the principate in the city, the
proconsul Arrian.[272] Besides a quaestor L. Axius Naso, no other senatorial
provincial official is recorded locally.[273] There must have been many
equestrian officials in the city. Recorded are a procurator provinciae
Baeticae, M. Cassius Agrippa, and a vilicus arcarius of the procurator ad
XX hereditatem in charge of collecting the inheritance tax.[274] In an unpublished inscription a tabellarius provinciae Baeticae, an imperial freedman, is recorded; he was involved in the work of the cursus publicus.[275]
There does not seem to have been a military force stationed at Córdoba. A
praefectus orae maritimae appears in a Cordoban inscription (CIL 2.2224),
but this inscription is no evidence that the coastal police force had a de-
tachment or headquarters in the city.[276] In a pacified province, the army
was usually not much in evidence.

As the provincial capital, Córdoba was the site of the provincial assembly, a body which met regularly to offer encomia to the Emperors, to
carry on the provincial imperial cult, and occasionally to complain to Rome
about the corruption and cruelty of various governors.[277] Apart from the
selection of provincial flamens, no activity of the assembly is locally recorded, not even the erection of a statue to an Emperor.[278]

4

ARCHAEOLOGY OF THE CITY

THE WALLS

Córdoba possessed an extensive wall. Its extent during the Empire can be accurately described, for a few actual remains have been discovered and the circuit of the Arab "Al-Medina" and "Villa" followed the Roman structure (see Map 8).[279]

On the north, the wall follows the Avenida del Generalísimo. Along this expanse, Sánchez de Feria reported remains in the Huerta de la Regina, especially in the Barrios de los Tejadores and de la Merced (A, B on Map 8).[280] On the east, the wall ran from the Puerta del Rincón (modern Plaza Ruiz Alda) to Cruz del Rastro at the river's edge, via the streets Alfaros, Calvo Sotelo, Diario de Córdoba, and San Fernando, popularly called "de la Feria." Along this stretch Santos Jener in 1948 identified a tower north of the calle Portillo (E), and reported remains near the Plaza San Salvador (F) and in front of the Santa Marta church (G).[281] On the south, the wall extended along the Guadalquivir; no sure remains are reported.[282] To the west, the wall followed the Huerta del Rey, then the Paseo del General Primo de Rivera and the Jardines de la Victoria, back to the Avenida del Generalísimo.

The wall was not always so large. Although Sentenach is certainly wrong to say that the southern portion is not Roman at all but Arabic, this segment is an addition after the wall of the Marcellan colony was built.[283] The remains of a wall that originally closed the town on the south have been identified. This wall, also attested in Arab times and elucidated by a recently discovered inscription mentioning a vicus Hispanus shows remnants in the gardens of the Colegio de Santa Victoria (C) and in the patio of the Museo Arqueológico (D).[284] The exact course of the wall cannot be traced, but the modern streets Cuesta Santa Ana, Pineda Saravia, and Naranjo fall along its path.

The history of the wall is not entirely clear. There can be little
doubt that, given the city's location, the site was walled from the beginning. Viriathus attacked the walls in the second century B.C., and they
played a part in events of 49 B.C. In 45 B.C. Caesar was again before the
walls (Bell. Hisp. 5). It is possible that he took up a position between
them and the river, which would prove that the lower wall was not yet built,
but despite Sentenach, it appears more likely that Caesar camped on the far
side of the Guadalquivir in order to cut off Cn. Pompey's coming to the aid
of his borther Sextus in Córdoba.[285] It does seem likely that Córdoba,
like Valentia, was originally built a short distance, about 400-600 meters,
away from the river; Caesar does seem to camp between the bridge and the
wall later in the campaign of 45 B.C. (Bell. Hisp. 33.1-2). The extension
of the wall to the river is attributable to Augustus' time on the occasion
of the colonial grant, when new territory was added; a new tribe was designated for the area, and a new orientation of buildings shows that a new
survey was carried out. Though unfortunately no direct archaeological
evidence confirms this hypothesis, it does explain the data that we
possess.[286]

TOWN PLAN

The old Marcellan town fits nicely on a typical grid pattern, whether
or not this grid actually goes back to Marcellus' time. The main gates,
in exactly the same location as those of the Arab city, were at the Puerta
de Gallegos (Bab-Liũn, the Lion Gate), Puerta de Osario (Bab-Arrumia, the
Gate of the Romans, i.e., Christians), Puerta del Rincón (Bab-Tolaitola,
i.e., the Gate of Toledo), Puerta de Hierro (Bab-el Hadid), and a gate of
unknown name at the Plaza Santa Ana.[287] The grid lay according to these
gates, with the axes running from the Puerta Osario to "Santa Ana" and from
the Puerta Gallego to the Puerta de Hierro (see Map 8). The orientation
of the grid can still be seen in some of the streets and lanes of Córdoba
and in the excavated remains in the calle Cruz Conde.[288]

The new town to the south lies on a different axis. The episcopal pal-
ace--formerly the Arab alcázar, the Visigothic ducal palace, and a Roman
structure--lies according to the new axis. In this section of the modern
city also, small lanes still reflect the grid pattern.[289] The gates in
this part of the town are the Puerta Piscatoria (Algeciras), the Puerta de
la Estatua (Bab-es-sura), so named from the lion statue over the gateway

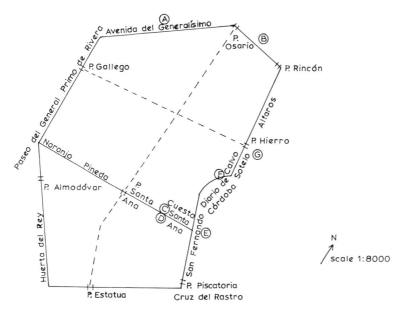

Map 8. Córdoba's wall and modern streets.
(Broken lines show axes of town plan)

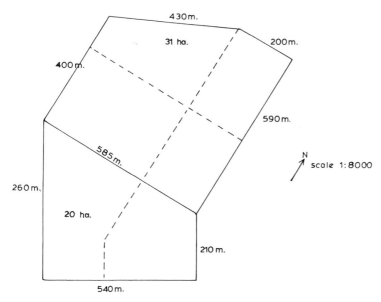

Map 9. Schematic sketch of Roman Córdoba.

to the stone bridge, and the Puerta de Almodóvar (Bab-Batalios).[290] The
main street ran from the Plaza Santa Ana to the bridge at the Puerta de la
Estatua.

The town itself was divided into vici, or neighborhood districts. A
vicus forensis, near the forum, and a vicus Hispanus, near the gate at the
Plaza Santa Ana (?), are epigraphically attested. Other vici are difficult
to identify; a vicus capite canteri probably refers to a vicus in Rome, not
in Córdoba, and the vicus turris was probably outside the walls.[291]

Córdoba was not unusually large. It is not surprising that it was a
larger than average Augustan colony, for a town existed at the site before
an Augustan colony was added. The measurements of the schematic town
plan (Map 9) show the size of the Marcellan colony as about thirty-one
hectares (76 acres) and that of the Augustan addition as about twenty
hectares (49 acres). The total size would be about fifty-one hectares
(125 acres). This is smaller than Tarraco in the Empire but still a
respectable size.[292]

STRUCTURES INSIDE THE CITY WALLS

Córdoba's forum, attested as early as the late second century B.C.
(Cicero Verr. 4.56), eluded secure identification for centuries. "Viejos
escritores cordobeses" had located it near the San Miguel church, and others
had put it at the Plaza de las Tendillas (formerly the Plaza de José Antonio
Primo de Rivera).[293] Now, however, thanks to the work of Santos Jener,
Vicent, and Marcos, there remains little doubt that the forum was in the
area around the modern streets Cruz Conde, Ramírez de Arellano, Góngora,
and Cabrera. Pavements of the forum were first found here in 1929, and new
discoveries were made in 1935, 1947, and in the 1970s. A large plaza and
monumental elements were identified; footing holes showed a pavement bor-
dered by a portico. In addition, the forenses inscription was found near
here at the corner of Góngora and Alvaro. Santos Jener found Campanian
pottery in a well below the forum; on this basis he dated the forum to Marcellus. Marcos speaks of a "late Republican" forum. Given the scarcity
of Republican architecture in the West, perhaps caution is in order in
dating this complex.[294]

A number of buildings should be associated with the forum complex, most
notably a basilica (attested in 48 B.C. by Bell. Alex. 52.2), a temple,
and a curia.[295] The temple is unrecorded. Wiseman locates the basilica

in the Plaza de las Tendillas, but he has no evidence. The curia has perhaps been identified on the site of the Colegio de la Asunción, where
Santos Jener and earlier writers report monumental columns, marble stairs,
and other remains.[296] So far, however, no certain connection with the curia
building has been made.

The forum was the center of public life, but there must have been other
markets. There is no continuity from ancient to modern times to help in
location of these. There is little evidence for Arab use of present market
location, much less Roman. The exception is the Plaza de la Corredera,
outside the walls to the east (12 on Map 10).[297] This marketplace goes
back at least to Arab times, but during Roman times it was a complex of
urban villas (see below).[298] Sánchez de Feria placed the port market complex (forum censorium) in the Huerta del Alcázar, on the basis of remains
of a large Roman building there. Santos Jener records a Roman wall forming
an angle with the north side of the Alcázar and then turned toward the interior of the edifice. He does not conjecture about the wall's purpose.
But at any rate some Roman buildings in this location are attested (3).[299]

Four baths may have been identified in Córdoba. Santos Jener sees bath
complexes both north (4) and south of the forum; in las Tendillas (José
Antonio) he reports capitals, walls, and foundations of a "notable monument"
(5). Azorín ascribes the remains of a large (9 m. x 10 m.) pool, pavement,
arches, and galleries found in the Plaza del Escudo and Plaza del Angel to
a bath complex (6). A lead water pipe leading here was found, as well as
a marble inscription that the author does not, unfortunately, publish.
Finally it can be noted that a dedication to Fortuna, a common subject of
commemoration at bath areas, was found in Santa Clara street. Santos Jener
also gives an inexact reference (without specifying a location) to "Republican baths" "semi-etrusco por sus decorados de barro cocido" that were perhaps destroyed by Caesar in the civil wars. Without more data it is impossible to evaluate this notice.[300]

There was evidently a complex of public buildings in the port area of
the city. Unpublished excavations in the Alcázar de los Reyes Cristianos
indicate an important building, perhaps part of the governor's administrative complex, praetorium (7)--although the residence of the governor was
presumably on the site of the later Visigothic ducal palace (47). As noted,
this whole waterfront area was busy with commerce and tax collection, and

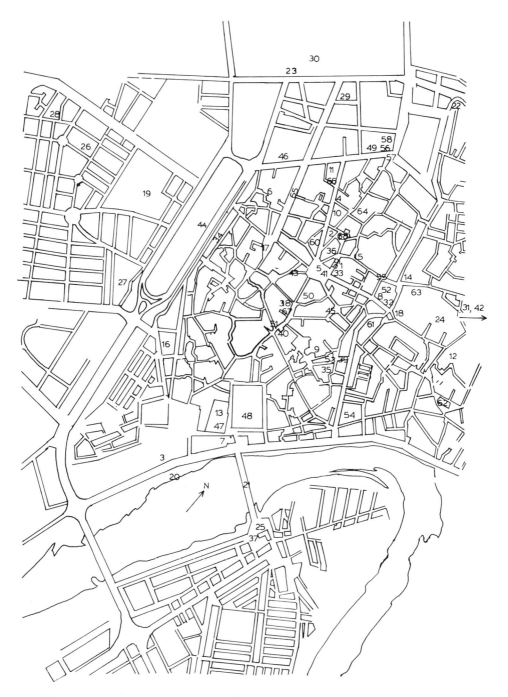

Map 10. Archaeological finds in Córdoba. (See legend)

LEGEND: MAP 10

Archaeological finds in Córdoba

Note: Many locations are approximate. Santos Jener 1955 p. 9 and p. 67
mentions a <u>Registro General</u> de <u>Hallazgos</u> <u>Arqueológicos</u> for Córdoba that
had 500 notations in 1951. I have been unable to locate and consult this
document.

1. Colegio de la Asunción	Marble steps: Tovar 1974 p. 90
2. Cruz Conde	Forum complex: Santos Jener 1955 pp. 98-102; 67; 1927.3 pp. 20-21
3. Huerta del Alcázar and Alcázar	column <u>in situ</u> at gateway; Roman wall in the area: Santos Jener 1927.3 p. 21
4. Cruz Conde	remains of bath complex: Santos Jener 1950 pp. 158-159; 1955 pp. 98-102
5. Plaza de las Tendillas (José Antonio)	capital, walls, foundations of a notable monument: bath: Santos Jener 1927.3 p. 19, cf. 1955 p. 72; Tovar 1974 p. 90
6. Plaza del Escudo	pool, pavement, arches, garlleries: Azorín 1923 pp. 89-91; Com. Mon. 1926.2 p.11
7. Ronda de Isasa	columns, pavement, etc., in patio of Christian Alcázar: Praetorium?: Blanco 1966.1 p. 24
8. Claudio Marcelo	temple: García y Bellido 1964
9. Plaza de Jerónimo Páez	steps in Museo Arqueológico patio
10. Cruz Conde 16	villa remains: Santos Jener 1946 p. 82
11. Cruz Conde 32	house remains: Santos Jener 1955 pp. 107-108
12. Plaza de la Corredera	villas: García y Bellido 1965 p. 184
13. Torrijos	portico with three bases <u>in situ</u>: possibly Syrian temple: Bosch Gimpera 1924 p. 220; Santos Jener 1952 p. 474
14. Ayuntamiento	house walls, mosaic, columns found near here: Fernández Chicarro 1953 p. 437
15. Conde de Torres Cabrera 1	column bases: Carbonell 1949 p. 87
16. Huerta del Rey	remains of aqueduct: Fernández Chicarro 1953 pp. 437-439
17. San Felipe	sewer: Com. Mon. <u>Anales</u> ... <u>Córdoba</u> 1926.2 p. 11
18. Joaquín Costa and Rodríguez Marín	steps: Santos Jener 1927.2 p.15, cf. 1955 p. 123
19. Avenida de Medina-Az-Zahra	remains of stadium?: Santos Jener 1955 p. 10
20. Ronda de Isasa	quay and 30 m. long structure: Tovar 1974 pp. 89-90 (citing Sánchez de Feria)
21. bridge over Guadalquivir	foundations of stone bridge: Torre 1922 pp. 95-96
22. north of the city	cemetery
23. Avenida de America	lead sarcophagus: Fernández Chicarro 1953 p. 439
24. east of the city	cemetery
25. south of the city	cemetery
26. Avenida de Medina-Az-Zahra	cemetery of northwest

27. Camino Viejo de Almodóvar   cemetery of southwest
28. Avenida Medina-Az-Zahra   large houses: Santol Jener 1955 p. 11
29. Pérez Galdós 4   capital, marble, paving, glass, ceramics: BRAH 80 (1921) p. 185

30. railroad station   roof tiles: Santos Jener 1927.3 p. 19
31. Muñices   roof tiles: Santos Jener 1927.3 p. 19
32. Claudio Marcelo   colossal marble statue: García y Bellido 1961.2 pp. 196-200

33. Plaza de las Tendillas   statue of Ceres: Ortí 1958 p. 40
34. Eduardo Dato   headless statue (Venus?): Santos Jener 1927.3 p. 21

35. Antonio del Castillo 1   half statue of marble (nymph?): Santos Jener 1927.2 p. 15

36. Plaza Bañuelos   mutilated marble statue of warrior: Santos Jener 1927.3 pp. 20-21

37. Campo de la Verdad   child's head of terra cotta: Santos Jener 1954.2 p. 298

38. Angel de Saavedra   marble Roman sculpture: Vicent 1973 p. 674

39. near "House of Seneca"   fountain sculpture: Santos Jener 1927.1 pp. 524-525

40. Angel de Saavedra   women's head of marble: Vicent 1973 pp. 674-675

41. Plaza de las Tendillas   bronze head of lion in Ibero-Roman style: Santos Jener 1927.4 p. 121

42. Plaza San Lorenzo   prow ornament: Blanco 1970 pp. 110-111
43. Sevilla   mosaic: Carbonell 1950 p. 90
44. Paseo de la Victoria   mosaic: Santos Jener 1927.2 pp. 13-14
   opus sectile: Vicent 1971 p. 174

45. Plaza de la Compañía   two mosaics: Com. Mon. Anales ... Córdoba 1926.1 p. 68 = Paraiso (Ornachuelo); Santos Jener 1955 p. 72
   opus sectile: Vicent 1971 pp. 171-173

46. Avenida del Generalísimo   Visigothic ducal palace; probably Roman governor's residence; cf. Castejón 1929 p. 259
47. Torrijos   Arab mosque; probably Roman temple

48. Cathedral
49. Avenida del Generalísimo   temple of Manes: Santos Jener 1955 p. 68; Jaén 1935 p. 39

50. Jesús y María   drum, capital, cornice: Santos Jener 1954.2 p. 297

51. Angel de Saavedra   columns of gray and pink granite: Vicent 1973 p. 675

52. Ayuntamiento   entranceway identified in foundations: Marcos 1977.2 p. 207

53. Ambrosio de Morales 7   traditional house of Senecas: Gálvez 1924 pp. 175-180; Blanco 1966.1 p. 18

54. San Fernando   aqueduct: Santos Jener 1955 pp. 124-125
55. Plaza San Salvador   steps of "amphitheater": Santos Jener 1950 p. 140

56. Avenida del Generalísimo   statue of Minerva: Espasa 1907 p. 591
57. Plaza de la Merced   mosaic in patio of the Hospicio: Santos Jener 1927.2 p. 13

58. Avenida del Generalísimo   crypt of Santo Eulalia in the Hospicio: Palol 1967 p. 134 n. 64

59. Diego de León   houses: Santos Jener 1955 p. 72
60. Manueles = ?Quero   bust of Commodus: Santos Jener 1955
                                        p. 72
61. Diario de Córdoba 19   graves: Santos Jener 1940 p. 438
62. Plaza de San Pedro   no buildings in Republican times; early
                                        imperial inscription: Marcos-Vicent-
                                        Costa Ramos 1977 pp. 199, 201
63. San Pablo   gateway of large blocks found next to
                                        temple in 1917: Marcos 1977.2 p. 205
64. Osario 1   Campanian pottery of Republican period
                                        but no evidence of structures until
                                        imperial times: Marcos 1977.3 p. 213
65. Gran Capitán   mosaics of house; Iberian or Ibero-Roman
                                        ceramics below with Campanian ware and
                                        a little sigillata: Marcos 1977.1
                                        p. 218
66. M. de Sandoval   Republican Campanian ware: Marcos
                                        1977.4
67. Angel de Saavedra   Naso inscription dedicated by vicus
                                        Hispanus: Vicent 1973 pp. 676-677;
                                        Knapp 1981
68. Plaza San Miguel   Naso inscription dedicated by vicus
                                        forensis: Contreras 1977 p. 392;
                                        Knapp 1981

was perhaps the site of the quaestorium and riverside forum. There is no
doubt that it was outside the walls in Roman times.[301]

Of temples, disappointingly little is known. Much useless speculation
has clouded the picture for centuries. The most persistent misapprehension
is that a temple of Janus existed where the cathedral/mosque now stands
(48).[302] As pointed out before, this mistake derives from a misunderstand-
ing of the milestones in the Patio de los Naranjos, in front of the cathedral
(CIL 2.4701, 4716); these milestones measure "ab Iano Augusto," an arch at
the border of Baetica and Tarraconensis. Janus Augustus has nothing to do
with a temple in Córdoba. Likewise the location of a "temple" to the Manes
on the Avenida del Generalísimo has no archaeological basis which I can
find (49).

On somewhat firmer ground rests speculation concerning other temples.
An inscription to various Syrian deities (AE 1924.14) can perhaps be related
to monumental remains nearby (13). The worship of the Magna Mater at Gran
Capitán and Góngora, attested by two inscriptions (CIL 2.5521; AEA 1968
pp. 93-95), points to a temple in the area. Nearby, an unpublished inscription from Plaza de los Doblas refers to Minerva and perhaps indicates her
temple there: a statue of the goddess is reported to have been found near
the modern hospicio (orphanage) in the vicinity.[303] Archaeological remains
raise the possibility of a temple to Hercules in the port complex: two
fragments of a frieze showing the labors of Hercules were found in the vicinity of the cathedral, and a statue of the demigod was found in the Alcázar. Some of the monumental remains in the area may belong to this
temple.[304] In the same area, a Roman temple must underlie the cathedral
(48), although as discussed above, a "temple" of Janus is unlikely. The
early Christian basilica of St. Vincent, intermediary between Roman temple
and Arab mosque, dates perhaps to the fifth century A.D.[305] Other remains,
even if of temples, are far too limited for conclusions to be reached
about them.[306]

By far the most spectacular archaeological discovery of recent years
in Córdoba is the excavation of the temple on calle Claudio Marcelo (8).
In 1955 Santos Jener reported the finds in the area (finds that had been
sporadically recorded for two hundred years and more); he related them to
a significant building but did not guess what it might have been.[307] García
y Bellido excavated the structure and concluded that the temple (for such
it turned out to be) was begun in A.D. 75-100 and finished under Nerva or

Trajan.[308] It is somewhat larger than the temple of Nîmes and is impressive
even in its present state of incomplete restoration. Perhaps it was dedicated to the imperial cult, although there is no direct evidence for this.
The time of construction would be right, for the imperial cult in Baetica
dates only from Flavian times. But a non liquet is in order.[309]

There must have been a theater in Córdoba, but its location remains
problematic. Amador de los Ríos placed it in the church of San Nicolás y
Felipe; others have supposed that the steps extant in the patio of the
Museo Arqueológico are part of the seating for this structure (9). De los
Ríos was apparently engaging in guesswork, and Marcos has cast doubt on
the "step" theory. The theater remains a mystery.[310]

Only a few urban villas have been discovered. There was a fine example
in the calle Cruz Conde (10), evidence of another in the same street (11),
of another near the town hall (Ayuntamiento) (14), and perhaps of another
in the calle Conde de Torres Cabrera (15). There is also the tradition
(from the thirteenth century) of the "house of Seneca" near the eastern
wall of the city (53): the likelihood that this really is the site of
Seneca's family town house is not great. Although the evidence for particular villas is slight, the distribution of the inscriptions helps to de-
fine the "residential" as opposed to the "public" areas of the city. The
official inscriptions--from dedication stones, statues, temples, etc.--
cluster as shown on Map 11. I suggest that the residential areas were the
"new town" south of the old wall, and the northeastern portion of the city.
Of course chance and the incidence of new building construction influence
the distribution of inscriptions, but over the centuries this distribution
has been maintained.

Water was a primary need of a city such as Córdoba. Remains of aqueducts
have been found in the Campo de la Verdad, across the bridge from the city,
along the eastern wall, and in the Huerta del Rey (16).[311] The water supply must have come from the Sierra Morena to the north and west of the city.
Another part of the water system, a sewer, was found in the calle San Felipe
in 1924 (17).

REMAINS OUTSIDE THE WALLS

Many of the most monumental structures of a Roman town were located
outside the walls. Córdoba's amphitheater, for example, has long been
placed at the Convent of San Pablo, just to the east of the city. Traces

of a building were found in 1730. More recently a series of steps was discovered (18) and remains were identified in the Plaza San Salvador (55).
Jaén and Santos Jener accept the location, and Wiseman (without citation!)
reports that bullfights were held there in Arab times. Marcos, in a vague
statement that "recientes exploraciones" have turned up new evidence,
questions the validity of the traditional location. He prefers a site to
the west of the city, where the gladiators were buried, but he can point
to no archaeological data to support his view. The amphitheater, like the
theater, remains unlocated.[312]

The port complex has already been alluded to. Market, temple, administration building--all were in the area where the Christian Alcázar and
the Alcázar gardens are now (3). Tovar in addition reports the quay and
a structure thirty meters long that were part of the port (20). To judge
from the amphorae from Córdoba in the Monte Testaccio in Rome, the port
did a thriving business.[313]

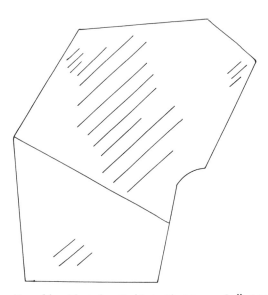

Map 11. Sketch of distribution of "official" inscriptions.

Close to the port was the stone bridge (21). Although the current superstructure is later, the foundation is Roman. L. Sáinz, the engineer who repaired the bridge in 1877, says that the Roman blocks at the foundation are like those in the foundations of the immediately adjacent wall.[314] There is no way to date the bridge archaeologically, and opinion is divided as to whether it is Republican or later.[315] Historical indications are that it was built by Caesar or later. In 48 B.C. (Bell. Alex. 59-60) there does not seem to have been a bridge over the Guadalquivir; if there had been Marcellus would not have had such a hard time getting back across the river after his engagement with Cassius Longinus. The lack of a bridge at that time is not surprising; from Córdoba to the sea there was no permanent bridge until the nineteenth century, except one built at Alameda del Obispo in A.D. 989 and later destroyed by a flood. The river is fordable in winter and presents even less of an obstacle in summer.[316] In 45 B.C., according to Bell Hisp. 5.1-5, Caesar built a bridge across the river and camped on the side away from Córdoba in order to cut off Cn. Pompey. The narrative implies that the bridge was near the town. According to Bell. Hisp. 33.1-2, Caesar crossed back over the bridge and camped between it and Córdoba; he was close enough to hear the roar of dissension inside the town. Therefore, the bridge as a wooden structure dates from Caesar's time. There is no way to say when it was rebuilt in stone.[317]

Along all major roads leading from Córdoba lay burial areas. For example, to the south of the city, across the river, the wealthy buried their own. To the east and north also there are signs of the tombs of the rich (25). Only to the west, along the "old road" to Almodóvar, are lower class tombs found in abundance; this location is also where the oldest graves have been uncovered. Here the burial area runs about a mile along the road and the gladiators' epitaphs have been found (27). Santos Jener made many discoveries here and in the burial area to the north near the Avenida de Medina-Az-Zahra (26). The northern burial area, which has produced the most interesting finds of recent years, follows the road leading from the Puerta Osario; the very name of that gate indicates the tradition of burial in the area (22). Finally, to the east from the Plaza del Salvador, another burial area has produced remains and inscriptions (24). Another large group of graves still farther to the east past the Arab Ajerquía quarter has been reported, but these reports are sketchy.[318]

For the living there were <u>villae</u> <u>urbanae</u> and <u>rusticae</u>. The most spectacular <u>villa</u> <u>urbana</u> yet discovered yielded the fine mosaics that are now
in the Christian Alcázar. Workmen in the Plaza de la Corredera (12) uncovered the pavings, and some were saved, although no systematic attempt
to explore the villa was possible. Other houses have been found in the
same area (31). The mosaics, at la Corredera at least, seem to date from
the second century A.D. To the north of the city, some remains (a capital,
marble paving, glass, ceramics) have been found at Pérez Galdós 4 (29),
and in the same area, roof tiles were discovered as the train station was
being built (30). To the west of the city there are remains of houses
among the graves; for example, a large house existed at Diego Serrano and
Palma Carpio (28). On the southwestern side of Córdoba, Castejón identified the palace where the tree planted by Caesar grew (Martial Epig. 9.62)
with the "Bala Moguit" or palace of "Mogueit el Rumi" in the gardens of
the Christian Alcázar. Today a plane tree, symbolic of Martial's <u>platanus</u>,
grows in a small commemorative plaza in the modern gardens. The identification nevertheless seems pure guesswork.[319]

Further from the city walls the countryside must have been dotted with
<u>villae</u> <u>rusticae</u>. An archaeological survey of the area is very much needed.
As of now only four country homes have come to my attention. Three kilometers north of the city, in the Cortijo del Alcaide, Vicent reports a
find; eleven kilometers east, in Alcolea, García y Bellido notes another;
at El Encinarejo de los Frailes (Villarrubia), Santos Jener records a third;
Bonsor gives the fourth at Alameda del Obispo. The remains at Venta de
Pedroches, two kilometers north of Córdoba, may be a fifth villa, but the
statue of Ceres and Proserpina, plus the altar found there, suggest a
shrine of some sort.[320]

Córdoba, its immediate environs, and its <u>territorium</u> were linked to the
rest of Baetica and Roman Spain by an extensive network of roads. The <u>Via</u>
<u>Augusta</u> followed a route from the Pyrenean border of Spain to Gades (Cádiz);
it passed through Córdoba. From Castulo it came south, touched Córdoba,
and then went on to Astigi to the southwest. The route through the city
of Córdoba was probably Puerta Hierro to Plaza de las Tendillas, south via
the Plaza Santa Ana to the patio de los Naranjos of the mosque, and through
the portion of the mosque built by Almanzor to the bridge. A total of
thirty-four milestones have been found at Córdoba, most of them brought by
the Arabs from outlying areas. Many (twelve) mention the <u>Via</u> <u>Augusta</u>

from mile sixty-two (CIL 2.6208) to mile eighty-three (CIL 2.4717). Of the twelve, eight are datable—three coming from the time of Augustus, three from that of Tiberius, and two from that of Nero. This portion of the Via Augusta was obviously built and maintained well in the first century A.D.

Another important road led north, leaving by the Puerta Osario for Mellaria and Augusta Emerita; it approximates the modern road to Villaviciosa. Remnants of the Roman paving have been found. To the south across the bridge another road led to Ulia and to the coast at Malaca (Málaga). To the southeast another brought the traveler to Ucubi (Espejo) and Iponoba (Baena). An alternate route to the Via Augusta led to Castulo and the upper reaches of the Guadalquivir. Finally, on the west, a road may have led from the Puerta Almodóvar or Gallego, along the north bank of the Guadalquivir, to Hispalis (Seville). This latter road is not mentioned in the itineraries, but probably did exist (cf. Caesar Bell. Civ. 2.20.6).[321]

PLASTIC ART

For a variety of reasons, the full account of the art of Roman Córdoba cannot yet be written. The following is an account of some of the major finds, but useful conclusions on the city's artistic and architectural history must await a thorough examination of artifacts currently held in the provincial museum and in private hands. Such an examination is beyond the scope of this discussion.

Plastic art was strong in Baetica. The main centers were at Italica, Córdoba, and Seville.[322] At Córdoba quite a number of statues have been found, although only one of an Emperor—and that in fragments.[323] Divinities have done better: Ceres, from the Colegio de la Asunción (33); Diana(?); Dionysus; Minerva (56); Venus (34); Vulcan; and a naiad or nymph (35).[324] In bas-relief, Thouvenot notes a number of pieces, including one showing the contest of Athena and Poseidon and another showing olive measuring.[325] Five members of the imperial family are represented by busts: Germanicus; Hadrian; Faustina, wife of Marcus Aurelius; Commodus; and, perhaps, Julia Domna.[326] Various other pieces of scupture have turned up from time to time: a female head, of the early Empire; a head of white marble, in the calle Angel de Saavedra (40); a bronze lion head in Ibero-Roman style, in the Plaza de las Tendillas (41); a young noble boy; a terracotta of a child's head and figure of a seated boy, in the Campo de la Verdad.[327]

A rather peculiar example of local monumental art is the prow of a
ship found in the Plaza San Lorenzo (42), now in the archaeological museum.
It was probably part of a column honoring a Cordoban who had distinguished
himself in naval warfare, but it may have been part of a rostrum. Its
style dates to the early Empire.[328]

Mosaics, of course, are a common type of art found in Córdoba. The
fine examples from the urban villa in the Plaza de la Corredera have already been noted; among them are depictions of Galatea, Polyphemus, Eros,
and Psyche. Fragments turn up constantly, in various places. At one point
a Roman mosaic was used as the floor in a local bar.[329]

Epilogue:

CHRISTIANITY AND LATE ANTIQUITY

The sources for a history of Córdoba during the Empire were scanty; those for the period from Constantine to the Arab conquest are practically non-existent. Spain, in many ways the _finis_ _mundi_ for an Empire engrossed in the problems of northern barbarians and eastern threats, is seldom mentioned in the fourth century, and the history of the fifth to early eighth centuries must be pieced together from less than satisfactory sources. Nonetheless, by using a combination of scanty evidence and induction, something can be said of Córdoba's history for this period.[330]

Christianity, for all its profound significance in Spanish history, made a rather slow start in the Peninsula. Little progress had been made before the fourth century, and it remained mostly an urban phenomenon with no mass appeal until the seventh. Before Constantine, no Christian writer is known. As would be expected of an urban sect, Christianity was stronger in the heavily urbanized province of Baetica than in other areas of Iberia. The number of martyrs shows this, as does perhaps the heavy representation of the south at the council of Iliberis (Elvira) (A.D. 306?), where eleven of nineteen bishops and representatives came from towns in Baetica.[331]

At Córdoba itself, early Christianity has left a few traces. The first Cordoban bishop mentioned is the famous Osius, later an influential adviser to the Emperor Constantine; his life sheds little light on the Córdoba of his day.[332] In the fourth century Córdoba was a center of anti-Priscillianism. The bishop Hyginus was one of the first to oppose the heresy--this same Hyginus was later excommunicated by the council of Caesaraugusta for having joined the heretics.[333] In later centuries the bishop of Córdoba is noted at various councils (see below), for example, at the third council of Toledo in 589. The report of attendance leaves no doubt that Córdoba was a bishopric in Visigothic times as well as earlier.[334] The

The metropolitan see in Baetica, however, was Hispalis, not Córdoba, during
most of late antiquity.

Córdoba had its martyrs as well as its bishops. During the Diocleti-
anic persecutions, Ascisclus and Zoilus died for their faith (Prudentius
Perist. 4.19), as did a Faustus, Januarius, and Martialis.[335] An inscription of a namesake of Ascisclus has been found in the cemetery to the west
of the city: [Ascis]clus fa[mulus Christi ... vixit an]nos ... (HAE 1404).

The archaeology of Christian Córdoba is as uninformative as the literary sources. The only bright spot is the existence of five sarcophagi of
fine quality, some whole and some fragmentary, that were imported to the
city in the Constantinian period. These artifacts show that the wealthy
of the Christian community had good taste and that the commercial links
between Córdoba and Rome, where the sarcophagi were made, were still
strong.[336] Apart from the sarcophagi, there is little to report. Vicent
has identified an extensive paleochristian cemetery to the north of the
city. The inscription cited above indicates one to the west as well.
Christian cemeteries might be expected on all sides of the city where there
were Roman cemeteries before.[337] Practically no remains of Christian edifices have been uncovered. Santos Jener gives a drawing of a crypt of
Santa Eulalia at the Hospicio (58). Induction allows the supposition that
there was a bishop's church. The antiquity of the mosaics and the chapel
in the current cathedral is unknown; the church of San Vincente was supposedly on this spot before the Arabs built their mosque. Only a few pieces
of decorative art in ceramic remain as reminder of the beauties of such
edifices.[338]

The secular history of Córdoba in late antiquity is vague, but one has
an impression of an important city, a center of political and economic life
in Baetica. For all of Spain, the fourth century A.D. is practically un-
documented. At the end of the third century the city was the capital of
the province. Sometime in the fourth century it ceased to be so and
Hispalis (Seville) replaced Córdoba as the pre-eminent city of the area.[339]
A comes Hispaniarum was at Córdoba in A.D. 317. Perhaps the silting up of
the Guadalquivir, making it essentially unnavigable beyond Seville, as it
is today, had something to do with the subsequent change of capital to
Hispalis. At any rate, Ausonius (Urb. 11.81-83), writing in the late
fourth century, recognized Hispalis as the more important city and the
capital.[340]

The barbarian invasions of the late third century did not hit the
cities of Baetica as hard as they hit those of Tarraconensis. Ausonius
paints a picture of prosperity, and there is no evidence that Baetican
cities contracted to within their original walls, as did so many towns in
the north. The imported Christian sarcophagi indicate a prosperous aristocracy. Wealth continued to be derived from the land, which was held in
smallish latifundia, while the nobles lived in the towns for the most part.
Commerce continued. Oil was once again exported, though this export industry had collapsed in the middle of the third century. Grain was also
shipped; the scant evidence points to an agricultural revival in the fourth
century. The only dark spot in this generally prosperous picture is the
decadence of the mining activity. Apparently the mines of Baetica showed
only a shadow of their former richness at this time.[341]

Culturally, Córdoba in the fourth century--and indeed for the rest of
late antiquity--leaves little mark. The sarcophagi, since they are not of
local manufacture, indicate wealth and taste, but not local artistic accomplishment. No architecture survives (only some trivial remnants of
Constantinian date), no sculpture, no evidence of famous writers--although
until the end of antiquity Córdoba basked in the light of its earlier
famous products the Senecas and Lucan (Sidonius Apollinaris Carm. 9.230-
258).[342]

The peace and prosperity of the fourth century were rudely shattered
by the barbarian invasions of the fifth. From October of A.D. 409, Germans entered the Peninsula in large numbers, and a two-year period of chaos
ensued.[343] The Siling Vandals entered Baetica under their king Fredbal,
and their defeat and extermination by the Visigothic king Wallia, in the
imperial service, provided only very temporary relief. The Asding Vandals,
now allied with the Alans, were forced to migrate from Galicia and took the
southern part of the Peninsula for their own in A.D. 422; in 425, Hispalis
fell to them. The fate of Córdoba is unknown. Probably one should assume
the worst. After the Vandal king Gunderic died in A.D. 428, his brother
Gaiseric came to the throne. Under Gaiseric, in 429, the Vandals were in-
vited to invade Africa by Boniface, a pretender to the purple. The cities
of Baetica, Córdoba included, were free again from barbarian control.[344]

The respite lasted only a few years. The Suevi had seized northwestern
Spain, and in 438 they invaded Baetica; in 441 they captured Seville and
(we assume) Córdoba. After an abortive attempt to eject them in 446,

Theodoric II of the Visigoths drove them out in 458-459. There is dispute
as to whether the Visigoths remained in Baetica or not. García Moreno
paints a picture of local resistance by the provincial nobility to Roman
and barbarian alike until the middle of the sixth century. But Thompson
presents strong evidence to the contrary; the Visigoths seem to have come
to Baetica to stay in 458. There is no record that the Germans withdrew
from the province after this date. Indeed a few brief notices from subsequent years seem to show that they were still there. Perhaps, as in Galicia, the old Roman provincial government continued to function at the be-
hest of and under the control of the barbarians. Settlement is another
matter. Few Goths settled in the south before the beginning of the seventh century. Evidence is scanty, but there is no reason to doubt that,
despite the late start, there were as many Goths in Baetica as in other
Spanish provinces by the end of the kingdom in 711.[345]

At the middle of the sixth century, the sources once again allow a
clearer view of events. In 550 or 551, Agila, recently crowned king of
the Visigoths, attacked Córdoba. The city had apparently regained its
independence at some point in the previous century, even though the Visigoths maintained control in Baetica in general. Agila made a tactical
blunder by desecrating the tomb of Saint Ascisclus outside the walls; the
Catholic Christians, incensed at this villainous deed by the Arian king,
soundly defeated his forces, and having   lost a son, his royal treasure,
and the better part of his army, he was forced to flee back to Augusta E-
merita (Mérida).

At this point, Justinian, Emperor in Byzantium, saw an opportunity to
recapture Spain for the Roman Empire. He struck a treaty with Athanagild,
a rival to Agila, and sent troops to Baetica to assist him in insurrection.
In the fact of this threat the Visigoths deposed Agila and elected Athanagild as king; Athanagild promptly did an about face and opposed the Byzantine encroachments. The areas of "independent" Baetica were now under Byzantine protection, and Athanagild had to try to capture the major cities.
Although Hispalis fell to him in about A.D. 567, at the very end of his
reign, his repeated attacks on Córdoba were always in vain.[347] Shortly
after Athanagild's death in 567, Leovigild became king of the Visigoths in
Spain. Córdoba, the long "rebellious" city, was high on his list of pri-
orities. In 572, as John of Biclanum, the best chronicler of his day, tells
it, Leovigild took the city by a night attack.

> Leovigildus rex Cordubam civitatem diu Gothis revellem nocte
> occupat et caesis hostibus propriam facit multasque urbes et [348]
> castella rusticorum multitudine in Gothorum dominum revocat.

The struggle for Córdoba was not quite finished, however. Sometime
soon after this victory Córdoba fell into Byzantine hands, for in A.D.
584, when Hermenegild, a son of Leovigild and a rebel against him, was driven from Seville by the king, he took refuge in Córdoba. Leovigild bribed
the Byzantine commander with 30,000 solidi (a tremendous sum) to hand the
errant son over. Hermenegild, betrayed by his supposed protector, took
refuge in a church but eventually surrendered and was taken prisoner. Leovigild celebrated his accomplishment by minting coins that read: CORDOBA
BIS OBTINUIT. Córdoba was now in Visigothic hands to stay.[349]

Under the Visigoths Córdoba virtually disappears from view once again.[350]
The only historical references mention the city as a minting place for various Visigothic kings and note Cordoban participation in various church
councils. The following kings minted at Córdoba and are given in chronological order: Reccared (A.D. 586-601), with the legend CORDOBA PIUS;
Suinthila (621-631); Sisenand (631-636); Chintila (636-640); Tulga (640-
642); Chindasuinth (642-653); Reccesuinth (649-672); Wamba (672-680); Erwig
(680-687); Egica (687-702); Wittiza (700-710).[351]

Of the church conclaves of the period, Mansi notes Cordoban participation at the second council of Seville (A.D. 619 or 620), the fourth council
of Toledo (633), and the sixth (638), seventh (646), eighth (653), thirteenth (683), and fifteenth (688) councils in that same town. Earlier, in
the sixth century, a bishop had been at the first council of Seville (590)
and at yet another council at Toledo (597). No light is thrown on the history of the city, however.[352]

Life under the Visigoths may not have been very different than life
would have been without them; the social and economic situation likely remained much the same. Visigoths were a small minority of the population,
and Romans maintained positions of power and influence even during periods
when a conscious effort was made by the kings to "Germanize" the ruling of
the land. The most striking developments, which most likely would have occurred had the Roman Empire continued to control the area, were the increase
in the number of fortified villas and the disaffection of the lower classes.
Details are lacking, but the villa-based, highly exploitative social and
economic structure that had already been prevalent in much of Spain now
dominated Baetica as well. Brigandage was rife; squabbling among the

Visigothic aristocracy continued unabated. An external menace would cause serious difficulties.[353]

Ultimately, Visigothic pride and ambition provided the opportunity for that menace to materialize. King Witiza died in 710, and the senatus of the kingdom elected Rodrigo as the new monarch. But Witiza's clan was dissatisfied with the choice and determined to regain the throne, with the help of foreign troops. The Arabs were at hand across the Strait of Gibraltar, in Africa. The fateful decision was made. Tariq brought a force of 12,000 Moslem troops across the strait in April of A.D. 711 to "help" the Witizan faction. On (perhaps) the twenty-third of July, 711, his forces met those of Rodrigo the king for a decisive battle at the Guadalete River. Treachery by the sons of Witiza removed the wings of the Visigothic army, and the center, fighting valiantly, was crushed. The Visigoths fled north with the Arabs right behind them. Córdoba, its bridge cut and its walls in ruins, fell easily to the Moslem army. It would rise again, as the capital of Moslem Spain, and one of the most magnificent cities of medieval Europe; but Roman Córdoba had come to its end.[354]

Appendix I:

Classical References to Córdoba

Anthologia Latina	409 = Seneca the Younger Epig. 9
	688.1
Appian	Ib. 48–50
	65–68
	Bell. Civ. 2.104–105
Ausonius	Ordo Nob. Urb. 84
Caesar	Bell. Civ. 2.19–21.5
[Caesar]	Bell. Alex. 49.1–64.3
	Bell. Hisp. 2.1–11.3
	12
	32–33.1
Cassius Dio	41.15
	41.24
	42.15.2–3
	43.32
	43.33
	43.39
	45.10
Cicero	Arch. 10.26
	Att. 10.31
	10.32
	10.33
	12.37a
	Verr. 4.56
Codex Theodosianus	9.1.1 = Codex Iustinianus 3.24.1
Columella	RR 7.2.4
Divisio orbis terrae	4 (Geographi latini minores, ed. A. Riese [Heilbronn, 1878] p. 15)
Eutropius	4.9
Hilarus	ex opere historico fragmentum 2.15 (Migne vol. 10 p. 642)
Johannis Biclarum	Chronica 2 (T. Mommsen, Monumenta Germaniae Historica vol. 11 p. 217)
Josephus	AJ 19.1.3
Julius Honorius	Cosmogr. A19 (Geographi latini minores, ed. A Riese [Heilbronn, 1878] p. 34)
Julius Obsequens	18
Isidore of Seville	Chronica 2 (T. Mommsen, Monumenta Germaniae Historica vol. 11)
	Historia Gothorum 45 (T. Mommsen, Monumenta Germaniae Historica vol. 11)

[Isidore]	De vir. ill. 5.14 (Migne vol. 83)
Itineraria Antoniniana	402.6
	403.4
	409.1
	412.6
	413.1, 5
	415.3
Itineraria Vicarell.	CIL 11.3281 line 10
	11.3282 line 10
	11.3283 line 10
	11.3284 line 11
Livy	45.5.1
	Per. 48
	111
Martial	Epig. 1.61.8
	9.61
	12.63.1-5
Martianus Capella	6.630
Martyrologium Hieronymianum	ad diem 5 Kal. Iul.
	ad diem 2 Id. Oct.
	ad diem 14 Kal. Dec.
Notitia Galliarum	I p. 573 (T. Mommsen, Monumenta Germaniae Historica vol. 9)
Pliny	HN 3.1.7
	3.1.10
	3.1.13
	3.1.14
	19.42.152
	34.2.4
Plutarch	Caes. 17
	Sert. 22
Polybius	35.2.2
Pomponius Mela	Chorogr. 2.6.88
Prudentius	Perist. 4.19-20
Ptolemy	Geog. 2.4.9
Rav. Cosm.	315.11
	315.15 (= 4.44)
Sallust	Hist. 2.28 (Maurenbrecher)
	2.70 (Maurenbrecher)
Seneca the Elder	Suas. 6.27
Seneca the Younger	Epig. 9 (Haase vol. 1 p. 263)
	Fr. 88
Sidonius Apollinaris	Carm. 9.230-258
Silius Italicus	Pun. 3.401
Strabo	3.2.1-3 (141C)
	3.4.9 (160C)
	3.4.19-20 (166C)
Suetonius	Aug. 51
	De Poetis ed. Roth p. 299
	De vir. ill. ed. Roth p. 301
Sulpicius Severus	Chronica 2.46.8
Valerius Maximus	9.1.5
Varro	Ling. 5.162

Appendix II:

Epigraphic Sources

The following is a list of inscriptions attributed to or concerning Córdoba. Find site is noted if it is other than Córdoba. Visigothic and most Christian inscriptions are not included.

CIL vol. 2
- 198*
- 199*
- 200*
- 1055 (Lora del Río)
- 1179 (Seville)
- 1200 (Seville)
- 1201 (Seville)
- 1347 add. (Ronda la Vieja)
- 1600 (Baena)
- 1637 (Carcabuey)
- 1694 (Tucci)
- 2026 (Anticaria)
- 2133 (Porcuna)
- 2191-2321
- 2348 (Torremolinos)
- 3272 (Castulo)
- 3278 (Linares)
- 3358 (Jaén)
- 4962.4
- 4963.9
- 4967.37
- 4976.14
- 5068 (Puebla de Alcocér)
- 5521-5537
- 5538 = HAE 165 = HAE 1003
- 6245.3
- 6252.20
- 6253.12-14
- 6254 II
- 6257.105

CIL vol. 6
- 10229 (Rome)
- 20768 (Rome)
- 34664 = 37898 (Rome)
- 38595 (Rome)

CIL vol. 8
- 21666 (Albulae)

CIL vol. 13
- 6869 (Mainz)

CIL vol. 15
- 3068 (Rome)
- 3994 (Rome)
- 4031 (Rome)
- 4099 (Rome)
- 4110 (Rome)
- 4117 (Rome)

Ephemeris Epigraphica
- 8.106
- 9.1075

L'Année Epigraphique
- 1908.148 = BRAH 52 (1908) pp. 453-456
- 1915.12
- 1916.41 (Narbonne) = ILG 586
- 1924.14 = HAE 2179 = AE 1974.371
- 1932.78
- ?1933.95 (Rome)
- 1934.24 = HAE 2052
- 1934.25 = HAE 2053
- 1951.46 (Volubilis)
- 1952.126 = HAE 323 = AE 1962.49
- 1952.127 = HAE 326 = AE 1962.53
- 1962.44
- 1962.45 = HAE 1832
- 1962.46 = HAE 1406, 1832
- 1962.47 = HAE 325
- 1962.48 = HAE 324
- 1962.49 = HAE 323
- 1962.50 = HAE 1407
- 1962.51 = HAE 1833

```
1962.52 = HAE 327
1962.53 = HAE 326 = AE 1952.127
1962.54 = HAE 1403
1962.55 = HAE 1408
1962.77 = HAE 1861
1965.58
1966.181 = HAE 2091
1971.178 = AEA 1971 p. 161
1971.179 = AEA 1971 p. 162
1971.180 = BRAH 1971 p. 180
1971.181 = BRAH 1971 p. 179
1971.182 = BRAH 1971 p. 181
1971.183 = BRAH 1971 p. 182
1971.184 = BRAH 1971 p. 183
1971.185 = BRAH 1971 p. 184
1972.276 = Habis 1972 pp.
   321-324
1972.277 = Habis 1972 pp.
   321-324
1974.370 = Tovar 1971
1974.371 = HAE 2179 = AE 1924.14
1974.372 = Habis 1974 p. 226
1974.452
```

Hispania Antiqua Epigraphica

```
 164 = 1002                        1595 = HAE 2094
 274                               1827
 275                               1828
 276                               1829
 277                               1830
 323 = AE 1952.126 = AE 1962.49   1831 = 1406 = AE 1962.46
 324 = AE 1962.48                  1832 = AE 1962.45
 325 = AE 1962.47                  1833 = AE 1962.51
 326 = AE 1952.127 = AE 1962.53   1856
 327 = AE 1962.52                  1857
 328                               1858 (cf. Corduba 1976 pp. 33-37)
 329                               1859
 330                               1961 = AE 1962.77
1001                               2046
1002 = 164                         2047
1004                               2048
1401                               2049
1402                               2052 = AE 1934.24
1403 = AE 1962.54                  2053 = AE 1934.25
1404                               2055
1406 = 1832 = AE 1962.46          2070
1407 = 1832 = AE 1962.50          2071
1408 = AE 1962.55                  2091 = AE 1966.181
1409                               2094 = AE 1595
```

Other sources (listed chronologically)

Fernández Franco, J. <u>Antigüedades romanas de España</u>. (c.1550) cited by M. Pilar Muro Meléndez-Valdés, "Inscripciones latinas de Córdoba recogidas por Fernández Franco," Tesis de Licenciatura, University of Seville, 1977: inscription number 42, pp. 162-164

<u>BRAH</u> 42 (1903) pp. 449-450

<u>BRAH</u> 52 (1908) pp. 453-456, 525 = <u>AE</u> 1908.148

<u>BRAH</u> 56 (1910) pp. 142, 451-453, 454-455

<u>Anales</u> ... <u>Córdoba</u> 1926 p. 11

<u>Anales</u> ... <u>Córdoba</u> 1927-28 pp. 14-15

<u>BRAC</u> 6 (1927) p. 526

Thouvenot 1973 (originally published 1940) p. 577

Santos Jener 1947 p. 93

Santos Jener 1955 p. 117

Vázquez de Parga 1958 pp. 28-29

Ortí 1958 p. 57

<u>AEA</u> 36 (1963) p. 172

<u>AEA</u> 41 (1968) p. 94

Vives, J. <u>Inscripciones latinas de la España romana</u> (Barcelona 1971) no. 1779

Vicent 1973 pp. 675-677

<u>Boletín del Instituto de Estudios Giennenses</u> 22 (1976) no. 90, p. 85

<u>Corduba</u> 1 (1976) pp. 15-27, 28-32, 38-40, 145-151

<u>Habis</u> 7 (1976) pp. 387-390

<u>Habis</u> 8 (1977) pp. 410-412, 417-418, 422-423, 445-450

Piernavieja, P. <u>Corpus de inscripciones deportivas de la España romana</u> (Madrid 1977) pp. 165-166

<u>Mélanges Casa Velázquez</u> 17 (1981) pp. 51-52 no. 7

<u>Phoenix</u> 35 (1981) pp. 134-141

Serrano Ramos, E., R. Atencia Páez. <u>Inscripciones latinas del museo de Málaga</u> (Madrid[?] 1981) <u>passim</u>

Appendix III:

Index to Inscriptions

Included are inscriptions from Córdoba and relating to Córdoba, by nomina and cognomina. The abbreviations are those used in the list of inscriptions in Appendix II. "Madrid file" refers to inscriptions not yet published, but recorded in the master file for the revision of the CIL (Deutsches Archäologisches Institut, Madrid). Names of consuls and emperors are excluded. [...] indicates a restored text; (...) indicates expansion of an abbreviation or an addition to create the normal spelling of a word.

NOMINA

	Abullia	N.1. Nigella	CIL 2.2255
N.	Abul[l]ius	Chr[e]st[us]	2254
L.	Acilius	L.[f.] Modestus	2234
T.	Acclenus	T.f. Qui. Centu[rio?]	2215
L.	Acxius	Nomentanus	HAE 2046
Q.	Aeclanus	Hermias	CIL 2.2203
	Aelia	Faustina	5524
	Aelia	Flaviana	2224
	Aelia	Vitalis	2209
	Elia	Memmesis	see Elia
	Elia	Vetustina	see Elia
L.	Aelius	L.f. Gal. Faustinus	5524
M.	Aelius	Modestus	HAE 2049
	Aemilia	D.1. Quarta	private collection
D.	Aemilius	D.1. Nicephorus Brattiarus	private collection
C.	Aemilius	Oculatus	MMAP 1947 p. 93
L.	Aemilius	L.1. Xanthus	MMAP 1958-61 pp. 28-29
M.	Aerarius	Telemac(h)us	AE 1971.181
L.	Afinius	L.1. Ata[...]	Madrid file
L.	Ai(milius)		CIL 2.4963.9
	Annaea	L.1. Prima	Corduba 1976 pp. 145-151
L.	Annaeus	L. [...]	Corduba 1976 pp. 145-151
Q.	Annedius	Q.1. Surillio	CIL 2.5526
	Annia	T.1. Helena	2215
Q.	Annius	Apronianus	3358
Q.	Annius	Fabianus	3358
C.	Annius	C.f. Lepidus Marcellus	5522
L.	Annius	Valens	HAE 1407 = 1832
	Antestia	).1. Iuniana	Madrid file
L.	Antestius	L.(f.) Ser. Sabinus	EE 9.1075
L.	Antistius	Rusticus	CIL 2.2242

	Antonius	Alchimus	CIL 2.2256
L.	Antonius	Constans	2257
M.	Anto[nius]	Heren[nianus]	2258
L.	Antonius	Saturninus	2257
C.	Antonius	[-.]f. Gal. Seranus	AE 1971.183
P.	Argentarius	).1. Faustus	Madrid file
	Asicia	Facunda	Madrid file
M.	Asicius	M.1. Pelops	Madrid file
A.	At(ilius)		CIL 2.4963.9
M.	Atilius	M.1. Apeles	HAE 1830
	Atinia	Q.1.	CIL 2.5527 = 5532
Q.	Atinius	Attic[us]	= Q. Minius Attic[us], CIL
			2.5527 = 5532
	Aufidius		CIL 2.2301
C.	Avilia	It[...]na	HAE 2053
	Aure[lia]		CIL 2.5528
	Aurelia	Leucothoe	1694
	Aurelia	Valeriana	2260 = 5529
	Aurelia	Valerina	5529
	Aurelius	Celerinianus	2261
M.	Aurelius	Marcellinus	Madrid file
	Aurelius	Stephanus	CIL 2.5521
L.	Axius	L.f. Pol. Naso	Phoenix 1981 pp. 134-141
	Acxius	Nomentanus	see Acxius
	Badia		CIL 2.2262
	Baebia	Venusta	6.34664
L.	Brutt(ius)	Barga Firmus	Thouvenot 1973 p. 576 no.1
Cn.	Cacius	Cn.C.1. Firmus	Madrid file
Cn.	Cacius	Cn.1. Quietus	Madrid file
Cn.	Cacius	Cn.1. Ursus	Madrid file
	Caecilia	Q.1. Firma	CIL 2.2272
	Caecilia	Tusculana	2264
	Caecilius	Crysantus	2263
M.	Caecilius	L.f. Qui. Severus	Madrid file
	Calpurnia	Tertulla Secundina	AE 1971.180
L.	Calpurnius	Salvianus	CIL 2.2265
	Calpurnius	Urbanus	2265
	Caninia	M.1. Secunda	2266
M.	Caninius	M.1. Alexander	2266
M.	Caninius	Chilo	2266
	Casius		HAE 2052 = AE 1934.24
M.	Cassius	M.f. Agrippa	CIL 2.2212
M.	Cassius	Pollio	2212
	Circia	C[l]eta	2268
	Claudia	Saturnina Tib.1.	Habis 1977 pp. 447-449
	Clipius		HAE 2052
	Clodia		Madrid file
	Clodia	Euporia	Anales ... Córdoba 1927-28
			p.14
	Clod(ius)	Augendus	CIL 2.2211
	Coelia	Ianuaria	AEA 1968 p. 94
L.	Cominius	L.f. Gal. Iulian(us)	HAE 2091 = AE 1966.181
	Cornelia		Madrid file

	Cornelia	Aletea	CIL 2.2272
	Cornelia	L.1. Danais	2296
	Cornelia	[F]au[s]tilla	2270
	Cornelia	L.1. Prima	2286
	Cornelia	C.1. Quarta	2271
	Cornelia	Severa	HAE 1832
	Cornelius	Africanus	CIL 2.2195
L.	Cornelius	L.f. Caranto	2286
[Cn.	Corne?]lius	L.f. [Gal.] Cinna	5525
	[C]ornelius	[?Cr]ocalus	BRAH 1903 p. 450
L.	Cornelius	L.1. Euhemerus	CIL 2.2272
M.	Cornelius	Fannianus	2252
C.	C(ornelius)	Olynthius	AE 1915.12
P.	Cornelius	Philoclis 1. Auctus	Habis 1977 pp. 410–412
L.	Cornelius	Primus	CIL 2.2286
	Cornelius	Restitutus	2195
Q.	Cornelius	M.f. Gal. Valerinus	3272
C.	C[osanus]		2220c
[C.	Cosanus	-.f.] Gal. [...]	2220a
C.	Cosanus	C.f. Gal. Rusticus	2220b
	Cur(iatius)	Innocentius	2211
Q.	Dasumius	Solux	CIL 2.2273
	Decetia	C.1. Rustica	Madrid file
	Decimius	Germanianus	CIL 2.2206
C.	Dillius	L.f.A.n. Ser. Aponianus	AE 1932.78
	Domitius	Isquilinus	CIL 2.2236
	Egnatia	Florentina	CIL 2.2274
	[Egnatiu]s	Faustinus	2205
	Elia	Memmesis	Est. Giennenses 1976 p. 85
	Elia	Vetustina	Est. Giennenses 1976 p. 85
	Etria	Parthenia	CIL 2.2275
	Fabia	Modesta Themisonis f.	Madrid file
	Fabia	Cn.f. Prisca	CIL 2.2249
M.	Fab[...]	Epor[ensis]	2251
M.	Fabius	Basileus	2221
Q.	Fabius	Q.f. Qui. Fabianus	1200
M.	Fabius	M.M.M.1. Gu[lus?]	AE 1916.41
C.	Fabius	Nigellio	CIL 2.2193, 2194
Sex.	Fabius	Phaeder	Habis 1977 pp. 417–418
	Fabius	Seneca	CIL 2.2249
M.	Fabius	Themison	Madrid file
	Fannia	M.1. Rhodine	HAE 1830
M.	Fannius	M.1. Rhodo	HAE 1830
A.	Fannius	Speudo	AE 1971.182
	Favonia	Res[tituta]	CIL 2.2276
M.	Favonius		2276
	Fl(avius)	Hyginus	2210
P.	Fron[ti]nus	Sciscola	2348
	[Fu]lcinia	L.f. [Pr]isca	AE 1971.185
L.	[F]u[l]cinius	Lalus	CIL 2.2308
L.	Fulcinius	Pacatus	AE 1971.185
C.	Furnius	C.f. Pap. Fortunatus	Madrid file

	Helvia	Tu[scilla?]	CIL 2.2279
M.	Helvius	M.f. Ser. Rufus	Habis 1976 p. 388
M.	Helvius	[Tuscus?]	CIL 2.2279
	Herennia	Q.l. Cretica	2281
	Herennia	Q.l. Lezbia	2281
	Herennia	Q.l. Palaestra	2281
Q.	Herennius	Q.l. Clarus	2281
	(Herennius?)	Montanus Rufi f.	2250
Q.	Herennius	Q.l. Phileros	2281
Q.	Herennius	Rufus	2250
	Hirria	L.f. Pa[...]	2282
	Iulia	C.Sex.l. Eunica	CIL 2.2284
	Iulia	T.f. Lybissa	2223
	Iulia	).C.l. Pusinna	2284
T.	Iulius	T.[f.]	2223
C.	Iulius	C.l.Sex.l. Athenidorus	2284
	Iul(ius)	Caninius	2211
L.	Iulius	M.f.Q.n. Gal. Gallus Mummianus	2224
L.	Iulius	Protogenes	2237
L.	Iulius	M.[f.] Qui. Saxio	2245
L.	Iulius	Tha[llus?]	2279
	Iunia	T.l. Clarina	Madrid file
	Iunia	Delicata	CIL 2.2271
	Iunia	-.l. Diutera	Madrid file
	Iunia	Genice	EE 8.106
	Iunia	Lycias	BRAH 1908 p. 45
	Iunius	Bassus Milonianus	CIL 2.2222
L.	Iunius	Bil(icus)	BRAH 1910 p. 454 (where read as Lunius)
C.	Iunius	Celadus	CIL 6.20768
	Iun(ius)	Germanus	CIL 2.2211
L.	Iunius	P.f. Ser. Paulinus	CIL 2.5523
L.	Iunius	Plato	BRAH 1908 p. 454
M.	Iunius	[L.f.] L.n. Gal. Terenti[anus] Servilius Sabinus	CIL 2.1347 add.
M.	Iuniu[s]	Ultimus	4976.14
	Iunius	Ursus	HAE 1595 = 2094
	Latinia	M.l. Da[...]	Madrid file
	Latinia	M.l. T[...]	Madrid file
M.	Latinius	M.[l.]	Madrid file
	Licinia	L.l. Aesiona	CIL 2.2223
	Licinia	L.l. Antioch(e, is)	2223
	Licinia	L.l. [T]yche	1201
L.	Licinius	L.l. Cogitans	1201
Q.	Licinius	Q.f. Ser. Rusticus	AE 1974.452
	[Li]cinius	C.l. Salvius	CIL 2.2307
M.	Licinius	Sodalis	2285
	Lollia	C.f. Maniliana	AE 1971.182
M.	Lucius	M.f. Ser.	CIL 2.2286
	Luclena	).).l. Grata	5526
M.	Lucretius	Marianus	2216

L.	Lucretius	Severus	CIL 2.1055
M.	Lucretius	Verna	2246
	Luria	C.l. Faustilla	5536
M.	Lutatius	M.f. Ser. Albanus	CIL 13.6869
M.	Ma[...]		CIL 2.2318
	Maia	P.f. Secunda	Habis 1977 pp. 445-447
	Manilia	Hilara	CIL 2.2288
L.	Maniliu[s]		2288
L.	Manius	L.f.	2289
L.	Manlius	A.f.A.n. Gal. Bocchus	2225
L.	Manlius	A.f. Cor. Canus	CIL 6.38595
P.	Minicius	Facundus	CIL 2.2294
Q.	Minius	Atticus	5527 = 5532
	Marcia	Antiocis	2292
	Marcia	Celsa C. Marci Celsi f.	2290
	Marcia	[P.] l. Fausta	Habis 1977 pp. 445-447
P.	Marcius	P.f. Ser.	Habis 1977 pp. 445-447
C.	Marcius	Celsus	CIL 2.2290
Q.	Marcius	Q.l. [Fulvus?]	2291
M.	Marcius	Niger Baxonensis	HAE 164
P.	Marcius	P.f. Ser. Pollio	Habis 1977 pp. 445-447
Q.	Marcius	Q.l. Eumolpus	Habis 1977 pp. 447-449
	Maria		HAE 1401
	Maria	Hellas	Habis 1977 pp. 422-423
	Maria	C.l. Hellas	AE 1974.372
Sex.	Marius		CIL 2.2269
Q.	Marius	Q.l. Eumolpus	Habis 1977 pp. 447-449
T.	Marius	Mercello Persinus	CIL 2.2226
	Messia(?)		HAE 1004 (read as Mussias)
C.	Messius	Rufinus	1637
	Munnitia		2052
	Mussia	Agele	274
	Mussia?	).l. Rosia	275 cf. Santos Jener 1955 p. 111
	Neria	). et T.l. Daphne	CIL 2.2296
	Neria	T.l. Firma	2296
T.	Nerius	T.l. Antigonus	2296
T.	Nerius	T.l. Asiaticus	2296
T.	Nerius	T.l. Hilarus	2296
	Norbana	Q.f. Quintilla	5068
	Num(isia)	Fra[tern]a	HAE 2053
C.	Num(isius)	Ae[ta]cinus	2053
C.	Num(isius)	Apa[...]aopi or Era[...]aopi	2053
L.	Numisius	Gaetulus	CIL 2.2298
C.	Num(isius)	Philem[on]	HAE 2053
C.	Nu(misius)	Sex(tianus)	2053
	Octavia		CIL 2.5534
	Octavia	[...]o	2238
	Octavia	Modestae l. Chloris	2238
	Octavia	T.C.l. Modesta	2238
C.	Octavius	Au[...] Felix	2238

C.	Octavius	C.l. Cuccio	CIL 2.2238
L.	Octavius	Licinianus Gal.	XII CAN 1973 pp. 675-676
C.	Octavius	Modestae l. Macer	CIL 2.2238
	(Octavius)	Octavi[an]u[s] Licinianus	XII CAN 1973 pp. 675-676
C.	Octavius	T.C.l. Primus	CIL 2.2238
C.	Octavius	Prot[us]	2238
	Octavius	Rufus	2204
*C.	Orvelius	L.f. Cn[...]	Ortí 1958 p. 57 (*false?)
C.	Papiriu[s]		AEA 1963 p. 172
Sex.	Papiri[us]		AEA 1963 p. 172
	Persia	L.f. Secunda	CIL 2.2247
L.	Persius	Di[ph]ilus	2239
	Petilia	).l. Comunis	Madrid file
	Petilia	T.l. Marta	CIL 2.2282
	Petilia	L.l. Sextia	Madrid file
L.	Petilius	L.l. Priamus	Madrid file
	Petroni(us, a)		HAE 326
	[Pomponi]a	T.l. Anu[s]	CIL 2.2240
	[Pomp]onia	[T.] f. O[pt]a[ta]?	2240
	Pomponia	Q.f. Tusca	2301
C.	Pomponius	C.l. Licinus	2300
[T.?]	Pomponius	Pamphilus	2240
	Porcia	Bassenia	5521
	Postumius	A.f. [P]ap. Acilianus	2213
L.	Postumius	).l. Barnaetus (or Barneus)	HAE 276, cf. Santos Jener 1955 p. 111
L.	Postumius	Bla[stus?]	CIL 2.2191
	Publicia	Marcia	BRAC 1927 p. 526
C.	Publicius		CIL 2.2230
P.	Publicius	Fortunatus	MMAP 1958-61 p. 29
	Publicius	Fortunatus T(h)alamus	AEA 1968 p. 94
A.	Publicius	[Ge]rmanus	CIL 2.2229
	Publicius	Valerius Fortunatus Thalamus	5521
	Quintia	L.l. Caletuche	Habis 1977 pp. 417-418
	Quintia	P.f. Galla	CIL 2.5522
L.	Quintius	L.l. Amphio	Habis 1977 pp. 417-418
	Rubria	Fau[st]ina	CIL 2.2303
[Q.]	Ru[fi]lius	L.f.C.n. [...]	2192
L.	Salvi[us	-.f.] Sedatus	HAE 1861
C.	Sar.	Acutius	CIL 2.5535
	Sempronia	Prixsilla	2304
	Sempronia	L.l. Secunda	5536
	Sempronia	Vitalis	2305
L.	Sempronius	C[...]	2241
	Sempronius	Donatus	Habis 1977 pp. 449-450
C.	Semproni[us	C.l.] Nigellio	CIL 2.2026
M.	Sempronius	M.l. Princeps	5536
	Sentia	Mapalia	5537
	Servilia	Nepotina	BRAH 1908 p. 454

Q.	Servilius	Q. [l.?f.?] Chryseros	HAE 277
	Servilius	Patriciensis	BRAH 1908 p. 454
	Servilius	Patricius	BRAH 1908 p. 454
	Setuleia	Isias	CIL 2.2306
	Situleia	Filumene	HAE 2055
L.	Stertinius	L.f. Hor. Maxumus	Habis 1977 pp. 410-412
	[St]lattia	).l. Salvia	CIL 2.2307
	[Sulpi]cia	Delphis	2289
	Sulpicia	L.f. Rufina	2308
	Trebia	Romana	CIL 2.2309
	Trebonia		Madrid file
	Vale[...]		CIL 2.2313
	Valeria	[...]	2311
	Valeria	Bastula	AE 1951.46
	Valeria	Felicitas	CIL 2.2312
	Valeria	C.f. Pa[e]tina Tuccitana	3278
	Valeria	Q.f. Prisca	2249
	Valeria	Quinta	2248a
C.	Valerius	Aestius	2310
C.	Valerius	Avitus	2253
C.	Valerius	[Dioph]ane(?)	2243
L.	Valerius	C.f. [K]apito	2242
	V(alerius)	Pate[rnus]	Mél. de l'Ecole Fran. 1918-19 p. 314
L.	Valerius	Poen[us]	CIL 2.2242
C.	Valerius	Zephyrus	2243
M.	Velcennius	Fortunatus	AE 1933.95
D. or P.	Vergilius	Amarantus	CIL 2.2215
	Vibia	Crocale	1600
	Vibia	P.l. Piale	HAE 2070
	Vibia	Prisciana	CIL 2.2263
Q.	Vi[b]i[us]	L[aetus]?	2207
Q.	Vibius	Laetus	2216
P.	Vibius	Protus	HAE 2070
	Ulpius	Helias	AEA 1968 p. 94
	Voltillia	Ne(?)[...]	AE 1971.182
	Volumnia	Spera[ta]	AE 1971.179
P.	Volumnius	Vitalis	AE 1971.179
	[...]	L.).l. Optata	CIL 2.2299
	[...]a	Berulla	2233
	[...]a	L.l. Thais	2316
	[...]ara	Flori l.	Madrid file
	[...]ius	M.f. Ser. Heres	HAE 1856
	[...]lia	Docime	CIL 2.2214
	[...]ria		2321
	[...]s	L.f. Men. [...]tus	2280

COGNOMINA

		[Acc]epta	HAE 1829 (possibly [rec]epta [in pace])
		Acco	AE 1915.12
	Postumius A.f. Pap.	Acilianus	CIL 2.2213
		[Acis]clus	HAE 1404
		Actius	327
C.	Sar.	Acutius	CIL 2.5535
	Licinia L.1.	Aesiona	2223
C.	Valerius	Aestius	2310
C.	Num(isius)	Ae[ta]cinus	HAE 2053
		Aetern(us)	MMAP 1947 p. 93
	Cornelius	Africanus	CIL 2.2195
	Mussia	Agele	HAE 274
		Agilio?	CIL 2.2297
		Aglavus	HAE 2048
M.	Cassius M.f.	Agrippa	CIL 2.2212
M.	Lutatius M.f.	Albanus	CIL 13.6869
	Antonius	Alcimus	CIL 2.2256
	Cornelia	Aletea	2272
M.	Caninius M.1.	Alexander	2266
		Alpius?	HAE 1408
		Alypus?	1408
		Amabilis	1408
		Amandus	325
D. or P.	Vergilius	Amarantus	CIL 2.2215
L.	Quintius L.1.	Amphio	Habis 1977 pp. 417-418
		Ampliatus	Corduba 1976 pp. 15-27
T.	Nerius T.1.	Antigonus	CIL 2.2296
	Licinia L.1.	Antioch(e, is)	2223
		Antiochis	HAE 1827
	Marcia	Antiochis	CIL 2.2292
	[Pomp]onia	Anu[s]	2240
C.	Num(isius)	Apa[...]	HAE 2053
M.	Atilius M.1.	Apeles	1830
		Apollonia	324
		Aprodisia	CIL 2.2248b
		Apronianus	3358
C.	Dillius L.f.A.n. Ser.	Apronianus	AE 1932.78
		Aris[tob]ulus	AEA 1960 p. 190 = HAE 1858
		Arrianus	AE 1974.370
		[Art?]ema	CIL 2.2235 (or [Phil]ema?)
T.	Nerius T.1.	Asiaticus	2296
L.	Afinius L.1.	Ata[...]	Madrid file
C.	Iulius C.1.Sex.1.	Athenidorus	CIL 2.2284
Q.	Atinius	Attic[...]	5527 = Q. Minius Atticus, CIL 2.5532?
Q.	Minius	Atticus	CIL 2.5532 = Q. Atinius Attic[...], CIL 2.5527?
C.	Octavius	Au[...] Felix	2238
P.	Cornelius Philoclis 1.	Auctus	Habis 1977 pp. 410-412
	Clodius	Augendus	CIL 2.2211

		Avitae [1.?]	CIL 2.2259
		Eucumene	
		Avitae 1. Phylara-	2259
		g[y]ris	
C.	Valerius	Avitus	2253
L.	Brutt(ius)	Barga Firmus	Thouvenot 1973 p. 576 n.1
L.	Postumius).1.	Barnaetus	HAE 276 (cf. Santos Jener
			1955 p. 111
M.	Fabius	Basileus	CIL 2.2221
	Porcia	Bassenia	5521
		Bassus	HAE 1832
	Iunius	Bassus Milonianus	CIL 2.2222
	Valeria	Bastula	AE 1951.46
	[...]a	Berulla	CIL 2.2233
L.	Iunius	Bil(icus)	BRAH 56 p.454 (read Lunius)
L.	Postumius	Bla[esus?]	CIL 2.2192 (or Bla[stus]?)
L.	Manlius A.f.A.n.	Bocchus	2225
	Gal.		
L.	Sempronius	C[...]	CIL 2.2241
	Quintia L.1.	Caletyche	Habis 1977 pp. 417–418
		Calt[...] Num(isi)	HAE 2053
		Calva(?)	CIL 2.2248b
	Iulius	Caninius	2211
L.	Manlius A.f. Cor.	Canus	CIL 6.38595
L.	Cornelius	Caranto	CIL 2.2286
		Carpophorus	2295
		Casius	HAE 2052
C.	Iunius	Celadus	CIL 6.20768
	[...] P.f. Se[r.]	[C]eler	CIL 2.2280
	Aurelius	Celerianus	2261
	Marcia	Celsa	2290
C.	Marcius	Celsus	2290
T.	Acclenus T.f. Qui.	Centu[rio?]	2215
		Cerinthus	HAE 1406 = 1832
M.	Caninius	Chilo	CIL 2.2266
	Octavia Modestae 1.	Chloris	2238
N.	Abul[1]ius	Chr[e]st[us]	2254
Q.	Servilius Q.	Chryseros	HAE 277
	[1.?f.?]		
[Cn.	Corne?]lius L.f.	Cinna	CIL 2.5525
	[Gal.]		
		Ciriacus	2267
	[I]unia T.1.	Clarina	Madrid file
Q.	Herennius Q.1.	Clarus	CIL 2.2281
	Circia	C[1]eta	2268
		Clipius	HAE 2052
L.	Licinius L.1.	Cogitans	CIL 2.1201 (or Cogitatus?)
		Communis	6253.13
	Petilia	Comunis	Madrid file
L.	Antonius	Constans	CIL 2.2257
		Conservata	HAE 1857
		Corinthus Sex.	CIL 2.2269
		Marii serv.	

	Herennia Q.1.	Cretica	CIL 2.2281
	Vibia	Crocale	1600
	[C]ornelius	[?Cr]ocalus	BRAH 42 p. 450
	Caecilius	Crysantus	CIL 2.2263
C.	Octavius C.1.	Cuccio	2238
	Lavinia M.1.	Da[...]	Madrid file
	Cornelia L.1.	Danais	CIL 2.2296
	Neria). et T.1.	Daphne	2296
	Iunia	Delicata	2271
	Sulpicia	Delphis	2289
		Demetrius	Madrid file
	(...) Dionisia	Denatiai	HAE 2051
		Diocles	CIL 2.2235
		Dionisia Denatiai	HAE 2051
C.	Valerius	[Dioph]ane[s]	CIL 2.2243
		Diophanes?	6254 II
		[Di?]otimus	2235 (or [Z?]otimus?
L.	Persius	Di[ph]ilus	2239
	Iunia -.1.	Diutera	Madrid file
	[...]lia	Docime	CIL 2.2214
	Sempronius	Donatus	Habis 1977 pp. 449–450
	[...] [Phyla]g[y]ri [E]ris 1.		CIL 2.2259
	[...] Avitae [1.?]	Eucumene	2259
L.	Cornelius L.1.	Euhemerus	2272
Q.	Marius Q.1.	Eumolpus	Habis 1977 pp. 447–449
	Iulia C.Sex.1.	Eunica	CIL 2.2284
	Clodia	Euporia	Anales ... Córd. 1927–28 p. 14
		[Eutyc]hianus	CIL 2.2214
		Fa[...]	CIL 2.2319
		Fabianus	1200
	(...) Hilarus	Fab(ianus)	6252.20
P.	Minicius	Faciundus	2294
	Asicia	Facunda	Madrid file
M.	Cornelius	Fannianus	CIL 2.2252
	Marcia [P.] 1.	Fausta	Habis 1977 pp. 445–447
	Cornelia	[F]au[s]tilla	CIL 2.2270
	Luria C.1.	Faustilla	5536
	Aelia	Faustina	5524
	Rubria	Fau[st]ina	2303
L.	Aelius L.f. Gal.	Faustinus	5524
	Egnatius	Faustinus	2205
		Faustus	HAE 2052
		Faustus	324
		Faustus Fausti	2052
P.	Argentarius).1.	Faustus	Madrid file
	Valeria	Felicitas	CIL 2.2312
		Felix	2234
C.	Octavius Au[...]	Felix	2238
		Festus	AE 1972.276
	Situleia	Filumene	HAE 2055
	Caecilia Q.1.	Firma	CIL 2.2272

Q.	Vibius	Laetus	CIL 2.2216
Q.	Vi[b]i[us] (?)	L[aetus] (?)	2207
L.	[F]u[l]cinius	Lalus	2308
C.	Annius C.f.	Lepidus Marcellus	5522
	Aurelia	Leucothoe	1694
	Herennia Q.l.	Lezbia	2281
L.	Octavius Gal.	Licinianus	XII CAN 1973 pp. 675–676
	(Octavius)	Licinianus	XII CAN 1973 pp. 675–676
C.	Pomponius C.l.	Licinus	CIL 2.2300
		Lucilla	5530 = 2287? = 2190?
		Lucil[l]a	2287 = 5530? = 2190?
		Lucrio	5531
	Iulia T.f.	Lybissa	2223
	Iunia	Lycias	BRAH 52 p. 454
		Ma[...]	CIL 2.2217
C.	Octavius Modestus l.	Macer	2238
	Lollia C.f.	Maniliana	AE 1971.182
	Sentia	Mapalia	CIL 2.5537
M.	Aurelius	Marcellinus	Madrid file
C	Annius C.f. Lepidus	Marcellus	CIL 2.5522
	Publicia	Marcia	BRAC 1927 p. 526
M.	Lucretius	Marianus	CIL 2.2216
		Marsiana (e?)	HAE 2071
	Petilia T.l.	Marta	CIL 2.2282
		Mascellio	2293
L.	Stertinius L.f. Hor.	Maxumus	Habis 1977 pp. 410–412
		Me[...]	HAE 1833
		Melitine	CIL 2.2295
	Elia	Memmesis	Est. Gienneses 1976 p. 85
T.	Marius	Mercello Persinus	CIL 2.2226
	Iunius Bassus	Milonianus	2222
		Missias	HAE 1004 (perhaps Messia)
	Fabia	Modesta	Madrid file
	Octavia T.C.l.	Modesta	CIL 2.2238
L.	Acilius L.f.	Modestus	2234
M.	Aelius	Modestus	HAE 2049
	(Herennius?) Rufi f.	Montanus	CIL 2.2250
L.	Iulius M.f.Q.n. Gal. Gallus	Mummianus	2224
		Munnitia	HAE 2052
		Myrtale	CIL 2.5533
		Nagilio?	CIL 2.2297 = Nigellio?
L.	Axius L.f. Pol.	Naso	Phoenix 1981 pp. 134–141
	Voltillia	Ne?[...]	AE 1971.182
		Nepos	CIL 2.2318
	Servilia	Nepotina	BRAH 52 p.454
		Ner[...]	HAE 1406
		Ner[...]	HAE 325
		Ner[...]	HAE 324

		Ner[...]	HAE 1833
		Nice	CIL 2.2247
		Nicephora	2231
D.	Aemilius	Nicephorus Brattiarus	private collection
		Ni[c]ias	CIL 2.2308
	Abullia N.1.	Nigella	2255
C.	Fabius	Nigellio	2193
C.	Fabius	Nigellio	2194
C.	Sempron[ius C.1.]	Nigellio	2026
		Nigellio?	2297 = Nagilio?
M.	Marcius	Niger	HAE 164
L.	Acxius	Nomentanus	HAE 2046
	(Octavius)	Octavianus Licinianus	XII CAN 1973 pp. 675–676
C.	Aemilius	Oculatus	MMAP 1947 p. 93
	[...] L.).1.	Optata	CIL 2.2299
	[...]a L.f.	Optata	3272
	[Pomp]onia [.]f.	O[pt]a[ta]	2240
	Hirria L.f.	Pa[...]	CIL 2.2282
	[...] Volt.	Pa[...]	2318
L.	Fulcinius	Pacatus	AE 1971.185
	Valeria C.f.	Pa[e]tina	CIL 2.3278
	[...]lus	Pagan[us?]	2233
	Herennia Q.1.	Palaestra	2281
	Pomponius	Pamphilus	2240
	Etria	Parthenio	2275
		[P]arthenius	Madrid file
	V(alerius)	Pate[rnus]	Mél. de l'Ecole Fran. 1918–19 p.314
	Servilius	Patriciensis	BRAH 52 p. 454
	Servilius	Patricius	BRAH 52 p. 454
L.	Iunius P.f. Ser.	Paulinus	CIL 2.5523
		Paullus	AE 1971.179
M.	Asicius Molo	Pelops	Madrid file
T.	Marius Mercello	Persinus	CIL 2.2226
Sex.	Fabius	Phaeder	Habis 1977 pp. 417–418
		[Phil?]ema	CIL 2.2235 (or [Art]ema?)
C.	Num(isius)	Philem[on]	HAE 2053
Q.	Herennius Q.1.	Phileros	CIL 2.2281
		[P]hiletura	2231
	(Cornelius?)	Philoclis	Habis 1977 pp. 410–412
		Philomusus	CIL 2.2300
		[Phyla]rg[y]ri 1. [E]ris	2259
	[...] Avitae 1.	Phylarg[y]ris	2259
	Vibia P.1.	Piale	HAE 2070
L.	Iunius	Plato	BRAH 52 p. 454
L.	Valerius	Poenus	CIL 2.2242
		Pollio	HAE 2052
M.	Cassius	Pollio	CIL 2.2212
P.	Marcius P.f. Ser.	Pollio	Habis 1977 pp. 445–447
L.	Petilius L.1.	Priamus	Madrid file

	Annaea L.l.	Prima	Corduba 1976 pp. 145-151
	Cornelia L.l.	Prima	CIL 2.2286
		Primigenius	2302
C.	Octavius T.C.l.	Primus	2238
L.	Cornelius	Primus	2286
M.	Sempronius M.l.	Princeps	5536
	[Fu]lcinia L.f.	[Pr]isca	AE 1971.185
	Fabia Cn.f.	Prisca	CIL 2.2249
	Valeria Q.f.	Prisca	2249
	Vibia	Prisciana	2263
	Sempronia	Prixilla	2304
		Probus Paull(i) l.	AE 1971.179
L.	Iulius	Protogenes	CIL 2.2237
C.	Octavius C.l.	Prot[us]	2238
P.	Vibius	Protus	HAE 2070
		Prudens	325
		Psechas	Corduba 1976 pp. 145-151
	Iulia).C.l.	Pusinna	CIL 2.2284
	[...]-.f.	Pyramus	2133
	Aemilia	Quarta	private collection
	Cornelia C.l.	Quarta	CIL 2.2271
Cn.	Cacius Cn.l.	Quiet[us]	Madrid file
	Valeria	Quinta	2248a
		Qui[n]t[i]l[ianus]?	2207
	Norbana Q.f.	Quintilla	5068
	Gallia	Quirina	2278
	[...] L.l.	Rast[orianus?]	CIL 2.2319
	[...] -.l.	Rast[orianus?]	2319
	Favonia	Res[tituta]	2276
	Cornelius	Restitutus	2195
	Fannia M.l.	Rhodine	HAE 1830
M.	Fannius M.l.	Rhodo	1830
	Trebia	Romana	CIL 2.2309
		Rome	HAE 1406
	Mussia).l.	Rosia	275 (cf. Santos Jener 1955 p. 111)
	Sulpicia L.f.	Rufina	CIL 2.2308
		Rufina Rufini f.	AE 1971.180
		Rufinus	AE 1971.180
C.	Messius	Rufinus	CIL 2.1637
M.	Helvius M.f. Ser.	Rufus	Habis 7 p. 388
Q.	Herennius	Rufus	CIL 2.2250
	Octavius	Rufus	2204
	Decetia C.l.	Rustica	Madrid file
L.	Antistius	Rusticus	CIL 2.2242
C.	Cosanus C.f. Gal.	Rusticus	2220b
Q.	Licinius Q.f. Ser.	Rusticus	AE 1974.452
		Sabinu[s]	Madrid file
L.	Antestius L.[f.] Ser.	Sabinus	EE 9.1075
M.	Iunius [L.f.] L.n. Gal.	Terenti[anus] Servilius Sabinus	CIL 2.1347 add.

	[St]lattia).1.	Salvia	CIL 2.2307
L.	Calpurnius	Salvianus	2265
	[Li?]cinia C.1.	Salvinus	2307
		Satur	HAE 1832
	Claudia Tib. 1.	Saturnina	Habis 1977 pp. 447–449
L.	Antonius	Saturninus	CIL 2.2257
L.	Iulius M.[f.] Qui.	Saxio	2245
		Scinti[ll]a Numisi	HAE 2053
P.	Front[i]nus	Sciscola	CIL 2.2348
		Secunda	2280
	Caninia M.1.	Secunda	2266
	Maia P.f.	Secunda	Habis 1977 pp. 445–447
	Persia L.f.	Secunda	CIL 2.2247
	Sempronia L.1.	Secunda	5536
	Calpurnia Tertulla	Secundina	AE 1971.180
L.	Salvi[us -.f.]	Sedatus	HAE 1861
	Fabius	Seneca	CIL 2.2249
		Seneca Tarq[...]	ZPE 1979 pp. 137–138
		Septumina	Madrid file
C.	Antonius -.f. Gal.	Seranus	AE 1971.183
	Cornelia	Severa	HAE 1832
M.	Caecilius L.f. Qui.	Severus	Madrid file
L.	Lucretius	Severus	CIL 2.1055
M.	Iunius [L.f.] L.n.	Servilius Sabinus	1347 add.
	Gal. Terenti[anus]		
	Petilia L.1.	Sextia	Madrid file
C.	Nu(misius)	Sex(tianus)	HAE 2053
M.	Licinius	Sodalis	CIL 2.2285
Q.	Dasumius	Solax	2273
		Sper[ata]	AE 1971.179
A.	Fannius	Speudo	AE 1971.182
		Stelenus	HAE 326
	Aurelius	Stephanus	CIL 2.5521
		Studiosus	Corduba 1976 pp. 15–27
		Suciob[...]	CIL 2.6253.12 (a name?)
Q.	Annedius Q.1.	Surillo	5526
		Syntrophilus	2241
	Latinia M.1.	T[...]	Madrid file
M.	Aerarius	Telemac(h)us	AE 1971.181
M.	Iunius [L.f.] L.n.	Terenti[anus]	CIL 2.1347 add.
	Gal.	Servilius Sabinus	
	Calpurnia	Tertulla Secundina	AE 1971.180
		Thaddaius	CIL 2.2232
	[...]a L.1.	Thais	2316
	Publicius	T(h)alamus	AEA 1968 p. 94
	Fortunatus		
	Publicius Valerius	Thalamus	CIL 2.5521
	Fortunatus		
L.	Iulius	Tha[llus?]	2279
M.	Fabius	Themison	Madrid file
		Titilicuta	CIL 2.2295
		Toubo	6254 II
		Trium[phalis](?)	Corduba 1976 pp. 38–40
		Trophime	CIL 2.5538

		[Tr]ophimus C.C.P. ser.	CIL 2.2229
	Pomponia Q.f.	Tusca	2301
	Helvia	Tu[scilla?]	2279
	Caecilia	Tusculana	2264
M.	Helvius	[Tuscus?]	2279
	Licinia L.l.	[T]yche	1201
L.	Annius	Valens	HAE 1407
	Aurelia	Valeriana	CIL 2.2260 = 5529
Q.	Cornelius M.f. Gal.	Valerinus	3272
		Veneris	2231
	Baebia	Venusta	CIL 6.34664
		Venustia	Madrid file
M.	Lucretius	Verna	CIL 2.2246
		Vetusta	Madrid file
	Elia	Vetustina	Est. Giennenses 1976 p. 85
	Aelia	Vitalis	CIL 2.2209
	Sempronia	Vitalis	2305
P.	Volumnius	Vitalis	AE 1971.179
M.	Iuniu[s]	Ultimus	CIL 2.4976.14
	Calpurnius	Urbanus	2265
Cn.	Cacius Cn.l.	Ursus	Madrid file
	Iunius	Ursus	HAE 1595
L.	Aemilius L.l.	Xanthus	MMAP 1958 pp. 28-29
C.	Valerius	Zephryus	CIL 2.2235
	Valeria	[...]	CIL 2.2311
		[...]anus L.l.	2316
		[...]auricius	Habis 1977 pp. 449-450 (cognomen?)
		[...]epor	CIL 2.2316
		[...]lus	2233
		[...]nus L.l.	2316
	Octavia	[...]o	2238
		[...]onus	2320
		[...]rus	2316
	Vale[...]	[...]sep[...]	2313
	[...]s L.f. Men.	[...]tus	2280

Notes

The English spelling of place names has been used when this is the most familiar to the reader (e.g., Seville instead of Sevilla--but not Cordova for Córdoba). Otherwise Spanish and ancient names have been employed.

1. Schulten 1959 vol. I pp. 221-224, 244-246; vol. II pp. 47-61; Abad 1975.

2. For a general treatment, Thouvenot 1973 pp. 23-54; Arribas 1963; Cuadrado 1967 pp. 147-165; Savory 1968.

3. Santos Jener 1958.2 p. 83; Savory 1968 p. 29 and, in general, pp. 28-33.

4. Santos Jener 1958.2 p. 84.

5. Savory 1968 pp. 81-83; Pellicer 1967 p. 42.

6. Neolithic remains, Santos Jener 1958.2 pp. 81-82, 85-88, 96. Flint hatchet heads come from Molino de Sansueña, calle Cruz Conde no. 12, and the Huerta de San Pedro: Santos Jener 1958.2 pp. 87-88.

7. Savory 1968 pp. 75-78. For other Neolithic activity see Savory pp. 90-96, 118-119; Muñoz 1969 p. 40.

8. Renfrew 1967 = 1973 p. 273.

9. Harrison 1977 pp. 69-71.

10. Renfrew 1967 = 1973 pp. 263-277; 1979 pp. 85-91.

11. The arrival of the first metal workers in the area is shadowy. According to Savory 1968 p. 147 and Blance 1961 p. 200, some tombs and "tholoi" in central Andalucía show a relationship to the Los Millares culture, which was centered in Almería. The Los Millares culture dates, according to calibrated carbon-14 figures, to c.3000 B.C. (Renfrew 1979 p. 91). The salient technological advance is the exploitation and use of copper deposits in the vicinity. See also Santos Jener 1958.2 p. 89.

12. Renfrew 1967 = 1973 p. 270.

13. Santos Jener 1955 p. 112; 1958.2 pp. 89-90 (beaker ware near Córdoba at the Cerro de la Sagrada Familia, in the Campo de la Verdad; = Harrison 1977 no. 211?). The account of the "Beaker culture" by Savory 1968 pp. 166-189 must be rejected in light of analyses such as that presented by Harrison 1977. On the intrusive nature of beaker ware in the Guadalquivir valley, see Harrison p. 70.

14. Renfrew 1967 = 1973 p. 273. For a nondiffusionist account of

southeastern Spanish prehistory, including a model for the natural evolution of the Los Millares and El Argar cultures, see Gilman 1976.

15. Harrison 1977 p. 72.

16. Renfrew 1979 p. 91.

17. Type of bronze: Savory 1968 pp. 212-213; Gilman 1976 pp. 309-310; in general, see Savory 1968 pp. 193-199.

18. Savory 1968 p. 199; cf. Arribas 1967 p. 106; Muñoz 1969 pp. 43-44.

19. On Carmona: Savory 1968 p. 199; Muñoz 1969 p. 41. Sites near Córdoba: Santos Jener 1958.2 pp. 91-92, 86, 90.

20. Santos Jener 1958.2 pp. 89-90.

21. Harrison 1977 p. 72.

22. Luzón 1973; Blanco 1969. These studies supplant Bernier 1963.

23. Luzón 1973 p. 35

24. Blanco 1969 pp. 123-125. Blázquez 1975.2 pp. 367-368 also sees ceramic evidence for an infiltration in the ninth-eighth centuries B.C. See also Savory 1968 pp. 232-236.

25. Blanco 1969 pp. 126-132, 141-142, 144-149.

26. Luzón 1973 pp. 29, 35.

27. There is no "Roman horizon" at Colina de los Quemados. The final Iberian phase is overlaid by remains from the Arabic (i.e., post-Roman) period. Luzón 1973 p. 35.

28. Blanco 1969 pp. 149-152.

29. Blanco 1969 p. 158; see also Blázquez 1979 p. 424, who attributes the new technology to peoples from the Meseta.

30. Blanco 1969 pp. 152-153 reports the find of a marvelous stela at Ategua in material dating to this same incised ware period. On it are pictured a warrior, with "carp's tongue" sword and round shield, and a chariot below. Perhaps the stela is indicative of a warrior element in this society. "Carp's tongue" swords are generally associated with the advanced Bronze Age culture of Andalucía. One has also been found near Córdoba at Palma del Río (Savory 1949 p. 153). Blázquez 1975.2 p. 360 discusses the evidence from the Colina and from Cabezo de San Pedro (Huelva) and postulates an influx from the Meseta in 700-600 B.C. See also Savory 1968 pp. 214-215.

31. Jaén 1935 p. 42; Blanco 1966.1 p. 21; Santos Jener 1955 p. 69. Santos Jener repeats the guess as to the outline of the city that was made by José de la Torre. Santos himself contends that the only firm fact in support of this supposition is an attestation of an Iberian town next to the Roman camp of 206 B.C. However, such a Roman camp, supposedly established by L. Marcius, is a figment of the imagination. I know of no reference to it or, a fortiori, to an Iberian town next to it. On Iberian statuettes found, see Jaén 1935 pp. 25-26.

32. Other native relics have been found in the burials at the Camino Viejo de Almodóvar in the outskirts of the modern city. Santos Jener 1955 p. 10 (pot, plates, urns), p. 18 (terracotta figurine); Carbonell 1924

pp. 441-443 (bust in relief). The Comisión de Monumentos de Córdoba 1926.1
p. 57 reported the remains of a prehistoric wall in the area of the cemetery "de la Salud."

33. Santos Jener 1958.2 p. 94. Various far-fetched etymologies are
given by Jaén 1935 p. 30. Schulten 1959 vol. II p. 50 and Santos Jener
1958.2 p. 94 defend a Punic origin and the equation of "Cord-" with
"Cart-," Punic for "city."

34. Livy 28.22.1 says that the native name of the Guadalquivir is the
Certis. Vowel substitution, as well as substitution of "d" for "t",
causes no linguistic problems; "Cord-" and "Cert-" can easily reflect
the same native word. For the -uba suffix see Untermann 1961 p. 17 and
map 16; Thouvenot 1973 p. 189 n. 3; Contreras 1977 pp. 375-377; Santos
Jener 1958.2 p. 94. Perhaps the name of a native from Castulo, Cerdubelo
(Livy 28.20.11), also retains the stem Cerd- = Cert-, although Albertos
1966 p. 86 thinks it a Celtic or at any rate an Indo-European root. The
suffix -belo is certainly native; Untermann 1975 vol. I.1 pp. 77-78.

35. Strabo 3.2.2 (C141) actually cites Munda as the "metropolis",
but he may have erred. Cf. Hübner 1900 p. 1223, Knapp 1977 p. 124 n. 71
on this question. "Metropolis" occurs with reference to Córdoba in some
manuscripts of Ptolemy 2.4.9 (see Ptolemy ed. Müller p. 117). The equation of Cord- with Tort-/Turd- assumes that the c to t change was possible
in Iberian or to the Latin ear; see also Schulten 1959 vol. II p. 50.

36. In general, Tovar 1961 p. 39, 55; Untermann 1975 vol. I.1 p. 78.
The only native inscription reported so far is a graffito on a sherd
found at Colina. The scratching, written in the "Iberian" script, and
reading (right to left) IRDE ... or IRTE ... , is insufficient evidence
for judging which writing system was used by the inhabitants. See
Bernier 1968; Blázquez 1975.2 p. 359.

37. Bernier 1968 p. 108 correctly emphasizes that Córdoba was at the
meeting point of Iberian, Turdetanian (i.e., the successors of Tartessian),
and Indo-European (i.e., Mesetan) cultures.

38. For a good summary of the role of Phoenicians in the Iberian Peninsula, Blanco 1967 pp. 167-197.

39. Blanco 1969 pp. 134, 136; Blázquez 1975 pp. 369-370. Other Punic
artifacts have been found in the cemetery of the Camino Viejo de Almodóvar;
Santos Jener 1948 pp. 211, 213; 1958.2 pp. 94-95.

40. Blázquez 1979 p. 423; Blanco 1969 p. 158.

41. Santos Jener 1958.2 p. 94. No solid evidence for this factory is
cited. The derivation of Corduba from Cort- = Cart- = Punic "city" is unlikely, as I noted above.

42. Arribas 1963 pp. 138, 149, 186-187; Tovar 1963; Blázquez 1979.
In general, see Savory 1968 pp. 239-259; Untermann 1961; Tovar 1961. Tovar
1963 sees Celtic roots in such Andalusian place names as Cartare, Maenake,
Obulco, and Saguntia, as well as evidence for Celtic overlordship of
Tartessos in the name of the Tartessian king Arganthonios (p. 360). Celts
in Andalucía remained ethnically identifiable until the first century A.D.
(p. 365). On archaeological remains of the fifth and fourth centuries
B.C., see pp. 368-370.

43. Blázquez 1979 pp. 422-423 identifies the "buried ware" round house

occupiers at Colina as Celtiberians. The date for these remains (eighth to sixth centuries B.C.) seems too early to allow this identification.

44. The basic work is still García y Bellido 1948.2. For a more general account, see Blanco 1967.

45. Arribas 1963 p. 44; Blázquez 1975.2 pp. 309-310.

46. Trías 1967.

47. Bernier 1963 p. 204 reports a red figure fragment, which he identifies as Attic, from the fourth century B.C. It was found in one of his trenches at Colina. The manner of these excavations makes the significance of this find uncertain.

48. No native's name is known from Córdoba. Jaén 1935 p. 34 mentions a "Cordoban chief" named Auraricus. This person seems to be imaginary; I have found no other reference to him, nor does he appear in Albertos 1966.

49. On the date of the abandonment of the Colina settlement see Luzón 1973 p. 35, p. 38 n. 35. Further out from Colina, Marcos 1977.4 pp. 225-226 has excavated another native site in the zone called Valladares. Here too, many pre-Roman and Arab remains came to light, but practically no Roman artifacts. Whatever native element there was in Córdoba has left little trace archaeologically or epigraphically. Contreras 1977 p. 393 can adduce only four "pre-Roman, Iberian" names in the epigraphy: Eunica (CIL 2.2284); Mapalia (CIL 2.5537); Caranto (CIL 2.2286); and Boccus (CIL 2.2225). Of these, Eunica is the normal Greek name and Mapalia may be Celtic (Albertos 1966 p. 147) or African; Caranto (Albertos p. 76) is Celtic, and Boccus is African (Albertos p. 56). Perhaps Clodius Turrinus, the friend of the elder Seneca, bears a native cognomen.

50. See n. 31 above. Contreras 1977 p. 388 n. 17 reflects Santos' thesis, and Chaves 1978 p. 17 n. 9 accepts it, following Vicent 1973 p. 673. Ruggiero 1900 p. 1208 thinks that Córdoba had its roots in the canabae of a legionary base.

51. Cf. the situation in the winter of 48-47 B.C.: Cassius Longinus, left in charge at Córdoba by Julius Caesar, dispersed his troops in various towns (Bell. Alex. 48).

52. On garrisons in Iberia, see Knapp 1977 pp. 15-18 (p. 17 on Ilipa).

53. The source for Strabo's account of the foundation of Córdoba seems to be Posidonius. Posidonius visited the Peninsula about 95 B.C. Presumably the Marcellan tradition goes back at least that far. See also Blanco 1966.1 p. 19; Vittinghoff 1952 p. 73 n. 1; Hübner 1900 p. 1221. Hübner earlier supposed that the foundation reference derived from Polybius (1867 p. 306). At any rate, it seems reasonable to assume that Marcellus was considered the "founder" of Córdoba by the end of the second century B.C. at the latest. Wiseman 1956 pp. 20, 29 is wrong to name Ti. Sempronius Gracchus as the founder in 179 B.C.

54. M. Claudius Marcellus Aeserninus was a quaestor in Ulterior in 48 B.C.

55. The name of this town seems to be Celtic and has nothing to do with Marcus Marcellus.

56. In general, Simon 1962 pp. 30-46.

57. Polyb. 35.1-4; Appian Ib. 49; Knapp 1977 p. 47.

58. Eutr. 4.9.2 (cf. Oxy. Per. of Livy 48); Polyb. 35.2.2 (wintering).

59. Some modern views are summarized by Contreras 1977 pp. 396-402. To these add Ortí 1958 pp. 35-36.

60. See Blanco 1966.1 p. 20; Wiegels 1973 pp. 563-564. Possibly Iliturgis should be added as another foundation: Knapp 1977 pp. 109-110.

61. Hübner 1867 p. 306; Bosch Gimpera 1935 p. 108; Vittinghoff 1952 p. 72; Ortí 1958 p. 36; García y Bellido 1959.1 pp. 451-452; H. Galsterer 1971 p. 9; Brunt 1971 p. 215; Griffin 1972 p. 18; 1975 p. 30; Tovar 1974 p. 87; Contreras 1977 pp. 394-396, 409; Wiegels 1973 p. 563 leaves the question open; Chaves 1978 pp. 18-19 prefers 169/168; Santos Jener 1950 gives 169 on p. 144 and 152 on p. 148.

62. Contreras 1977 pp. 395-396 contends that, had the town been founded in 169/68, Livy would have mentioned it. But the notice on the foundation of Gracchuris is retained only in an epitome; although the actual text of Livy is extant, it makes no mention of Gracchuris. This shows the inherent danger of arguing from silence. For Contreras' further statement that Marcellus wintered at Córdoba in 169/68, I can find no evidence. Wiegels' point (1973 p. 563), that few soldiers would have been available for settlement in the midst of the wars of the period, seems inconclusive.

63. Wiseman 1956 pp. 20, 29 and Ortí 1958 pp. 38-39 favor a citizen colony; cf. Contreras 1977 p. 402, who is uncertain whether citizen or Latini are involved at Córdoba.

64. Latin colony: H.Galsterer 1971 p. 10; Wiegels 1978.1 p. 205. Vicus etc.: Hübner 1867 p. 306; 1900 p. 1221; Marchetti 1922 p. 877; Van Nostrand 1937 p. 137; Thouvenot 1973 p. 184; Knapp 1977 pp. 120-121. Conventus: cf. Wilson 1966 p. 16; Blanco 1966.1 p. 22; Griffin 1975 p. 30; expressly rejected by Contreras 1977 p. 408. Thouvenot 1973 p. 189 calls Córdoba an oppidum, but this term has no legal meaning and cannot be used to describe the status of a town.

65. Vittinghoff 1952 p. 73 n. 1, followed by H. Galsterer 1971 p. 9 n. 20. See also Hübner 1900 p. 1223, who seems to take the cohorts as a local muster.

66. Wilson 1966 p. 16 n. 8; Griffin 1972 p. 18; Thouvenot 1973 p. 141; Brunt 1971 p. 216 n. 4; Wiegels 1973 p. 564.

67. Carteia's foundation as a Latin colony in 171 B.C. (Livy 43.3) does not compromise Strabo's statement; only the area along the Guadalquivir valley is meant by "in this area." Cf. H. Galsterer 1971 p. 9 n. 21. It is true that ἀποικία can have much the same neutral meaning as oppidum in Latin. ἀποικία could here mean only "settlement", but Strabo does not use the term promiscuously and appears to have selected it here because he thought that Córdoba had been founded with a special status.

68. This possibility is not given sufficiently serious consideration by Knapp 1977 pp. 120-122.

69. All founded in the 120s B.C. Wiegels 1974; Knapp 1977 pp. 125-131 (Valentia); 131-139 (Palma and Pollentia).

70. For conventus and Latin colonies, the lists at Kornemann 1900.1 pp. 514-418; 1900.2 p. 1183.

71. Levick 1967 p. 69; Hatzfeld 1919 p. 294; Brunt 1971 p. 215. For general aspects of conventus, Sherwin-White 1973 pp. 225-227.

72. Cives Romani existed in Latin colonies, for many of the chief men would be Roman citizens per magistratum. Of course, Roman businessmen would also be there in some number.

73. Knapp 1980.2 and below.

74. For the Carteian inscription, see Woods 1969.

75. Citizens: Wilson 1966 p. 16 (veterans); H. Galsterer 1971 p. 15; Contreras 1977 p. 383. Romans and Italians: Wiegels 1973 pp. 563-564. Hybridae: Blanco 1966.1 pp. 20-21 (rejected as not "select" enough by Contreras 1977 pp. 383-384). On the loose meaning of Romaioi (not strictly "Roman citizens" only), see Brunt 1971 p. 215 (Romans and Italians) and Knapp 1977 p. 138.

76. Local aristocracy and auxiliary veterans: Contreras 1977 p. 383; Blanco 1966.1 p. 21. The attempt to find evidence of these natives in the prosopography of Córdoba fails: Contreras 1977 p. 393 and above n. 49.

77. Cf. Levick 1967 pp. 69-72.

78. Cf. the example of Pisidian Antioch, Levick 1967 pp. 75-76.

79. Santos Jener 1955 fig. 17; Blanco 1966.1 p. 25; 1976 p. 140.

80. Vicent 1973 pp. 676-677. (1) L(ucio) Axio L(uci) f(ilio) Pol(lia tribu) Naso(i) / q(uaestori), trib(uno) milit(um) / proleg(ato), decem- vir(o) stlit(ibus) iud(icandis) / vicani vici Hispani. (2) L(ucio) Axio L(uci) f(ilio) Pol(lia tribu) N[ason](i) / q(uaestori), tri(buno) / militum prol(egato), / decemvir(o) stlitibus iu(dicandis), / vican(i) vici forensis. The first was found in the street Angel de Saavedra; the find site of the second is near the ancient forum (Contreras 1977 p. 392). The stones are themselves statue bases. On the inscriptions see Knapp 1981.

81. For other urban vici in towns of the Empire, the list in ILS 3.2 p. 673. On the setting up by vici of inscriptions honoring persons, cf. the well-attested activity of the vici in Pisidian Antioch (Levick 1967 p. 76). For vici in Spain, see Rodríguez Neila 1976.2.

82. Cf. Contreras 1977 pp. 391-392, who sees the vicus Hispanus as a remnant of the original settlement, as does Rodríguez Neila 1976.2 p. 117.

83. Castejón 1964 pp. 372, 375.

84. Blanco 1966.1 pp. 21-22 accepts the dipolis on the evidence of the wall and the Arab city. Tovar 1974 p. 87 n. 74 accepts it on the basis of the vici inscriptions, plus the coloni et incolae of CIL 2.2222, 2226 (from Córdoba). But Tovar's interpretation of the incolae is surely false; Henderson 1953 p. 140; Wiegels 1978.2 p. 658. Incolae have nothing to do with the remnants of a native, noncitizen population in a town; every town had incolae. Tovar's comparison of Córdoba and the known double community at Emporion is also inappropriate; there is no indication that the Cordoban native and immigrant settlements were hostile. See Wiegels 1978.2 p. 658.

85. In general: Levick 1967 pp. 69-71; Salmon 1969 p. 169 n. 29. Minturnae (a citizen colony in 209 B.C.): Sherwin-White 1973 p. 80 n. 4. Salonae: Wilkes 1969 pp. 223-225; Knapp 1980.2.

86. For these wars see Bosch Gimpera 1935 pp. 89-144; Simon 1962 pp. 87-142; Knapp 1977 pp. 30-32.

87. <u>Anth</u>. <u>Lat</u>. 409 (Riese). The authenticity of this epigram may be doubted, as by Blanco 1966.1 p. 18, who considers it a rhetorical exercise of the late Empire and argues that its spirit is wholly alien to Seneca (p. 19 n.6), and C. Prato 1964 p. VIII; however, on the basis of word se-lection and style, it seem likely to be genuine. See Stauber 1920. Au-thenticity is not decided by Ortí 1958 p. 54; Rozelaar 1976 p. 82 n. 5 rejects Prato's caution and accepts the poem's authenticity. The histori-cal value of the epigram is considerable. In view of the historical bent of Seneca's father, I suppose that Seneca learned something of Córdoba's local history from him. Livy may also be a source (cf. Blanco 1966.1 p. 19). The events seem to be narrated in reverse chronological order, beginning with the civil war. The entire epigram runs as follows:

> Corduba, solve comas et tristes indue vultus,
> Inlacrimans cineri munera mitte meo.
> Nunc longinqua tuum deplora, Corduba, vatem,
> Corduba non alio tempore maesta magis:
> Tempore non illo, quo versis viribus orbis
> Incubuit belli tota ruina tibi,
> Cum geminis oppressa malis utrimque peribas
> Et tibi Pompeius, Caesar et hostis erat;
> Tempore non illo, quo ter tibi funera centum
> Heu nox una dedit, quae tibi summa fluit;
> Non, Lusitanus quateret cum moenia latro,
> Figeret et portas lancea torta tuas.
> Ille tuus quondam magnus, tua gloria, civis,
> Infigor scopulo: Corduba, solve comas,
> Et gratare tibi, quod te natura supremo
> Adluit Oceano: tardius ista doles!

88. Blanco 1966.1 p. 30 dates it to 141 B.C., with no evidence. He later dates it to the civil war.

89. Military activity: Simon 1962 pp. 68-142; Blanco 1966.1 p. 33; Thouvenot 1973 p. 126. Situation in 145 B.C.: Appian <u>Ib</u>. 65; Knapp 1977 pp. 30-31

90. Appian <u>Ib</u>. 65 (144 B.C.), 66 (143 B.C.). Knapp 1977 pp. 202-203; Thouvenot 1973 pp. 126-127. Blanco 1966.1 p. 30 supposes that, earlier in the Viriathic war, Plautius (commander in 146 B.C.) also used Cór-doba as a headquarters. For such action, there is no explicit evidence.

91. Thouvenot 1973 p. 189 even considers Córdoba to have been the headquarters for Romans in the Viriathic war. If so, then at least in 145 B.C. it was abandoned in favor of Urso.

92. For a detailed discussion of this coin, its type and date, Chaves 1978 pp. 43-88; Knapp 1980.1.

93. The inscription <u>CIL</u> 2.2227, in which an Egnatuleius Seneca appears as a quaestor, is not from Córdoba but from Tarraco. No other quaestor is attested at the town. See Knapp 1979. For Roman quaestors minting in local towns, Mommsen 1860 pp. 374-375. It is impossible that Q stands for q(uinquennalis).

94. A Cn. Iulius Mento appears in Livy 4.26.1 as consul in 431 B.C. However, the true reading is C. not Cn., as Ogilvie 1965 p. 575 shows. Mento is thus not an examples of a Cn. Iulius.

95. See Crawford 1969.

96. MRR vol. 1 p. 552.

97. Hildburgh 1921 pp. 162-163.

98. Crawford 1969 p. 86 n. 184 for the hoard. Also Hildburgh 1921.

99. MRR vol. 1 p. 538, 539 n. 4; Thouvenot 1973 p. 189.

100. On the events of the war see Schulten 1923 p. 1748-1751.

101. Sallust Hist. 2.70 (M); Plutarch Sert. 22.2; Val. Max. 9.1.5; MRR vol. 2 p. 98.

102. Support for Metellus: Gabba 1954 p. 93 (for); Wilson 1966 p. 31 n. 3 (against). "Culte du chef": Etienne 1958 p. 113. Clientele: Etienne 1958 p. 105. There are only four Caecilii in Cordoban prosopography; perhaps few received grants of citizenship from him. Cf. Cicero Arch. 26. This episode is perhaps the origin of Ortí's statement (1958 p. 41) that Cordoban poets accompanied Cornelius Balbus to Rome, for which I can find no evidence.

103. Blanco 1966.1 p. 30.

104. Maurenbrecher ad loc. relates this earthquake to one in Italy in 77/76 B.C. and dates the Cordoban earthquake to these years as well. An earthquake in Italy would be unlikely to have a "sister" earthquake in Iberia, however. It is best to date the disaster only generally to Metellus' period of command. The Sierra Nevada to the south of Córdoba are susceptible to earthquakes: Schulten 1959 vol. 1 p. 292.

105. MRR vol. 1 p. 180.

106. Sutherland 1939 p. 119.

107. Cf. Knapp 1977 pp. 119-120.

108. Blanco 1966.1 p. 22.

109. Griffin 1972 n. 4; his name "advertises a connection with some Roman Claudius--perhaps the founder of Corduba." Kajanto 1965 p. 184 takes the cognomen as Latin in origin, but it is very uncommon and could hide a native root.

110. Griffin 1972 pp. 4-5; 1975 p. 30; Wiegels 1972 n. 214.

111. Cordoban origin: Blanco 1966.1 pp. 28-29 (pro); Castillo 1965 n. 336 (con).

112. Cf Albertini 1923 pp. 21-22.

113. Caesar Bell. Civ. 1.38 with 2.19.3. Other reports are secondary: Eutr. 6.20.2; Orosius 6.15.6; Livy Per. 110, 111; Dio 41.23.

114. One of these was the legio vernacula (Bell. Civ. 2.20.4). See Yoshimura 1963.

115. Bell. Civ. 2.18.4: 180,000 sesterces (45,000 denarii); 20,000 pounds of silver (1,680,000 denarii at 84 denarii to the pound); 120,000 modii of grain, at three sesterces per modius. On these rates of conversion, Knapp 1977 pp. 167, 169 n. 15. These exactions accord well with the

yield of booty brought back from Spain in the early second century B.C.; that booty, over sixteen reported years, averaged about 2,750,000 denarii per year. Knapp 1977 pp. 167-169.

116. Bell. Civ. 2.19.2-3. This conventus must not be confused (as Tovar 1974 p. 87) with the later conventus iuridici which are judicial assize districts. The cohortes colonicae are not from Córdoba (cum eo casu venissent) and so are no proof that Córdoba was a colony at this time (as Vittinghoff 1952 p. 73 n. 1 and H. Galsterer 1971 p. 9 n. 20). See above on Córdoba's status. This episode offers proof, if any is needed, that Córdoba was walled at this time.

117. Dio 41.24.2; Cicero Att. 6.6.5.

118. Location uncertain but somewhere in Lusitania: Tovar 1974 pp. 254-255.

119. This is the only mention of Córdoba's basilica. So far no archaeological remains have been securely linked to this structure, which would have been near the forum, since it was a center of litigation and general business.

120. Cf. CIL 2.2265; Castillo 1965 p. 47 n. 85.

121. Castillo 1965 p. 21 n. 44 does not make this connection. Notice that Clodius Turrinus before (Seneca Contr. 10.4.16) and Sex. Marius after (Dio 58.22.2; Castillo 1965 p. 125 n. 235) are Cordubenses and the richest men in the province as well. This is another indication of Córdoba's prosperity.

122. Other plotters: Manilius Tusculus (Bell. Alex. 53.2); L. Racilius (52.2, 53.3) and L. (Iuventius) Laterensis (53.4)(apparently not provincials); L. Licinius Squillus (52.4); Q. Sestius (55.5).

123. Bell. Alex. 57.4-5; 59.1. Dio 42.15.2 also notes that Cordobans participated, as does Livy (Per. 111); both probably just follow Bell. Alex. here.

124. On Aeserninus, see Dio 42.15; Münzer 1899 p. 2770.

125. I have followed the narrative of Caesar's continuator in giving this account of events at Córdoba in 49/48 B.C. Although there is an obvious bias in Caesar's favor, the validity of the outline of historical fact can be accepted. There is no other source against which the Caesarian account can be checked, however.

126. Dio 43.29.3; cf. Cicero Fam. 9.13.1.

127. Wealth: Bell. Alex. 55.2; Bell. Hisp. 33.3-4. Annii in the south: Castillo 1965 n. 35-51a; Quin(c)tii: Castillo 1965 n. 287-288. Scapula: Kajanto 1965 p. 255. There are only four Scapulae in CIL 2 and none from Baetica. Dio: the codex Mediceus manuscript gives κύιντον, which need not be a mistake for κυιντιον as Reimarus emends. Indeed the whole name is corrupt, with 'L' giving κύιντον σκιπίωνα. Cf. Wilson 1966 p. 38 n. 4.

128. See also Syme 1958 p. 785.

129. Dio 43.30.4-5; Cicero Fam. 6.18.2; Bell. Hisp. 1.3.

130. Date (46 B.C.): Bell. Hisp. 2.1; plot in which P. Curtius lost his life: Cicero Fam. 6.18.2; events: Dio 43.28.31.

131. Bell. Hisp. 1.3 speaks as though a number of towns opposed Cnaeus; Dio 43.28.31 says that only Ulia was loyal to Caesar.

132. Appian Bell. Civ. 2.103: 27 days to Spain; Strabo 3.4.9: 27 days to Obulco; Suetonius Div. Iul. 57: 24 days to Spain; Orosius 6.16: 17 days to Saguntum.

133. Bell. Hisp. 1.3-4; Dio 43.28.32.

134. Strabo 3.2.2 twice puts Munda where Córdoba should be. See Mommsen 1893 p. 613 (= 1909 p. 67); Schulten 1940 p. 160.

135. Bell. Hisp. 5-31; Dio 43.28.34-38; cf. Florus 2.13.77-85 and Schulten 1940. At one point, a supply train from Córdoba destined for Cnaeus was intercepted by Caesar, who took men and animals to his camp: Bell. Hisp. 11.1.

136. Bell. Hisp. 32-34; Dio 43.28.38-39; Appian Bell. Civ. 2.104. Sex. Pompey fled to Citerior: Cicero Att. 12.37.4; Florus 2.13.86.

137. There is no way to tell which side the Annei took, despite Rostbach's attempt (1894) to divine Pompeian sympathies. See Griffin 1975 p. 31.

138. Suetonius Div. Iul. 28: Caesar gave gifts to towns in Spain.

139. Martial Epig. 9.61 speaks of a plane tree planted by Caesar in Córdoba. Of course he could have planted it as quaestor in 69 B.C. or as propraetor in 61, but I am inclined to date the famous tree to his stay at this time. Plutarch Caes. 17.2 records that Caesar had his first epileptic seizure while at Córdoba. This event is also not closely datable.

140. Cicero Fam. 10.31.5: 16 March 43 B.C. On Sex. Pompey, Dio 45.10.

141. Pollio and Córdoba: Griffin 1972 pp. 5-6.

142. Most recently, Tovar 1974 pp. 87-88. Also, e.g., Hübner 1900 p. 1222; Vittinghoff 1952 p. 72; Blanco 1966.1 p. 36. Refuted by Galsterer-Kröll 1972 p. 97.

143. García y Bellido 1959.1 p. 451. Hübner 1900 p. 1222; 1867 p. 306; Ruggiero 1900; Kornemann 1900.1 p. 527; Grant 1946 p. 4; Marchetti 1922 p. 877; cf. H. Galsterer 1971 p. 10 n. 26, who does not rule out the possibility.

144. Entirely against Pompeians: Griffin 1972 p. 18, who also rejects the argumentum ex cognomine; Contreras 1977 pp. 406-407. H. Galsterer 1971 p. 10 n. 23 also rejects the cognomen argument, and Galsterer-Kröll 1972 provides extensive evidence.

145. Knapp 1977 p. 123.

146. Unfortunately the evidence of Seneca the Elder is unhelpful here. His use, at Contr. 1 praefatio 11, of colonia mea (intra coloniam meam me continuit) in reference to his experience during the civil wars is inconclusive, for the passage was written in A.D. 37-41, when Córdoba was undoubtedly a citizen colony. Likewise his reference at Suas. 2.18 to Statorius Victor as municeps meus might only be the loose use of the term municeps, meaning "fellow townsman." If so, the reference provides no evidence for a municipal status for Córdoba. It is to be regretted that Seneca makes no clear reference to Córdoba as a colony at an early date; he does to Tarraco in a context datable to 26-25 B.C. (Contr. 10 praefatio 14).

147. Isid. <u>Etym</u>. 15.1.71.

148. Gades had been made a <u>municipium</u> <u>c</u>. <u>R</u>. in 49 B.C.: H. Galsterer 1971 p. 17 n. 5. On the other towns, H. Galsterer 1971.

149. The tribes at Spanish towns tell much of previous status. The Sergian tribe is the tribe of Latin towns before 45 B.C.; Carteia (Woods 1969) sets the pattern. No town with the Sergia is attested as having a different status (Hispalis, Italica, Córdoba, Tucci, Ucubi, Urso, Hasta), and two towns attested as allied (<u>civitates</u> <u>foederatae</u>) before 45 B.C., Gades and Epora, are both in the Galerian tribe, not the Sergian.

150. Perhaps "Regia" refers to the family of Marcius Rex, the family of Caesar's grandmother: H. Galsterer 1971 p. 22 n. 53. Caesar also traced his ancestry back to Ancus Marcius and to the Alban kings (Dio 43. 43.2-3; Suetonius <u>Div</u>. <u>Iul</u>. 6.1). The cognomen may refer to Hasta's having once been the seat of a king (cf. Hippo Regius in Numidia). Could "Regia" have some peculiar pertinence to <u>hasta</u>? As for Caesar as patrician, it is true that he did not emphasize his noble status and even assumed the tribunician authority in 48 B.C. (Dio 42.20.3, 44.4.2). His pride in his ancient <u>gens</u> might still lead him to choose <u>patricia</u> as cognomen for a foundation. Galsterer-Kröll 1972 p. 67 n. 128 rejects a connection between Genetiva and Venus Genetrix.

151. Galsterer-Kröll 1972 pp. 59, 96 deduces a Caesarian or early Augustan date.

152. Clupea is a Colonia Iulia P[...], and Thabraca is a Colonia V(...) P(...). <u>Paterna</u> is a common cognomen and is the abbreviated word designated by P(...) in many cases. See the list in Galsterer-Kröll 1972. At one time "Patricia" was thought to lurk in Barcelona's name (Colonia Iulia Augusta Pat(...) Faventia Barcino), but an inscription discovered in the 1960s established the usual Pat(erna) instead of Pat(ricia): Balil 1968 p. 156 n. 1; H. Galsterer 1971 p. 27 n. 112. In general, a good history of <u>cognomina</u> is Galsterer-Kröll 1972 pp. 44-45.

153. Ortí 1958 p. 39 thought that all veterans were patricians and so Marcellus' "veteran settlement" in 152 was named after them! Contreras 1977 pp. 383-384, 387 and Chaves 1978 p. 20 relate the epithet to the "select" nature of the Romans at the foundation. So early an origin for the cognomen is properly rejected by Blanco 1966.1 p. 21 and Hübner 1867 p. 306. Marcellus, as a plebeian, would hardly choose such a name: Vittinghoff 1951 p. 73 n. 1.

154. Vittinghoff 1951 p. 73 n. 1.

155. Augustan source: H. Galsterer 1971 p. 10; Vittinghoff 1952 p. 73 n. 1 makes a comparison with Augustus' use of the name <u>vicus</u> <u>patricius</u> in his colony at Pisidian Antioch; however, the <u>vici</u> there are modeled on those of Rome and so have nothing to compare with Córdoba's name, unless it be thought that the epithet was inspired by a <u>vicus</u> name in Rome. Marcellus: Griffin 1972 p. 19.

156. <u>Patricius</u> as an adjective for Pater is not widely attested, but consider <u>Lydus</u> <u>de mens</u>. 4.1 (quoting Antistius Labeo): here Ianus Pater (as is the normal epithet: Otto 1918 p. 1176) is called Ianus Patricius. The adjective Patricius is not, however, attested in relation to Liber Pater or his cult. In partial defense of the idea it can be pointed out that other divine epithets appear in the area--for example, Urso Colonia Genetiva from Venus Genetrix (Genetivus is also attested for Apollo) and

Sacili Martialium from Mars. There was some connection between Caesar and
the cult of Liber Pater: Servius on <u>Ecl</u>. 5.29. Names of gods as cognomens
were only common in the period 124-118 B.C. and after Caesar's death:
Galsterer-Kröll 1972 p. 98.

157. Henderson 1942 pp. 12-13. H. Galsterer 1971 p. 19 questions the
double colony but offers no alternative explanation of the tribes. The
implications of the tribes, combined with a discussion of other evidence,
is to be found in Knapp 1980.2. Veterans are accepted by most scholars,
e.g., Vittinghoff 1952 pp. 72-73; H. Galsterer 1971 p. 10. Schulten's
emendation of Strabo 3.2.2 (ἡ Βαῖτις) to Κόρδυβα , presumably because
of the reference to a veteran settlement, is unnecessary.

158. Carthago Nova had <u>IIIIviri</u> when it was in the Sergian tribe (<u>CIL</u>
2.3408 and H. Galsterer 1971 p. 29 n. 131). It was later a colony and so
had <u>IIviri</u>. It seems clear that Carthago Nova was a citizen or Latin <u>muni-</u>
<u>cipium</u> for a time and then was converted to a colony, surely with the ad-
dition of veterans as the coinage of the town shows (Vives y Escudero 1924,
<u>Atlas</u> pl. 130). The Galerian tribe was acquired when the colony was
founded. In the case of Urso, perhaps the <u>urbani</u> (Pliny <u>HN</u> 3.3.12: <u>Col-</u>
<u>onia Genetiva Urbanorum</u>) were enrolled in the new tribe (Galeria: <u>CIL</u>
2.5442, rejected as an Ursonensis on insufficient grounds by Hübner), while
the old citizens remained in the Sergian tribe (<u>CIL</u> 2.5441).

159. Vives y Escudero 1924, <u>Atlas</u> pl. 165. The connection between the
type and a veteran settlement is not absolutely certain but very plausible
(cf. Knapp 1980.1). Likewise, the veterans need not have come in a new
<u>deductio</u>. The coinage of Italica shows a "standards" type (Vives y Escu-
dero 1924, <u>Atlas</u> pl. 168 and Chaves 1973), but there is no evidence in the
tribal designation of the town, which remained in the Sergia for its entire history, of a formal addition of soldiers. The origin of the "standards" type may relate to Italica's long history of military importance.
It is also possible that soldiers were settled <u>viritim</u> instead of by de-
ductio.

160. Córdoba's <u>deductio</u> is not mentioned as a "jointly settled city"
by Strabo 3.2.15, along with Augusta Emerita, Pax Augusta, and Caesaraugusta, because it was an addition to an existing colony. (It must be ad-
mitted, however, that there is no explicit evidence for an Augustan colony--
only inference based on the material I have presented.) Surely Etienne
1958 p. 393 is wrong in attributing the priestly emblems on Córdoba's
coinage to a symbolization of the refoundation of Córdoba. The sacred
implements pictured (Vives y Escudero 1924, <u>Atlas</u> pl. 165) symbolize
Augustus' priestly offices (Knapp 1980.1).

161. Knapp 1980.1.

162. Cohen 1880 vol. 1^2 p. 150 n. 605, accepted as evidence by Hübner
1867 p. 307; H. Galsterer 1971 p. 10; Wiegels 1972 n. 228; Tovar 1974 p.
89. Chaves 1978 pp. 163-164 rightly does not list the coin; Grant 1946
p. 220 and n. 14 seems to doubt Cohen's report. Ritterling's surmise
that the <u>V Alaudae</u> was settled at Córdoba is wrong (1925 p. 1566 line 46),
as is Hübner's suggestion that cohorts from Cassius Longinus' <u>legio</u> V
were settled (1900 pp. 1222-1223). How García y Bellido 1959.1 p. 453
came to the idea that the <u>II Alaudae</u> and <u>X Gemina</u> were settled is unknown.
There is one slim hope for identifying (one of) the legion(s). By odd
coincidence, a scrap of evidence points to the <u>legio</u> <u>XV</u>! L. Manlius Bocchus, honored as a duovir at Córdoba (<u>CIL</u> 2.2225), also records the

office of <u>tribunus</u> <u>militum</u> in the fifteenth legion. He probably held this office before his Cordoban post. Castrén 1975 p. 52, following Gabba, has noted how in new military colonies ex-centurions and <u>tribuni</u> <u>militum</u> were often given positions of authority. If Bocchus is an example, perhaps we may suppose that a fair number of men of the fifteenth legion were settled at Córdoba--although not all, since the coins of Augusta Emerita tell us that some, at least, were settled in that Augustan colony. This bit of evidence cannot be pressed far, however.

163. Cohen even gives his coin as XV, which others have interpreted as two separate numbers, X and V. Cohen's version confirms the misreading derives from a misinterpretation of the upside-down R and A on the reverse of the coin.

164. On the PERM CAES AUG coinage and a visit by Augustus, Grant 1946 p. 220.

165. Masdeu 1784 nn. 396-397; Ortí 1958 pp. 46-47. Agrippina was the patroness of Seneca the Younger, although this relationship need not have anything to do with the patronage of Córdoba exercised by her grandfather Agrippa.

166. <u>CIL</u> 2.4701, 4703, 4704, 4706-4709, 4711.

167. For local accents, see Cicero <u>Arch.</u> 26.10 for Córdoba and <u>SHA</u> <u>Hadr.</u> 3.1 for Italica. The <u>pingue</u> ... <u>atque peregrinum</u> language of <u>Arch.</u> 26.10 may reflect the native element (Wilson 1966 p. 31 n. 2). Although Carnoy 1906 tries to identify a "Spanish" Latin (cf. Griffin 1972 p. 13 n. 46), there is little evidence for a Baetican dialect of that language.

168. Griffin 1972 p. 15.

169. Vibius Severus: Tacitus <u>Ann.</u> 4.13; for these men, see Alföldy 1969, with full citations.

170. On these men, see below.

171. On this reorganization, see Wiegels 1978.1; Bosworth 1973.

172. <u>CIL</u> 2.4724, first reported by Alfaro at the beginning of the seventeenth century; it had disappeared by the beginning of the eighteenth.

173. Santos Jener 1950 p. 159; 1955 p. 141; García y Bellido 1964 pp. 164-165.

174. Hübner ad loc. Montenegro 1978 p. 321 likewise considers it a milestone. For a similar milestone, <u>CIL</u> 2.4725.

175. L. Dasumius probably provides money in his will for building at Córdoba.

176. Henderson 1953.

177. Liebenam 1900 pp. 252-263; Manni 1950; H. Galsterer 1971 pp. 57-58; Rodríguez Neila 1978.2.

178. Suffect <u>duoviri</u> were possible, so the exact number of men who held the office between, say, 15 B.C. and A.D. 285 is impossible to determine. More than six hundred, at any rate, even assuming that some men held the office more than once.

179. On Italica see Thouvenot 1973 p. 212 and n. 6. Unfortunately duovirs did not sign coins at Córdoba as they did, for example, at

Carthago Nova. The duovirs are mentioned in a number of contexts: a date (nn. 3-4, 9-10, ?11-12); a plaque dedicated to them (nn. 5, 7); a statue dedicated by Cordubenses (nn. 8, 14); a dedicator of a statue (nn. 13, 15); a statue authorized by another town (n. 1); a statue of a provincial flamen (n. 6); a gravestone (n. 2).

180. Liebenam 1900 p. 257(with n. 2)-260; H. Galsterer 1971 p. 56.

181. Quinquennales occur at Tarraco, Barcino, and Carthago Nova in Tarraconensis, and at Osset and Iluro in Baetica (CIL 2 p. 1168). On their duties, H. Galsterer 1971 p. 56.

182. Ensslin 1954; Sachers 1954.

183. Cf. Rodríguez Neila 1978.2 pp. 207-208, who thinks that CIL 2.5525 refers to two offices, praefectus and IIvir aed. pot., and takes IIvir aed. pot. as a nonsimplified way to say "aedile". In a town with IIIIviri this would make sense, but I find it implausible in the case of Córdoba, where the aediles form a separate college distinct from the IIviri.

184. Grant 1946 p. 158. Most recently Rodríguez Neila 1978.2 p. 210 n. 40 attributes the coin to Córdoba.

185. Liebenam 1900 pp. 263-265; Sabbatucci 1954; Degrassi 1956.

186. The "Seneca Tarq." attested at CIL 2.2227 is in fact a Seneca from Tarraco: see Knapp 1979. In all of Baetica 56 aediles are attested by CIL; 101 come from Tarraconensis and a mere 12 from Lusitania. Cf. Rodríguez Neila 1978.2 pp. 207-208.

187. Only five towns show quaestors in CIL 2; of the fourteen examples, eight come from Tarraco (H. Galsterer 1971 p. 56). On local quaestors in general, see Liebenam 1900 pp. 265-273. Castrén 1975 p. 51 observes that quaestors are absent from Pompeian records and suggests that it must have been an insignificant office in the town.

188. Rodríguez Neila 1978.2 p. 205.

189. CIL 2.2227 is from Tarraco, not from Córdoba. See note 186 above. This quaestor was the only one recorded in Baetica.

190. Cf. CIL 2.6278 line 24.

191. My analysis of over 250 local cursus from the West shows that only about six percent of the duovirs advanced to the tribunate, while about twelve percent reached the first step in an equestrian career.

192. Wiegels 1972 n. 278.

193. Wiegels 1972 n. 296.

194. For general material on municipal magistrates, Broughton 1965; Langhammer 1973.

195. Liebenam 1900 pp. 226-238, 241-252.

196. Cf. Castrén 1975 p. 55.

197. Liebenam 1900 pp. 248, 480. In Pompeii the four vici were voting districts for the popular assembly (Castrén 1975 pp. 79-82). Might the attested Cordoban vici also have been voting districts?

198. Chevallier 1974. Vittinghoff 1973 and Nierhaus 1964 also provide valuable leads.

199. The mileage of the vase and the <u>Itineraria</u> <u>Antoniniana</u> do not agree. On Ad Aras, Tovar 1974 p. 100 and <u>IA</u> 413.4.

200. Similarly, the <u>mansio</u> Ad Herculem, halfway between Gades and Mergablum (<u>IA</u> 408.3.12). Perhaps this too was a territorial boundary. See also Thouvenot 1973 p. 484.

201. For summaries of information concerning these towns, Tovar 1974.

202. On Augusta Emerita with territory in another province, Wiegels 1976 p. 258.

203. Albertini 1923 p. 90 on the conventus boundary.

204. Nierhaus 1964, followed by Wiegels 1976 p. 267. Chevallier 1974 rejects watersheds as boundaries too hastily. On watersheds as boundaries in Africa see Broughton 1929 p. 77.

205. Modern administrative divisions--civil and ecclesiastical--are the result of the Reconquest and so, even though they bear a resemblance to ancient divisions, they should not be used as hard evidence; continuity is slight or nonexistent. However, the boundary of the modern <u>partidos</u> <u>juridicales</u> of Posadas and Córdoba correspond closely, on all sides except the north, with the boundaries I have suggested. Epigraphy tells us nothing, nor does numismatics--the coins of Córdoba circulate too far beyond its territory. Milestones are useless since they do not measure from the city.

206. Córdoba may not have been large enough to warrant such prefects: H. Galsterer 1971 p. 23 estimates Merida's size at 20,000 km^2, while Córdoba, with the boundaries I suggest, would be at most 4,000 km^2. See also Wiegels 1976.

207. For Astigi, Ponsich 1979 p. 11 fig. 3; for Orange, Dilke 1974.

208. López Ontiveros 1974.

209. Ponsich 1974; 1979.

210. Strabo 3.2.1; Pliny <u>HN</u> 3.1.10. On economic life in general, Chaves 1978 pp. 125-149.

211. Wiegels 1972 n. 299.

212. In ancient toponomy we find "Mari-" names all along the modern Sierra Morena: mons Mariorum near Río Tinto (<u>IA</u> 432; Ptolemy 2.4.12), Mariana near Valdepeñas (<u>IA</u> 455), and the mons Marianus itself, which is probably the Cerro Muriano, sixteen miles northeast of Córdoba. The name has nothing to do with <u>moreno</u> (brown) or with the Moors; a semitic root is unlikely, although it has been suggested (Carbonell 1953 p. 106). See also Schulten 1959 vol. 2 pp. 245-246, 314-315; Sandars 1905 p. 315. Workings at Cerro Muriano go back 5,000 years (Santos Jener 1958.2 pp. 89-90; Carbonell 1953 p. 107). Evidence of smelting came to light in the Colina settlement of pre-Roman Córdoba. On Marius, Blanco 1966.1 p. 27.

213. Analysis of the bronze in Córdoba's coins has not produced any clear results; it cannot at this point be related to this specialty bronze for which Córdoba was famous. (I owe thanks to F. Chaves for this information.) Schulten's idea that the <u>aes</u> <u>Cordubense</u> was an attempt to imitate Corinthian bronze is unprovable (1959 vol. 2 pp. 314-315), as is his idea that it was the bronze for which Tartessos was famous (1959 vol. 2 pp. 327-328). Pliny only remarks that it was especially good for making coins.

214. Schulten 1959 vol. 2 pp. 272-281 does not mention Córdoba specifically with reference to silver coins.

215. On copper, Wiseman 1956 p. 59. The Almadén quicksilver ore may have been shipped through Castulo; cf. CIL 2.3270, where a via quae per Castulonensem saltum Sisaponem ducit is mentioned. A lead ingot with the inscription C P T T CAENIORVM, found at Alcaracejos, refers to four Caenii and has nothing to do with the involvement of C(olonia) P(atricia) in the lead trade: Schulten 1959 vol. 2 p. 294.

216. AE 1971 n. 181. A similar collegium exists at Milan: CIL 5.5892, 5847. There are only five examples of the nomen Aerarius in Schultze 1904 and no other in CIL 2. The man had taken his nomen from his work upon gaining his freedom. This work is not the "aerarius" of early Roman political history; it denotes a worker in metals, usually bronze and copper. Ruggiero 1895 lists nine others in CIL. Waltzing 1895 vol. 1 p. 358 n. 6, 454; Mommsen at CIL 5 pp. 635, 1191; Santero 1978. This Cordoban association may be equivalent to a collegium fabrum et centonariorum. On socii = collegium, Waltzing p. 340. This collegium aerariorum is comparable to the confectores aeris who made the dedication to T. Flavius Augusti libertus Polychrysus, a procurator montis Mariani, at CIL 2.1179.

217. Octavius might seem a peculiar name for an imperial freedman, but see Weaver 1965.

218. Pliny HN 33.139 also mentions embossed vasa anaglypta, and the scholia on Iuv. 9.145 gloss curvus caelator as laborosi anaglyptarii. Otherwise the word anaglyptarius occurs only in Ambrose. Caelatores, a subdivision of sculptors, are mentioned by Quint. Inst. orat. 2.21.9; cf. DE 2.1 (1900) p. 34 (Loewy).

219. For speculation on the system of agricultural exploitation in Andalucía, Mangas 1978.

220. Bell. Hisp. 8, cf. Strabo 3.2.5; Schulten 1959 vol. 2 pp. 119-120.

221. Schulten 1959 vol. 2 pp. 437-438, 510-511; Broughton 1973.

222. Seneca's wealth was probably in land: Griffin 1972 p. 6. He perhaps refers to estates at Córdoba in NQ 3, praef. 2: Griffin 1975 p. 2 n. 6. Little work is being done in rural archaeology in the province of Córdoba. Perhaps eventually M. Ponsich will be able to provide the sort of information that he has so ably made available for the lower Guadalquivir. On dispensatores, see DE vol. 3 p. 1920 (Vulic) and RE 5.1 (1903) p. 1189-1198 (Liebenam). The dispensator is the second highest man in the household financial administration, after the procurator and over the vicarii. If the Felix of CIL 2.1198, a dispensator for the imperial patrimonium, is the same as the Felix of CIL 2.2234, then the Cordoban was an imperial, not a private, administrator. But Felix is a very common name, and it seems more likely that he was a slave dispensator of his master L. Acilius Modestus.

223. Strabo 3.2.1 also attests Córdoba's importance as a trading center. The town's name is second only to that of Astigi on amphorae fragments from Monte Testaccio: Marchetti 1922 p. 780. On amphorae and trade, see Callender 1965 and Beltrán Lloris 1970. Callender p. 127 n. 587 records the names Valerius Pate[rnus] and Valerius Valerianus, who exported from Córdoba. A Valerius Paternus appears on another Cordoban inscription, Albertini 1918-19 p. 314.

224. Cf. CIL 15.3994, 4110, 4117, 4099, 4031, dated A.D. 153-227, which record export of produce from imperial estates. The pagus Augusti attested by CIL 2.2194 perhaps suggests imperial estates. On Córdoba as a customs and excise station, see Callender 1965 p. 229 n. 1484. One Cordoban merchant has been identified by Grenier 1937 p. 471 and n. 29; he associates an M. Fadius, noted as a Cordoban merchant on ILG 586, with the Fadii attested on amphorae from Monte Testaccio (CIL 15.3856-61, A.D. 149). However, the man at ILG 586 is a Fabius, not a Fadius; Grenier and subsequent works (e.g., Thouvenot 1973 p. 270) have misquoted the stone. Therefore a link between the two pieces of evidence is lacking.

225. García y Bellio 1959.3 (Severan date); Sotomayor 1964 and Vicent 1961 (early to mid fourth century). A marmorarius signuarius is attested by Vázquez 1958 p. 29.

226. CIL 2.2211. The exact nature of this collegium is uncertain. It probably had something to do with house construction. They appear at Rome, Villa Magna (Africa), Antium, and Narbo. See Waltzing 1895 vol. 4 pp. 45, 89 (with further literature cited). Hübner's explanation of this inscription is not to the point. One other fraternity may lurk in the abbreviations in an unpublished inscription from Córdoba that begins GENIO C C L H COLONIAE PATRICIAE. (My thanks to J. Castro for permission to mention this inscription before publication.)

227. Coactor: L. Persius Diphilus was a broker of some sort, perhaps a coactor argentarius involved with auctions (CIL 2.2239; RE 4.1 (1900) pp. 126-127; DE 2.1 (1900) p. 314). Grammaticus Graecus: Domitius Isquilinus lived to 101 years of age, as CIL 2.2236 notes (cf. another long-lived grammaticus at CIL 2.5079--he lived to 70). Isquilinus taught advanced literature; he was not a litterator, or elementary teacher (cf. Suetonius Gramm. 4). His cognomen suggests a Roman origin. DE 3 (1922) pp. 564-565 lists five other grammatici Graeci. Aurifex: See Thouvenot 1973 p. 265, citing Gaius Inst. 3.147. Musicarius: CIL 2.2241. The meaning of this word is not entirely clear. Lewis and Short s.v. call it "a maker of musical instruments"; the Oxford Latin Dictionary s.v. says "one who has charge of music," which is close to TLL's "qui musicam tractat." The word appears only in inscriptions and only seven times. The age (15) and apparent slave status of Syntrophilus point to a musical performer of some sort, the type of pretty boy brought in by Trimalchio in the Satyricon. Purpurarius (CIL 2.2235): these men, Diocles and Diotimus, were handlers of purple dye (cf. CIL 11.1069a). In general, see RE 23.2 (1959) pp. 1998-2020 (Schneider) and DS vol. 4.1 pp. 769-778 (Besnier). Most purpurarii are from Italy and the East. In the West, they are attested only in Raetia (CIL 3.5824) and perhaps at Narbo (CIL 12.4507-4508) and in Gaetulia (Mela 3.104?). Diocles is possibly directly related to a Roman enterprise, for CIL 6.9843 records a Diocles who is a freedman of T. Livius T.1. Philoxenus purp(urarius). Reinhold 1970 p. 54 n. 3 cites CIL 2.2235 as evidence for "unrestricted accessibility to purple throughout the Roman Empire" in the second century A.D. See also Schulten 1959 vol. 2 p. 374. Medicus: CIL 2.2237, 2348, AE 1971.181; the medicus was the practical, everyday doctor (or a military physician). He was usually a slave or a freedman, as, by their names, these Cordobans appear to be (L. Iulius Protogenes, P. Frontinius Sciscola, Telemachus). Sciscola was a town doctor (medicus c(oloniorum) c(oloniae) P(atriciae)). In general, see Scarborough 1969 pp. 109-121. Sarcinatrix: González 1981 no. 7, pp. 51-52. Vestiarius (CIL 2.2240): clothiers are rarely mentioned except in inscriptions. See DS vol. 5 pp. 760-761 (Chapot). Freedmen were

usually engaged, as apparently here. Ostiarius (HAE 326): although no other doormen appear in CIL 2, they are attested in Rome and elsewhere. On the job of ianitor see RE 18.2 (1942) p. 1665 (Schneider). CIL 2.2244 may hide a profession in [.]ementricus, but no satisfactory resolution is at hand. Van Nostrand 1937 pp. 200-201 discusses professions represented in Roman Spain, including some from Córdoba.

228. Local ceramics found: Santos Jener 1955 p. 24.

229. Cf. Syme 1958 p. 839.

230. On the Senecae, see Griffin 1975, Castillo 1965 no. 31; Wiegels 1972 no. 213 (Mela); Castillo 1965 no. 32, Wiegels 1972 no. 214 (Seneca fils); and Castillo 1965, Wiegels 1972 nos. 95 and 192 (Gallio); Wiegels 1972 no. 78 (Lucan) with further citations. With the exception of the elder Seneca, the family members show little interest in their hometown and may have seen it only infrequently. On this family see also Griffin 1972 p. 4.

231. Dillius Aponianus: Castillo 1965 no. 136; Wiegels 1972 no. 70; Syme 1958 p. 593 n. 2. Dillius Vocula: Castillo 1965 no. 137, Wiegels 1972 no. 71. Aponius Saturninus: Castillo 1965 no. 60; Syme 1958 p. 875; Wiegels 1972 no. 129 prefers Italica. On the Aponii in Baetica, Castillo 1965 pp. 385-386. Of course certainty is impossible in ascription of all of these men to Córdoba, since so much depends on conjectural relationships.

232. Castillo 1978 p. 227; Wiegels 1972 no. 109 is more cautious.

233. Castillo 1965 nos. 52, 53; Wiegels 1972 no. 40.

234. A new fragment of the testamentum throws doubt on the identity of the testator. See Eck 1978. On Dasumii, Syme 1958 pp. 784-785; Wiegels 1972 no. 64. Wiegels 1972 no. 65 attributes a Cordoban origin to Dasumius' adopted son P. Dasumius Rusticus. This is unlikely. Likewise Rusticus' adopted son, L. Dasumius Tullius Tuscus (Wiegels 1972 no. 66), was not a native Spaniard, nor was his son M. Dasumius Tullius Varro (Wiegels 1972 no. 67).

235. Castillo 1965 no. 39; CIL 2.5522.

236. Wiegels 1972 no. 47a.

237. Cf. Wiegels 1972 no. 243, who does not relate Clodius directly to Córdoba.

238. L. (?)Annaeus Seneca: Wiegels 1972 no. 215. Annaeus Mela: Wiegels 1972 no. 213. The close friendship between Annaeus Serenus and Seneca the Philosopher speaks for a Córdoban origin for Serenus. He was an equestrian. (Wiegels 1972 no. 215. But see Griffin 1972 p. 15 for a more conservative interpretation.)

239. Castillo 1965 no. 282; Blanco 1966.1 p. 36; Wiegels 1972 no. 318 records the possibility, based on Postumius' enrollment in the Papirian tribe, that the man came from Astigi, the only town in Baetica in that tribe. His grandson Paulus P.f. Postumius Acilianus appears as a praefectus cohortis in Britain under Antonius Pius. He is related to Postumia Aciliana Baxo(nensis), recorded at CIL 2.2060 = ILS 5496. Of the women involved with the Senecae, Acilia, wife of Mela, was a Cordoban, but the exact origin of Helvia, Seneca the Elder's wife, is uncertain. See also Griffin 1972 p. 8.

240. Wiegels 1972 no. 299. Another possible equestrian from Córdoba is M. Cassius Agrippa, a procurator Augusti (Wiegels 1972 no. 238). Likewise, a praefectus orae maritimae, L. Iulius Gallus Mummianus, attested on an inscription from Córdoba (CIL 2.2224 = ILS 6905), may be from the city itself (Wiegels 1972 no. 273). That L. Manlius Bocchus, a tribunus militum in the early first century A.D. (CIL 2.2225), is actually from Córdoba is doubtful, despite Wiegels 1972 no. 296.

241. Regulus: PIR² A.397; Wiegels 1972 no. 210 (considered an equestrian); Castillo 1978 p. 226. Other Aemilii from Córdoba are recorded by Vázquez 1958 pp. 28-29 and by Santos Jener 1947 p. 93. Calpurnius Salvianus (taken as an equestrian by Wiegels 1972 no. 236) was related to the Q. Calpurnius Salvianus who was involved in the plot against Cassius Longinus recorded at Bell. Alex. 52-53; he is very likely the L. Calpurnius Salvianus mentioned in CIL 2.2265, from Córdoba.

242. Women of this rank could be honored on their own merits: cf. CIL 2.3272.

243. Thouvenot 1973 p. 678 with CIL 2.2348. This doctor perhaps had more to do with the gladiators attested in large numbers (see below). For the evidence on artisans see above. For freedmen in Córdoba see Mangas 1971.2 pp. 285-290.

244. Mangas 1971.2 pp. 171-174 gives a list.

245. To judge by the concern of the Christians, the Jewish population in Baetica must have been greater than the few inscriptions indicate. On Jews in the area, Santos Yanguas 1978; Koch 1977; Thouvenot 1973 p. 186 n.5.

246. García y Bellido 1963.1 p. 73; García y Bellido 1962 pp. 67-74, with previous bibliography; cf. Thouvenot 1973 p. 271. A Syrian is also recorded as a gladiator: Marcos 1976 pp. 15-27.

247. Del Río Oliete 1978. Greeks as gladiators: HAE 1406; Marcos 1976 pp. 15-53.

248. Germans: HAE 323; AE 1971.179. Gaul: HAE 1408. Flamens: AE 1971.183; HAE 2091. Romans: HAE 1861; Vázquez 1958 p. 29. Mithra: CIL 2.5521; Blanco 1968 p. 94. Incolae are attested at CIL 2.2222 and Masdeu no. 665.

249. On the gladiators, García y Bellido 1960.1; Piernavieja Rozitis 1968; Marcos 1976 with full bibliography. A ludus Hispanus is attested by CIL 2.4519 (Barcelona): see Marcos 1976 pp. 33-37. Thouvenot 1973 p. 798 supposes that a school existed at Córdoba.

250. Griffin 1972 p. 13. Of antiquarian interest is Varro's notice (Ling. 5.162) that Cordobans used the word cenaculum for a "dining room", just as some Latin towns still did in Varro's day.

251. Arias Abellán 1978 presents a sound, succinct analysis of the perils of working with life-span figures. On pp. 194-195 there is a good summary of previous bibliography on the topic.

252. Silvanus: in an inscription in a private collection in Córdoba. Minerva: in an unpublished inscription. I thank J. Castro for permission to mention its reference to Minerva. Genii: Genius (CIL 2.2192); Genius oppidi Sabetani (CIL 2.2193); Genius Pagi Augusti (CIL 2.2194); Genius (Ortí 1958 p. 57, possibly false); Genius C C L H C P (see note 226 above).

Blanco 1966.1 p. 32: there is no evidence to support his reference to
Janus Augustus. The "temple of Janus" that has been traditionally located
at the site of the mosque is imaginary. It is based on early misinterpre-
tations of the milestones found there, which bear reference to mileage ab
Iano Augusto, a site on the border of Baetica and Tarraconensis near Andú-
jar. A cult of Janus Augustus has therefore nothing to do with the bridge
across the Guadalquivir located nearby; on the god Janus and bridges see
the critique of Nierhaus 1964 pp. 211-212. Likewise, Blanco's reference
to Volturnus is incorrect; the dedication to this god has a local reference point (see below).

253. Aphrodite: AE 1924.14; Nemesis: CIL 2.2195; Fortuna: CIL 2.
2191. The origin of the goddess Salpina, mentioned at HAE 2051, is uncertain. On Nemesis in Spain, García y Bellido 1960.2.

254. Syrians: García y Bellido 1962; 1963.1 p. 73 n. 48; Bendala
Galán 1978 pp. 219-220 with earlier bibliography. Mithra: García y
Bellido 1948.1; 1971.2 pp. 143-144 (statue of Mithra); Cybele and Attis:
Blanco 1968 pp. 93-95; CIL 2.5521. The taurobolic altar from Córdoba is
the finest found in Spain. A possible terracotta of Attis is reported by
Thouvenot 1973 p. 805. Fortunatus: Vázquez 1958 p. 29. CIL 2.2306 may
be evidence of the Isis cult in the city. On eastern religions in general,
García y Bellido 1967.

255. Fons: Vázquez 1958. Underworld: HAE 2051, cf. Fita 1908 p.
454. Magic: HAE 2051.

256. In general on the priesthoods, see Fiske 1900 pp. 113-126; Ladage
1971; H. Galsterer 1971 p. 59. On augurs, Ladage 1971 pp. 53-54.

257. CIL 2. 1347 add., 5523. Both men had been duovirs at Córdoba.
On pontifices, Ladage 1971, esp. p. 55; Fiske 1900.

258. Fiske 1900 p. 120.

259. Flamens: CIL 2.1347 add.; CIL 2.2195; Thouvenot 1973 p. 576 n.
1 (flamen Augustalis and dedication to Mercurius) CIL 2.5523 (flamen perpetuus); AE 1971 n. 185 (flaminica). Imperial cult: Fiske 1900 pp. 113,
120; CIL 2.2105 (Urgavo) mentions a flamen sacrorum publicorum, an example
of a nonimperial flamen, on which cf. Ladage 1971 p. 55. On the local
popularity of the cult, Sutherland 1934 p. 33 and n. 15. Terms: Jarrett
1971 pp. 526-527; Fiske 1900 pp. 113-114; Ladage 1971 pp. 80-82. Nemesis
dedication: CIL 2.2195.

260. Ladage 1971 pp. 87-93, 99, 104, 106; Jarrett 1971 p. 526.

261. On seviri, Etienne 1958 pp. 251-281; Ladage 1971 p. 96. On magistri Larum, cf. Etienne 1958 p. 282.

262. Castro 1977 pp. 447-449.

263. See n. 252 above.

264. Muñoz Coello 1976 p. 388.

265. E.g., Fiske 1900. The flamens are from Aurgi (Jaén) (CIL 2.2220b
with Knapp 1980.2). Celti (Peñaflor) (CIL 2.2221), Iporca (Constantina)
(AE 1971.183), Seria (Jerez de los Caballeros?) (Vicent 1973 pp. 675-676),
and Ilurco (Piños Puente) (HAE 2091).

266. Seneca Contr. 1 praef. 1; Griffin 1972 p. 6. Blanco 1966.1 p. 34

notes that a Marcellus was instructor of the elder Seneca and other Cordobans, but I can find no source for this statement. Is the rhetor, Mar-
ullus, meant?

267. Latro: Seneca Contr. 1 praef. 22, 24; 1 praef. 13; 2.4.12-13; 9
praef. 3. Victor: Seneca Suas. 2.18; Contr. 10.15-16; possibly of Etrus-
can origin--Griffin 1972 p. 4.

268. Seneca: Griffin 1975; Lucan: Ahl 1976. Martial: Cordoban poet:
Epig. 12.63.6-13; possible visit: Epig. 9.61; Castillo 1978 p. 227. For
other educators in Spain, García Iglesias 1975.

269. On the date of the reorganization, Albertini 1923 pp. 25-32 and
Henderson 1953 p. 141 (27 B.C.); Syme 1969 (16-13 B.C.); Van Nostrand 1916
pp. 95-97 and Grant 1946 pp. 134, 220 (15-14 B.C.). Full bibliography at
Wiegels 1976 p. 280 n. 33.

270. On the basis of Pliny HN 3.1.10, Hübner thought that Córdoba's
conventus was divided into two segments by the conventus of Astigi (see
the map at the end of CIL 2, Suppl.). Detlefsen 1870 rejected this interpretation. Most scholars have followed the interpretation of Detlefsen; e.g., Albertini 1923 p. 89, Van Nostrand 1916 p. 109. See also
Prieto 1973.

271. CIL 2, Suppl. p. LXXXVII, rejected by Albertini 1923 p. 50. Cf.
Thouvenot 1973 p. 169 n. 5.

272. An inscription discovered in 1968 and first published in 1971
(Tovar 1971, Vicent 1973) bears an epigram by this man in Greek. An as-
tonishing amount of controversy has been generated concerning this poem
and its relationship to the famous Arrian of Nicomedia. Of the discussions
(Fernández Galiano 1972, Robert 1973, Marcovich 1973, Burkert 1975, Peck
1976, Bosworth 1976, SEG 1976-77 no. 1215, Marcovich 1976, Koenen 1977
and Tovar again 1975) those of Tovar, with the corrections of Burkert, are
fundamental. No entirely satisfactory solution to the problem of the identity of the poem's author seems possible. For other proconsuls and imperial
officials in Baetica, see Alföldy 1969.

273. Vicent 1973.

274. CIL 2.2214. This vilicus arcarius worked for the imperial administration, either under a procurator at Rome or in the provinces. A number of procurators ad XX hereditatum are known from Baetica: see Pflaum
1960 p. 1330. In general, see Wachtel 1966.

275. J. Castro has kindly allowed me to cite this inscription before
its publication.

276. Etienne 1958 p. 129 n.6.

277. Hardy 1946. Perhaps CIL 6.31267 = ILS 103 indicates that there
was a mechanism for achieving and communicating provincial consensus even
before the assemblies were instituted as part of the introduction of the
imperial cult in Flavianic times.

278. Unless ILS 103 is credited to an assembly of some sort; a golden
statue of Augustus was set up in the forum Augusti at Rome. Dedications
to emperors at Córdoba are of unknown authorship (CIL 2.2197, Augustus;
CIL 2.2198, Germanicus; Com. Mon. Anales ... Córdoba 1926.1 p. 11, Claudius; Santos Jener 1955 p. 117, Pertinax; AE 1971 n. 184, Philipp), or by
a town (CIL 2.2200, Cornelia Salonina, wife of Gallienus, by Córdoba; CIL

2.2199, Gallienus and Valerianus, by Córdoba; CIL 2.2201, Aurelian, by
Astigi), or by an individual (Blanco 1968 p. 94, Severus Alexander).

279. Castejón 1929 p. 259 notes that the Arab wall follows the Roman,
although on p. 263 he says that no trace of the actual Roman wall survives;
Tovar 1974 p. 90; Blanco 1966.1 pp. 21-22. Blanco 1966.1 p. 24 cautions
against taking all of Castejón's identifications at face value, for Castejón was perhaps too quick to distinguish Arab from Roman on the basis of
the typology of stone building blocks used in the walls. Also on the
walls: Sentenach 1918; Jaén 1935.

280. Cited Thouvenot 1973 p. 383 n. 2.

281. Santos Jener 1948 p. 217; 1950 p. 140. A map of the portion of
this wall and modern buildings is at p. 143. Sentenach 1918 p. 208 locates
a tower at the Ermita de la Aurora, which I have been unable to locate.
Is it the same tower Santos speaks of?

282. Schulten considered a wall found at the northwest corner of the
Alcázar to be the Roman foundation of a gateway. Castejón 1929 pp. 276-277
doubts this. The basilica of San Vincente backed onto the wall: García
Rodríguez 1966 p. 263.

283. Sentenach 1918 p. 210. Jaén 1935 p. 39 n. 1.

284. Santa Victoria: de la Torre 1922 confirms Sentenach's report
(1918 p. 208 n. 1). Museo: Castejón 1964 p. 373 n. 12.

285. Sentenach 1918.

286. Blanco 1966.1 p. 24 is premature in having the wall reach to the
river in Caesar's time. Torre 1922 p. 87 correctly rejects such a wall.
Contreras 1977 p. 393, on the other hand, is too early in attributing a
double town to Marcellus; at best the area between the original southern
wall and the river was settled in a haphazard and informal way. The ir-
regularity in the Marcellan plan on the northern side is due to a seasonal
stream, long since buried, that ran there.

287. These gates have all been destroyed since the eighteenth century:
Castejón 1929 pp. 271-273. Sentenach 1918 p. 208 incorrectly identifies
the Puerta de la Estatua with the Plaza Santa Ana: see Castejón p. 271 and
below.

288. Cf. Thouvenot 1973 p. 410, Tovar 1974 pp. 90-91.

289. Castejón 1929 p. 279. The palace is set askew from the orientation of the mosque because the palace, along with the basilica of St. Vincent, which the mosque replaced, was aligned on the old town plan.

290. As noted above, Sentenach 1918 p. 208 incorrectly identified the
Puerta de la Estatua. A. Blázquez 1914 p. 462 cites the chronicle of
Ajbar Machmua pp. 23-24 to show that this puerta was thirty codos (cubits)
or less from the river. This puts the puerta 12.5-17.0 meters from the
river, depending on whether the codo real (= 0.574 m.) or the codo geome-
trico (= 0.418 m.) is used. Blázquez misidentified the Puerta de la Estatua with the Puerta Algeciras (Piscatoria). Castejón 1929 p. 271 calls
the Puerta Piscatoria the Porta Pescatoria, but I find no ancient reference
to a gate of this name. For other Arab gates in this area see Castejón
pp. 276-277.

291. On vicus Hispanus and vicus forensis, see the discussion above,

p. 13-14. The forensis inscription was found near the forum at the streets Góngora and Alvaro; the Hispanus stone comes from near Santa Ana, in the calle Angel de Saavedra. On the vicus forensis, cf. the district called forenses in Pompeii that P. Willems, Les élections municipales à Pompei (Amsterdam 1877) p. 87 (cited by Rodríguez Neila 1976.2) and Castrén 1975 p. 73 n. 4, place near the forum. Rodríguez Neila 1976.2 pp. 111-118, esp. 117, attributes the vicus capite canteri to Córdoba, but I think that intrinsically unlikely. He also mentions a vicus Patricius for which I can find no evidence except at Rome and Psidian Antioch. The vicus turris is where the tres coronae martyrs were buried and therefore probably not in the city: Thouvenot 1973 p. 316. Likewise the pagus Augusti was not within the walls (CIL 2.2194, cf. Blanco 1966.1 p. 26). Another extra-mural vicus was Secunda, across the bridge in the modern Campo de la Verdad. It was at the second milestone from the Cordoban forum (i.e., a mile from the forum). The name is attested only from Arab times but must be Roman: Castejón 1929 p. 287.

292. Augustan colonies: Wiegels 1976 p. 262. Tarraco had c.60 hectares within its walls: Alföldy 1978 p. 588.

293. Jaén 1935 p. 38 (quoted); Thouvenot 1973 p. 409; Wiseman 1956 p. 198 (who is very unreliable in his account of Roman Córdoba); Blanco 1966.1 p. 25; Tovar 1974 p. 90.

294. Forum: Santos Jener 1946 p. 82; 1947 p. 90; 1955 pp. 98-102 (Constantinian material found), 115-117 with fig. 47 p. 115. Campanian ware: Santos Jener 1947 p. 93. Late Republican date: Contreras 1977 p. 391 and n. 25 citing correspondence with A. Marcos. Republican architecture: Ward-Perkins 1970. I was shown a monumental wall, excavated recently and as yet not published, in the vicinity of the church of San Miguel. Perhaps this large building will prove to be part of the forum complex.

295. On the typical basilica-forum-temple complex that we might expect to find at Córdoba, Ward-Perkins 1970.

296. Santos Jener 1955 p. 67; Wiseman 1956 p. 198. The discoveries in calle Mármol de Bañuelos--walls of a large building, column bases, drums, and a Corinthian capital--may be related: Santos Jener 1927.3 pp. 20-21. In a house between here and calle de San Alvaro, workers found statue remains and destroyed them: pp. 20-21.

297. Locating finds on a map is very difficult because streets have changed names and old landmarks, buildings, and so on have disappeared. It is essential to consult the 1811 map, the first made of Córdoba in modern times. This plan has been republished by M. A. Ortí Belmonte 1924-28 (1930) p. 117. In 1851 Montis y Nolasco published an updated version of the 1811 map. In 1855 Dionisio Casanal produced a city plan with altitude lines included. I have not seen this map. Castejón 1929 p. 268 n. 2 says that a new map was in preparation in 1928-29, but he had not then seen it. My plan is drawn after a new map published for the Caja Provincial de Ahorros de Córdoba by Editorial Almax, Madrid, in 1977. This is the best map available. The map retains the street names from the Franco years. At present some of these street names are being changed yet again, back to those of the pre-Franco era. My Map 10 uses the "Franco" names since most maps available now print those.

298. Castejón 1929 p. 285.

299. Santos Jener 1927.3 pp. 20-21; 1927.1 p. 522.

300. Santos Jener 1955 pp. 140-141.

301. Tovar 1974 p. 90, citing Castejón.

302. Tovar 1974 p. 90; Blanco 1966.1 p. 32.

303. Espasa 1907 p. 591.

304. Santos Jener 1927.1 pp. 521-531; Sánchez de Feria 1772 p. 109. A column, apparently in situ, located in the Alcázar wall between the fortress and the garden. I have seen no speculation as to its attribution. In all, a temple to Hercules in this area must remain highly uncertain.

305. García Rodríguez 1966 p. 263.

306. A drum, capital, and cornice of Constantinian date were found at calle Jesús y María at the convent (50); near here columns of grey and rose granite were found in the calle Angel de Saavedra (51). Outside the walls, a statue of Ceres or Proserpina, walls, and an altar found at Venta de Pedroches, two kilometers from Córdoba, perhaps point to a temple there: Santos Jener 1927.3 p. 19.

307. Santos Jener 1955 pp. 121-141; 1950 pp. 137-143, 147 he records previous bibliography.

308. Provisional note: García y Bellido 1961.1 pp. 371-375; full report, 1964 p. 164. Bellido groundlessly relates the "Nerva restituit" inscription (CIL 2.4724) to the construction of this temple. He published the ceramics and other finds in the excavations in 1970. Alas no inscriptions or even numismatic evidence were found to help date the structure. Blanco 1970 pp. 120-123 dates the architectural pieces to Trajanic-Hadrianic times by their style. Santos Jener 1950 p. 154 had guessed at Augustan times; in 1953 pp. 175, 176 (Santos Jener 1955) he guessed at a Nîmes-like temple, perhaps built to Augustus by Marcellus, the son-in-law of Augustus!

309. García y Bellido 1964 p. 164; reconstruction: 1964 pp. 158-159; 1970 p. 3. Cult: Etienne 1958 p. 222; Thouvenot 1973 p. 417 notes that Córdoba, as a provincial capital and with the numerous dedications extant to provincial flamens, could be expected to have a temple to the imperial cult. Jaén 1935 p. 39 locates a temple of Augustus at the Ermita del Amparo. This seems to be speculation based on the discovery there of a dedication to Augustus (Augusto sacrum): CIL 2.2197.

310. Thouvenot 1973 p. 427 cites de los Ríos. Marcos kindly shared his views with me in conversations.

311. Fernández Chicarro 1953 p. 435; 1955 pp. 337-339. J. Castro mentioned in conversation that he had seen clear evidence of an aqueduct in construction sites and homes north of the city. Santos Jener 1955 p. 58 postulates a collecting reservoir.

312. San Pablo location: Santos Jener 1927.2 p. 15; 1955 pp. 122-123; Jaén 1935 p. 38; Wiseman 1956 p. 94. Location rejected: Marcos 1976 p. 49; 1977.2 p. 205-206. Some sort of entrance has been found in the foundations of the Ayuntamiento (Santos Jener 1950 p. 161 n. 3), but this has nothing, it seems, to do with the amphitheater (Marcos 1977.2 p. 207). Two other identifications hardly deserve mention because they are so tenuous: Santos Jener 1955 p. 10 identified remains as perhaps of the stadium in 1934 in the Facultad de Veterinaria building to the west of the city. Jaén 1935 p. 39 placed this structure in the area of the Avenida de la Victoria

(Paseo de la República Argentina/ General Primo de Rivera), without evidence. Jaén also, in a flight of fancy, identified a "naumaquia" at the crest of the molino de Martos.

313. Tovar 1974 pp. 89-90, citing Sánchez de Feria.

314. Sáinz y Gutiérrez 1894 cited by Torres 1922 p. 95 n. 11. But note that Ajbar Machmua p. 35 (cited by A. Blázquez 1914 p. 463) says that the bridge was rebuilt by Arabs with stone from the Roman wall in A.D. 719-720.

315. A. Blázquez 1914 p. 460, citing Sáinz. Sentenach 1918; Torre 1922 pp. 95-96. Sentenach p. 210 claims that some mouldings are Trajanic and show restoration from that period. Date: Republican: A. Blázquez 1914 p. 457; Sentenach 1918; later: Delgado (cited by Blázquez p. 457); Torre 1922; Jaén 1935 p. 41.

316. Torre 1922 p. 93. Ford: Ajbar Machmua, an Arab writing in A.D. 718, notes that the river is fordable in winter. Cited by Castejón 1929 p. 263.

317. Sentenach 1918 p. 209 is wrong to interpret Bell. Hisp. 51 as Caesar merely repairing the cut bridge.

318. Bridge: Santos Jener 1955 p. 12 identifies wealthy tombs; Jaén 1935 p. 39 says that a "poorman's" cemetery was here, but cites no evidence. Almodóvar: Santos Jener 1955 pp. 8, 9, cf. fig. I and plan I. Medina-Az-Zahra: Santos Jener 1955 pp. 109-110. Ostiario: García y Bellido 1959.3 pp. 7-8; Santos Jener 1955 pp. 11-12; Jaén 1935 p. 39; Vicent 1963 p. 210 (Huerta Machaquito); a lead sarcophagus was found near the train station (23), Fernández Chicarro 1953 p. 439. Salvador: Santos Jener 1955 p. 11; 1940 p. 438 (three lead sarcophagi found at no. 19 calle Diario de Córdoba); Torre 1922 p. 94 (sepulcher at later Puerta de Plasencia).

319. Plaza de la Corredera: García y Bellido 1965; Blanco 1959; 1961. See also note 329 below. West side: Tovar 1974 p. 91. Diego Serrano: Santos Jener 1955 p. 11 and fig. 44. Martial: Castejón 1964 p. 386 n. 44; Dolç 1953 p. 47 does not try to localize the domus referred to. Pérez Galdós: BRAH 80 p. 185. Train station and calle Muñices: Santos Jener 1927. 3 p. 19.

320. Alcaide: Vicent 1964-65 pp. 220-222; Gorges 1979 p. 249 no. 6. Alcolea: García y Bellido 1963.2 p. 172; Gorges 1979 p. 248 no. 2. Villarrubia: Santos Jener 1955 p. 46 (fourth century A.D. date); Gorges 1979 p. 251 no. 16. Pedroches: Romero de Torres 1909; Gorges 1979 p. 251 no. 12. Alameda: Gorges 1979 p. 248 no. 1.

321. Roads: in general see Thouvenot 1973 p. 479. Via Augusta: CIL 2 Suppl. pp. 627-628; Miller 1916 p. 179; Torre 1922 pp. 94-95; CIL 2.4701-4733, 6208. Augusta Emerita: Miller 159-160. Malaca: Miller p. 160. Castulo: Miller p. 180; Itineraria Antoniniana 403. Hispalis: see the map at Miller pp. 175-176. On the building and repair of roads, Herzig 1974.

322. Thouvenot 1973 p. 607.

323. Found at the temple on calle Claudio Marcelo (32). García y Bellido 1961.2 pp. 196-200 = 1961.1 p. 374. A marble statue of a warrior was found in Cruz Conde (36), but destroyed by the workmen. Perhaps this was of an Emperor. Santos Jener 1927.3 pp. 20-21.

324. Ceres: P. Ruano, in his Historia de Córdoba, reports a statue of Ceres found in this Colegio in 1735 (Ortí 1958 p. 40); note the statue of

Ceres or Proserpina found at Venta de Pedroches (Santos Jener 1927.3 p. 19).
Diana (?): Thouvenot 1973 p. 576. Dionysus: Thouvenot 1973 p. 583. Minerva: Thouvenot 1973 p. 580, from Gómez Moreno; Espasa 1907 p. 591 says
that this statue was found in a house next to the Hospicio on Avenida del
Generalísimo (56). Venus (?): headless statue in calle Eduardo Dato (Santos Jener 1927.3 p. 21). Vulcan head: Blanco 1975. Naiad: Santos Jener
1927.2 p. 15 (photo p. 16); 1927.1 pp. 523-524 = 1927.4 pp. 106-107; found
at calle Antonio del Castillo no. 1. A statue of Melpomene is also attested: Fernández Chicarro 1955 p. 322. Vicent 1973 p. 674 reports an uniden-
tified marble sculpture found in calle Angel de Saavedra (38). For sculpture in general, Poulsen 1933, García y Bellido 1949, Blanco 1976, and
works cited at Thouvenot 1973 p. 570 n. 1.

325. Thouvenot 1973 pp. 586, 590. A fountain sculpture, perhaps of Am-
phitro, was found near the "house of Seneca" (39): Santos Jener 1927.1 pp.
524-525. Thouvenot 1973 p. 806 (vegetal design); p. 804 ("cueillette des
olives" and young man holding flowers).

326. Germanicus: Thouvenot 1973 p. 592. Hadrian: Etienne 1958 p.
475. Faustina: Etienne p. 477. Commodus: Etienne p. 478 n. 7 doubts its
authenticity, but Thouvenot p. 594 accepts it as authentic; Santos Jener
1955 p. 72 records a bust of Commodus found in Manueles street. Julia Domna (?): Thouvenot p. 595.

327. Female head: Thouvenot 1973 p. 601. White marble head: Vicent
1973 pp. 674-675. Lion head: Santos Jener 1927.3 p. 21. Terracottas:
Santos Jener 1954.1. A terracotta antefix of a tragic mask, probably part
of the tomb of Publicia Marcia, whose tombstone was found there, was found
in the Escuela de Veteranía in 1927: Santos Jener 1927.1 pp. 525-526.
Various cornices, capitals, and ornamentations are recorded: Thouvenot
1973 pp. 612, 627; Santos Jener 1927.3 p. 21; Blanco 1970 pp. 116-119 (a
small fountain from Huerta Cardosa).

328. Blanco 1970 pp. 110-111; Santos Jener 1927.3 p. 21. Note the
prow with Triton on a victory monument at Convenae: MacKendrick 1972 p.92.

329. Corredera (12): see above n. 319. The bar was in the Plaza de
la Compañia (45): Com. Mon. Anales ... Córdoba 1926.1 p. 68. Four-seasons,
victory in chariot: Thouvenot 1973 pp. 643-644, 647 and n. 3. Other mosaics have been found at Plaza de las Tendillas (5), Santos Jener 1927.3
p. 21; calle Sevilla (43), Carbonell 1950 p. 90; Plaza de la Merced, in the
Hospicio (57), Santos Jener 1927.2 p. 13 = (?) 1927.4 p. 106; Instituto Nacional de Enseñanza, Santos Jener 1927.2 p. 13; Paseo de la Victoria, Santos
Jener 1927.2 pp. 13-14; calle Valladares and calle Sevilla (43), Com. Mon.
Anales ... Córdoba 1926.2 p. 11; "La Higuerilla" area (14), Fernández Chicarro 1953 p. 437. Opus sectile has been noted at Avenida del Generalísimo
25 (46), Vicent 1971-73; Avenida del General Primo Rivera 17 (44), Vicent
p. 174. For a general treatment see now Blázquez 1981.

330. In general, Thompson 1969; 1976; 1977; 1978; Stroheker 1974.

331. The council's being held in the south must have led to an over-
representation of local bishoprics. On Christianity, Blázquez 1978 pp.
259-264; Díaz y Díaz 1973. On Elvira, FHA 8 pp. 59-60.

332. On Osius see FHA 8 pp. 56-59; Thouvenot 1973 pp. 331-341, 793;
Clerq 1954; Turner 1911. He also is noted as Córdoba's bishop at the council of Serdica in A.D. 344: FHA 8 p. 66. He was not buried in the

Basilica de San Pereto on Mallorca, as a misreading of an epitaph had previously suggested: Palol 1967 p. 10 n. 17.

333. Priscillianism: Chadwick 1976. Hyginus: Sulpicius Severus
Chron. 2.46.7–47.3.

334. Orlandis 1977 p. 236.

335. Zoilus had had a good Christian education as a child, so he is
evidence for at least two generations of active Christians in Córdoba:
Thouvenot 1973 pp. 320, 792. A certain Dion "prefect of Córdoba" (praeses?)
presided at the condemnation of Ascisclus (Dozy 1961). Dion's official
position is something of a puzzle. Vives 1942 no. 324 gives a Cordoban
dedication to the five martyrs mentioned. On martyrs, Thouvenot 1973 p.
315 and n. 3.

336. On the sarcophagi and their Roman origins, Palol 1967 pp. 288–290,
297–300 with earlier bibliography. Cf. also Thouvenot 1973 pp. 662, 663,
665, with bibliography at p. 808.

337. Cemeteries: Palol 1967 p. 281; Vicent 1961; García y Bellido
1963.2. Epitaphs from Córdoba are numbers 161–166, 508–509 in Vives 1942.

338. Thouvenot 1973 pp. 656, 658; Palol 1967 pp. 253–255, 258–267, 269,
271. Christian inscriptions from Córdoba are given by Vives 1952 nos. 161–
166, 324, 339, 395, 417 and 508–509.

339. Albertini 1923 pp. 123–124.

340. Guadalquivir: Schulten 1959 vol. II p. 13—but on p. 52 he notes
that in the eleventh century a boat could travel to Córdoba. *Comes* at Córdoba: *C. Theod.* 9.1.1, cf. 12.1.4 (ed. Mommsen pp. 430, 663). Note also
Ausonius *Urb.* 11.84, which lists Córdoba among the important cities of the
Roman world.

341. García Moreno 1978 p. 300; Stroheker 1974 p. 587.

342. Cf. Ortiz Juárez 1959.

343. Stroheker 1974 p. 595; Orlandis 1977 pp. 22–26.

344. Bury 1928 pp. 103–105, 113–114, 117–118; García Moreno 1978 pp.
300–301; Orlandis 1977 pp. 26–32; Thompson 1976 p. 24.

345. Thompson 1977 pp. 3–6 with Hydatius 123; 1978 pp. 4–9; García Moreno 1978 pp. 301–304 with citations. On continued economic activity during
this period, García Moreno 1973.2. Baetica seems to have escaped the ravages of *bacaudae*: Stroheker 1974 p. 600; Thompson 1977 p. 29.

346. Orlandis 1977 p. 91; García Moreno 1977 p. 303; Thompson 1969 pp.
16–17; Isidore H. G. 45–46 (FHA 9 p. 135).

347. Stroheker 1939 p. 135; 1963 = 1975 pp. 209, 213; Orlandis 1977 p.
91 with *Chron. Caesaraug.* p. 223 (A.D. 568) = FHA 9 pp. 141–142. Athanagild died in 567; so the *Chron.* must have the date wrong. This episode
makes one wonder if Córdoba was indeed captured in earlier wars, for the
sources only mention the taking of Seville.

348. Ioh. Biclar. *Chron.* p. 213 = FHA 9 p. 153. Thompson 1969 pp. 60–
61; Orlandis 1977 p. 95. The notice of John of Biclarum indicates peasant
revolts in the area as well, but cooperation with the rebellious Cordobans
is "very doubtful": Thompson p. 61.

349. Stroheker 1939 pp. 146-147, 183-184; 1963 = 1975 pp. 213-214, 218; Thompson 1969 pp. 68-73. See FHA 9 pp. 186-187. Coin: FHA 9 p. 193. Thompson pp. 320-328 (esp. 321-322) tries to make a case for the Byzantines never having actually occupied Córdoba. True, they are never explicitly mentioned as in possession of the city, but who was opposing Athanagild when he unsuccessfully attacked the city? Why did Hermenegild surrender as soon as the Byzantines were bought off? A picture of Byzantine troops milling about Seville and Córdoba in these years, but never actually being garrison forces, seems unrealistic. The argument that the interior towns of Baetica were not in Byzantine hands, and therefore Seville and Córdoba could not have been, is weak (Thompson p. 322). Would not the Byzantines first try to control the major river cities, even if other towns were ignored? At any rate, there is no doubt that Byzantine troops operated freely in the area of Córdoba during this period, whether or not they actually garrisoned the city.

350. Of Visigothic building, scant record remains except stray column capitals, such as those reused in the mosque. One reference survives to a palace built by king Rodrigo that was called "a caldeis vallat Ruderici", according to the Cronica de Alfonso III (Rotense) ed. Ubieto p. 20.

351. Citations for coins: FHA 9 pp. 230, 281, 289, 294, 297, 308, 323, 341, 358, 372, 377.

352. Seville: Mansi 10.555-570 = FHA 9 p. 252. Among other things, a boundary dispute between Astigi and Córdoba was settled, and the unjust transfer of a priest from Italica to Córdoba was discussed. See also Thompson 1969 p. 305. Toledo: Mansi 10.641C-643C = FHA 9 p. 287. A Visigothic bishop of Córdoba attended--one Leudeficus or Leodefredus. He also attended the sixth Toledan council in 638 (Mansi 19.671A = FHA 9 p. 293). He is the first Visigothic bishop of Córdoba on record. A Roman, Agapius, was perhaps the first bishop appointed by a Visigothic king, Reccared. He (Agapius) was a disaster, for he was apparently totally unfamiliar with, or indifferent to, ecclesiastical obligations. He attended the III Toledo and I Seville councils, and died in about A.D. 619. Thompson 1969 pp. 110, 164. He was not the only unsatisfactory bishop that Córdoba had; another was found guilty of "carnal sin" in the time of Isidore of Seville (Thompson p. 304 n. 3). For the seventh council of Toledo, see Mansi 10.763-774 = FHA 9 p. 304; Leufredus was represented by another church official. At the eighth council, the Cordoban bishop was in attendance. Perhaps he was not a Visigoth, for the Visigothic bishops seem to be listed by name: Mansi 10.1221E-1222D = FHA 9 p. 314. A bishop named Mumulus represented Córdoba at councils thirteen (Mansi 11.1075C-1076A) and fifteen (Mansi 12. 21-22C = FHA p. 362). His name may betray a Roman, but Visigoths also certainly assumed such names.

353. García Moreno 1978 p. 307. One additional piece of information on Córdoba has come to us by accident from this period. We can assume that there was a large Jewish population at Córdoba--perhaps as a result of commercial acitivity in the city. When the Arabs took the city, they gave the task of guarding it to these Jews (Orlandis 1977 p. 83). Sisebut (king A.D. 612-621) addressed a letter to the bishop and civil authorities at Córdoba concerning the treatment of Jews (Thompson 1969 pp. 139, 305). As to Christians--perhaps the Catholic Hermenegild persecuted Arians (Thompson p. 80). The only other evidence we possess for Visigothic acitivity at Córdoba is the notice that Egica (687-702) issued legislation on escaped slaves from the city in the year 702: Thompson pp. 272-273.

354. Thompson 1969 pp. 249-250; Orlandis 1977 pp. 289-290.

Bibliography

Abad Casals, L. 1975. El Guadalquivir, vía fluvial romana. Seville

Abbott, F.F., A.C. Johnson. 1926. Municipal Administration in the Roman Empire. Princeton.

Acuña Fernández, Palomar. 1975. Esculturas militares romanas de España y Portugal. Rome.

Ahl, F. 1976. Lucan: an Introduction. Ithaca, N.Y.

Albertini, E. 1923. Les divisions administratives de l'Espagne romaine. Paris.

---. 1912. "Les étranges résidants en Espagne à l'époque romaine," Mélanges Cagnat (Paris) 297-318.

---. 1918-19. Mélanges de l'Ecole Française de Rome 37. 314.

Albertos Firmat, M. L. 1966. La onomástica personal primitiva de Hispania Tarraconense y Bética. Salamanca.

Alföldy, G. 1969. Fasti Hispanienses. Wiesbaden.

---. 1978. "Tarraco," RE Suppl. 15. 570-644.

Amador de los Ríos, José. 1879. "Monumentos latinobizantinos de Córdoba," Monumentos Arquitectónicos de España vol. 4. (Madrid).

Arías Abellán, C., Arcadio del Castillo Alvarez. 1978. "Estudio sobre metodología demográfica. El caso de una ciudad Andaluz en época romana," Actas, I Congreso Historia de Andalucía (Córdoba, 1976) (Córdoba) 193-201.

Arías Irene, A. 1949. "Materiales epigráficos para el estudio de los desplazamientos y viajes de los españoles en la España romana," Cuadernos de Historia de España 12 (Buenos Aires) 5-50.

Arribas, A. 1967. "La edad del bronce en la península ibérica," in Las raíces de España, ed. J.M. Gómez Tabanera (Madrid) 85-108.

---. 1963. The Iberians. London.

---. 1959. "Urbanismo del bronce primitivo," Zephyrus 10. 81-128.

Azorín, F. 1923. "¿Las termas romanas de Córdoba?" BRAC 2. 89-91.

Balil, A. 1961. La ley gladiatoria de Itálica. Madrid.

---. 1968. "Rectificaciones," AEA 41. 156-157.

---. 1965. "Riqueza y sociedad en la España romana (siglo III-I a.d.J.C.,"
    Hispania 25. 323-366.

Beltrán Lloris, M. 1970. Las ánforas romanas en España. Zaragoza.

Beltrán Martínez, A. 1950. "Las teorías de M. Grant sobre las monedas de
    Cartagena y otras españoles," Cong. Nat. Arq. I (Almería, 1949)
    (Cartagena) 291-294.

Bendala Galán, M. 1978. "Documentos de interés en la Bética para el
    estudio de las religiones orientales en Roma," Actas I Congreso
    Historia de Andalucía (Córdoba, 1976) (Córdoba) 211-221.

Bernhardt, R. 1975. "Die Entwicklung römischer amici et socii zu
    civitates liberae in Spanien," Historia 24. 411-424.

Bernier, J. 1966. Historia y paisaje provincial. Córdoba. (Not seen)

Bernier, J., F. J. Fortea. 1963. "Niveles arqueológicos del valle del
    Guadalquivir," BRAC 34. 199-206.

---. 1968-69. "Nuevo gráfito ibérico de Corduba," Zephyrus 19-20. 105-108.

Blance, B. 1961. "Early Bronze Age Colonists in Iberia," Antiquity
    35. 192-202.

Blanco, A. 1967. "La colonización de la península ibérica en el primer
    milenio antes de Cristo," in Las raíces de España, ed. J.M. Gómez
    Tabanera. (Madrid) 167-197.

---. 1968. "Documentos metroacos de Hispania," AEA 41. 91-100.

---. 1975. "Ein Kopf des Vulcan in Córdoba," MM 16. 263-266.

---. 1976. "Die Kunst Hispaniens in der Principatzeit," ANRW 2.12.3.

---. 1959. "Polifemo y Galatea," AEA 32. 174-177.

---. 1961. "Polifemo y Galatea en Córdoba," BRAC 32. 376-378.

---. 1962. "Polifemo y Galatea en Córdoba," Oretania 19. 168-170.

---. 1966.1. "Séneca y la Córdoba de su tiempo," Actas del Congreso
    de Filosofía II (Córdoba) 17-38.

---. 1966.2. "Séneca y la sociedad romana," Cuadernos Hispanoamericanos
    no. 194. 218-234.

---. 1972. "La Sevilla romana. Colonia Julia Romula Hispalis," Historia
    del urbanismo sevillano (Seville) 3-22.

---. 1970. "Vestigios de Córdoba romana," Habis 1. 109-123.

Blanco, A., R. Corzo Sánchez. 1976. "El urbanismo romano de la Bética,"
    Symposion de ciudades augusteas I (Zaragoza, 1976) (Zaragoza) 137-162
    (139-141 on Córdoba).

Blanco, A., J. M. Luzón. 1966. "Mineros antiguos españoles," AEA 39.
    13-88.

Blanco, A., J. M. Luzón, D. Ruiz Mata. 1969. "Panorama Tartésico en
    Andalucía oriental," V Symposium internacional de prehistoria penín-
    sular (Jerez de la Frontera, 1968) (Barcelona) 119-162.

Blázquez, A. 1912. "Camino romano de Sevilla a Córdoba," BRAH 61. 465-471.

---. 1914. "El puente romano de Córdoba," BRAH 65. 457-465.

Blázquez, J. M. 1978. "La Bética en el bajo imperio," Actas I Congreso de Historia de Andalucía (Córdoba, 1976) (Córdoba) 255-278.

---. 1975.1. Castulo I. Madrid.

---. 1981. Mosaicos romanos de Córdoba, Jaén y Málaga. Madrid.

---. 1979. "Projección de los pueblos de la meseta en Turdetania y Levante," Actas II Coloquio sobre lénguas y culturas prerromanas de la península ibérica (Tübingen, 1976) (Salamanca) 421-434.

---. 1975.2. Tartessos y las orígines de la colonización fenecia en occidente. Salamanca.

Bleicken, J. 1974. "In provinciali solo dominium populi Romani est vel Caesaris," Chiron 4. 359-414.

Bonsor, G. 1931. The Archaeological Expedition along the Guadalquivir. New York.

Bosch Gimpera, P. 1924. "Divinidades sirias en una ara encontrada en Córdoba," BRAC 3. 219-236.

Bosch Gimpera, P., P. Aguado Bleye. 1935. "La conquista de España por Roma," in Historia de España ed. R. Menéndez Pidal. (Madrid) 1-283.

Bosworth, A. B. 1976. "Arrian in Baetica," GRBS 17. 55-64.

---. 1973. "Vespasian and the Provinces. Some Problems of the Early 70s A.D.," Athenaeum 51. 49-78.

Boulvert, G. 1964. Les esclaves et les affranchis impériaux sous le haut-empire II. Aix-en-Provence.

Broughton, T. R. S. 1965. "Municipal Institutions in Roman Spain," Cahiers d'Histoire Mondiale 9. 126-142.

---. 1973. "Oil-producing Estates in Southern Spain," Akten des VI Internationalen Kongresses für Griechische und Lateinische Epigraphik (Munich, 1972) (Munich) 475-476.

---. 1929. The Romanization of Africa Proconsularis. Baltimore.

Brunt, P. A. 1971. Italian Manpower 225 B.C.-A.D. 14. Oxford.

Burkert, W. 1975. "Nochmals das Arrian-Epigramm von Córdoba," ZPE 17. 167-169.

Bury, J. B. 1928. The Invasions of Europe by the Barbarians. London.

Buttrey, T. V. 1960. "The 'Pietas' denarii of Sextus Pompeius," NC. 83-101.

Caamano, J. M. 1972. "Los Aelii en la península ibérica," BSAA 38. 133-163.

Callender, M. H. 1965. Roman Amphorae. Oxford.

Camacho, J. M. 1950. "Literatura de Córdoba: literatura romano-cordobesa," BRAC 21. 241-255.

Canto, A. M. 1974. "Inscripciones inéditas andaluzas I," Habis 5. 221-235.

Carbonell, A. 1949. "Antigüedades cordobeses." BRAC 20. 85-90.

---. 1950. "Antigüedades cordobeses," BRAC 21. 89-93.

---. 1924. "Contribución al estudio de la prehistoria cordobesa: estela ibérica de Córdoba," BRAC 3. 441-443.

---. 1927. "Contribución al estudio de la prehistoria cordobesa," BRAC 6. 413.

---. 1953. "Notas sobre antecedentes romanos y otros de las minas de Cerro Muriano," BRAC 24. 106-108.

Carnoy, A. 1906. Le Latin d'Espagne d'après les inscriptions. Brussels.

Castejón, R. 1929. "Córdoba califal," BRAC 8. 255-339.

---. 1962. "Discurso de contestación al ingreso de Don Victor Escribano Uceley," BRAC 33. 162-163.

---. 1964. "Nuevas identificaciones en la topografía de la Córdoba califal," Actas del I Congreso de Estudios Arabes e Islámicos (Madrid) 371-389.

Castillo, C. 1978. "Colaboración y rebeldía de los cordobeses frente al poder de Roma," Actas I Congreso de Historia de Andalucía (Córdoba, 1976) (Córdoba) 223-229.

---. 1974. "Hispanos y Romanos en Corduba," Hispania Antiqua 4. 191-197.

---. 1973. "El progreso de la epigrafía romana de Hispania, 1967-72," Emerita 41. 107-127.

---. 1965. Prosopographia Baeticae. Pamplona.

Castrén, P. 1975. Ordo populusque Pompeianus. Acta Inst. Rom. Finlandiae 8. Rome.

Castro Sánchez, J. 1977. "Cinco inscripciones funerarias de Córdoba," Habis 8. 445-450.

Chadwick, H. 1976. Priscillian of Avila. Oxford.

Chantraine, H. 1967. Freigelassene und Sklaven im Dienst der römischen Kaiser. Studien zur ihrer Nomenklatur. Wiesbaden.

Chapman, R. 1981. "The Megalithic Tombs of Iberia," in Antiquity and Man, Essays in Honour of Glyn Daniel, ed. J. D. Evans, et al. 93-105.

Chaves Tristán, F. 1978. La Córdoba hispano-romana y sus monedas. Seville.

---. 1973. Las Monedas de Itálica. Seville.

Chevallier, R. 1974. "Cité et territoire," ANRW 2.1 (Berlin) 649-784.

Clark-Maxwell, W. G. 1899. "The Roman Towns in the Valley of the Baetis'" Arch. Journ. 56. 243-306.

Clerq, V. C. de. 1959. "Osio de Córdoba y los orígenes del priscilianismo," BRAC 30. 301-308.

---. 1954. Osius of Córdoba. A Contribution to the History of the Constantine Period. Washington.

Cohen, H. 1880. Description historique des monnaies. 2nd ed., vol. 1. Paris.

Collantes de Terán y Delorme, F., C. Concepción Fernández Chicarro y de Diós, D. E. Woods. 1967. Carteia. Madrid.

Comisión Provincial de Monumentos Históricos y Artísticos (also cited as Comisión de Monumentos de Córdoba). 1927-28. "Nota del gobierno civil sobre hallazgos arqueológicos," Anales de la Comisión Provincial de Monumentos Históricos y Artísticos 25.

---. 1926.1. "Relación de la riqueza monumental y artística de la provincia de Córdoba," Anales de la Comisión Provincial de Monumentos Históricos y Artísticos 55-81.

---. 1926.2. "Resumen de Actas y trabajos: hallazgos arqueológicos," Anales de la Comisión Provincial de Monumentos Históricos y Artísticos 10-12.

Contreras de la Paz, R. 1970. "De la Córdoba romana: el sino trágico de los cordobenses en la Roma del siglo I a.d.J.C.," Omeya 14 no pagination. (Not seen)

---. 1977. Marco Claudio Marcelo, fundador de Córdoba. Córdoba.

---. 1969. "Quinto Cecilio Metelo Pío, proconsul de la provincia Ulterior (79-72 a.d.J.C.)," Omeya 13 no pagination. (Not seen)

Corzo Sánchez, R. 1973. "Munda y las vías de comunicación en el Bellum Hispaniense," Habis 4. 241-252.

Costilla, M. A. 1925. "Excursiones arqueológicas en diversos sitios de las provincias de Segovia y de Córdoba," Memorias de la Junta Superior de Excavaciones y Antigüedades 71. 4.

Crawford, M.H. 1969. Roman Republican Coin Hoards. London.

Cuadrado Díaz, E. 1967. "Un pueblo prehistórico hispano: Los Iberos," in Las raíces de España, ed. J. M. Gómez Tabanera. (Madrid) 143-166.

Degrassi, A. 1959. "L'amministrazione della Città," in Guida allo studio della civiltà romana antica, ed. Ussani and Arnaldi. Vol. 1 (Naples) 301-330.

---. 1956. "Duoviri aedilicia potestate, duoviri aediles, aediles duoviri," Studi in onore de A. Calderini e R. Paribeni (Milan) 151-155.

Deininger, J. 1965. Die Provinziallandtage der römischen Kaiserzeit von Augustus bis zum Ende des dritten Jahrhunderts n. Chr. Vestigia 6. Munich.
---. 1964. "Zur Begründung des Provinzialkultes von Augustus bis zum Ende des II Jh. n. Chr.," MM 5. 167-179.

Delgado, A. 1871-76. Nuevo método de clasificación de las medallas autónomas de España. Madrid.

Detlefsen, D. 1870. "Die Geographie der Provinz Baetica bei Plinius," Philologus 30. 265-310.

Dias de Riba, P. 1627. De las antigüedades y excelencias de Córdoba.

Díaz y Díaz, M. 1973. Cuadernos de Estudios Gallegos 28. 277.

Dilke, O. A. W. 1974. "Archaeological and Epigraphic Evidence of Roman Land Surveys," ANRW 2.1 (Berlin) 564-592.

Dolç, M. 1953. Hispania y Marcial. Barcelona.

Domergue, C. 1965. "Les Planii et leur activité industrielle en Espagne sous la République," Mél. Casa Vel. 1. 9-25.

Dozy, R. 1961. Le Calendrier de Cordoue. New ed. by Ch. Pellat. Leiden.

Dreizehnter, A. 1975. "Pompeius als Städtegründer," Chiron 5. 213-245.

Duncan Jones, R. P. 1977. "Age-rounding, Illiteracy, and Social Differen-
    tiation in the Roman Empire," Chiron 7. 333-354.

Eck, W. 1978. "Zum neuen Fragment des sogenannten Testamentum Dasumii,"
    ZPE 30. 278-286.

Ensslin, W. 1954. "Praefectus iure dicundo," RE 22.2. 1313-1315.

Espasa, J., ed. 1907. "Córdoba," Enciclopedia Universal Ilustrada vol.
    15 (Barcelona) 587-593.

Etienne, R. 1958. Le culte impérial dans la Péninsule Ibérique d'Auguste
    à Dioclétien. Paris.

---. 1973. "Les syncretismes religieux dans la Péninsule Ibérique à l'
    époque impériale," Travaux de Centre d'Etudes Superieures Spécialisé
    d'Histoire des Religions de Strasbourg (Paris) 153-163.

Fernández Chicarro y de Diós, C. 1953. "Actividades arqueológicas en
    Andalucía," AEA 26. 435-443.

---. 1954. "Inscripciones alusivas a la prima invasión de Moros en la
    Bética en el siglo II de la era," I Congreso Arqueológico del Mar-
    ruecos Español (Tetuán) 413-419.

---. 1955. "Noticiario arqueológico de Andalucía," AEA 28. 322-341.

Fernández Galiano, M. 1972. Emerita 40. 47-50.

Fernández Nieto, J., J. Fortea, J. M. Roldán. 1968-69. "Una nueva in-
    scripción del Museo Arqueológico de Córdoba," Zephyrus 19-20. 169-173.

Fiske, G. C. 1900. "Notes on the Worship of the Roman Emperors in Spain'"
    HSCP 11. 101-139.

Fita, F. 1908. "Las puertas del sueña. Nueva lápida votiva de Córdoba,"
    BRAH 52. 453-456.

Fortea, J., J. Bernier. 1970. Recintos y fortificaciones ibéricos de la
    Bética. Salamanca.

Gabba, E. 1954. "Le Origini della Guerra Sociale," Athenaeum 32. 41-114,
    293-345.

Galsterer-Kröll, B. 1972. "Untersuchungen zu den Beinamen der Städte des
    Imperium Romanum," Epigraphische Studien 9. 44-145.

Galsterer, H. 1971. Untersuchungen zum römischen Städtewesen auf der
    Iberischen Halbinsel. Berlin.

Galsterer-Kroll, B., H. Galsterer. 1972-73. "Neue Inschriften aus Köln,"
    Kölner Jahrbuch 13. 92-101.

Gálvez, R. 1924. "La casa de Séneca," BRAC 3. 175-180.

García Iglesias, L. 1975. "La enseñanza en la Hispania romana," Hispania
    Antiqua 5. 121-134.

García Merino, C. 1970. "La ciudad romana de Uxama," BSAA. 383-440.

García Moreno, L. A. 1978. "Andalucía durante la antigüedad tardía (ss. V-VII). Aspectos socioeconómicos," Actas I Congreso Historia de Andalucía (Córdoba, 1976) (Córdoba) 297-307.

———. 1973.1. "Colonias de comerciantes orientales en la Península Ibérica. Siglos V-VII," Habis 3. 127-154.

———. 1973.2. "Organización militar en la península ibérica—ss. V-VII," Hispania 33. 5-22.

———. 1976. "Sobre la sociedad de la península ibérica entre el reino de Tolosa y el de Toledo (c.507-569), Actas VI Cong. Internac. Estud. Clas. (Madrid, 1976).

García Rodríguez, C. 1966. El culto de los santos en la España romana y visigoda. Madrid.

García Ruiz, E. 1967. "Estudio lingüístico de las defixiones latinas no incluidas en el corpus de Audollent," Emerita 35. 55-89.

García Villada, Z. 1929. Historia eclesiástica de España. Vol. 1. Madrid.

García y Bellido, A. 1959.1. "Las colonias romanas de Hispania," Anuario de Historia del Derecho Español 29. 417-517.

———. 1948.1 "El culto a Mitras en la península ibérica," BRAH 122. 283-349.

———. 1963.1. El Dístylo sepulcral romano de Ilipula (Zalamea). Anejos de AEA III. Madrid.

———. 1959.2. "El elemento forastero en la Hispania romana," BRAH 144. 119-154.

———. 1949. Esculturas romanas de España y Portugal. Madrid.

———. 1970. Los hallazgos cerámicos del área del templo romano de Córdoba. Madrid.

———. 1948.2. Hispania Graeca. Barcelona.

———. 1960.1. "Lápidas funerarias de gladiatores de Hispania," AEA 33. 123-144.

———. 1965. "Los mosaicos romanos de la plaza de la Corredera en Córdoba," BRAH 157. 183-195.

———. 1960.2. "Némesis y su culto en España," BRAH 147. 119-147.

———. 1956-61. "Noticiario arqueológico hispánico V (1956-61)," AEA 241-245.

———. 1960.3. "Noticiario arqueológico," AEA 33. 169-172, 188-191.

———. 1963.2. "Noticiario arqueológico," AEA 36. 170-177.

———. 1971.1 "Novedades epigráficas. Inscripciones romanas de Córdoba, Navarra, Estremadura, Portugal, Cádiz, Ciudad Real, Málaga, y Murcia," BRAH 168. 179-205. (Córdoba, 179-184).

———. 1971.2 "Un nuevo Mithra Tauroktonos," AEA 44. 142-145.

———. 1969. "Orígenes y formas de las colonias romanas de Hispania," Cuadernos Hispanoamericanos no. 238-240. 382-387.

———. 1967. Les religions orientales dans l'Espagne romaine. Leiden.

---. 1963.3. "Sarcófago cristiano hallado en Córdoba en 1962," AEA 36. 170-177.

---. 1958. "El sarcófago del Brillante de Córdoba," Zephyrus 9. 237-241.

---. 1959.3. "El sarcófago romano de Córdoba," AEA 32. 3-37.

---. 1962. "Syrios en el pantheon hispano-romano," Zephyrus 13. 67-74.

---. 1961.1. "El templo romano de Córdoba," BRAC 32. 371-375.

---. 1964. "El templo romano de Córdoba," Oretania 157-165.

---. 1961.2. "Un toracato del 'tipo hierapytna' en Córdoba," AEA 34. 196-200.

Gilman, A. 1976. "Bronze Age Dynamics in Southeast Spain," Dialectical Anthropology 1. 307-319.

Gómez Moreno, M. 1912. Materiales de arqueología española. Vol. 1. Madrid.

González, J. 1981. "Inscripciones inéditas de Córdoba y su provincia," Mél. Casa Vel. 17. 38-54.

Gorges, J.-G. 1979. Les Villas Hispano-romaines. Paris.

Grant, M. 1946. From Imperium to Auctoritas. Cambridge.

Griffin, M. 1972. "The Elder Seneca and Spain," JRS 62. 1-19.

---. 1975. Seneca: A Political Biography. Oxford.

Grenier, A. 1937. "La Gaule romaine," in An Economic Survey of Ancient Rome, ed. T. Frank. Vol. 3 (Baltimore) 385-644.

Hardy, E. G. 1946. "The Provincial Concilia from Augustus to Diocletian," Studies in Roman History I (London) 236-283.

Harrison, R. 1977. Bell Beaker Cultures of Spain and Portugal. Bulletin 35. American School of Prehistoric Research.

Hatzfeld, J. 1919. Les trafiquants italiens dans l'orient hellenique. Paris.

Henderson, M. I. 1942. "Julius Caesar and Latium in Spain," JRS 32. 1-13.

---. 1953. Review of Vittinghoff 1952 (below), JRS 43. 140.

Herzig, R. 1974. "Probleme des römischen Strassenwesens. Untersuchungen zu Geschichte und Recht," ANRW 2.1 (Berlin) 593-648.

Heuten, G. 1935. "Les divinités capitolines en Espagne," Revue Belge de Philologie et d'Histoire 12. 549-558.

Hildburgh, W. L. 1921-22. "A Find of Ibero-Roman Silver at Cordova," Archaeologia 2nd series, 22. 159-184.

Hiller von Gaertringen, F., E. Littmann, W. Weber, O. Weinreich. 1924. "Divinidades sirias en una ara encontrada en Córdoba," BRAC 3. 219-236.

Holder, A. 1893-1916. Alt-celtischer Sprachschatz. Leipzig.

Hübner, E. 1867. "Corduba," CIL 2 (Berlin) 306-307.

---. 1892. "Corduba," CIL 2 Suppl. (Berlin) 886.

---. 1900. "Corduba," RE 4.1. 1221

Jaén, A. 1935. Historia de la ciudad de Córdoba. Madrid.

Jarrett, M. G. 1971. "Decurions and Priests," AJPh 92. 513-538.

Kajanto, I. 1965. The Latin Cognomina. Helsinki.

---. 1968. "The significance of non-Latin cognomina," Latomus 27. 817-834.

Knapp, R.C. 1977. Aspects of the Roman Experience in Iberia, 206-100 B.C. Valladolid.

---. 1980.1. "The Coinage of Corduba Colonia Patricia," Annali di Istituto Italiano di Numismatica (forthcoming).

---. 1980.2. "La epigrafía y la historia de la Córdoba romana," Anuario de Filología 5. 61-71.

---. 1981. "L. Axius Naso and 'Pro legato'," Phoenix 35. 14-38.

---. 1979. "One Less Seneca for Corduba," ZPE 36. 137-138.

Koch, M. 1977. "Zur fruhen judischen Diaspora auf der iberischen Halbinsel," Revista de la Universidad Complutense 26. 225-254.

Koenen, L. 1977. "Córdoba and no end," ZPE 24. 35-40.

Kornemann, E. 1900.1. "Coloniae," RE 4.1. 514-587.

---. 1900.2. "Conventus," RE 4.1. 1183-1200.

Kubitschek, W. 1882. De Romanorum tribuum origine ac propagatione. Vienna.

Ladage, D. 1971. "Städtische Priester-und Kultämter im lateinischen Westen des Imperium Romanum zur Kaiserzeit." Ph.D. diss. University of Cologne.

Langhammer, W. 1973. Die staatsrechtliche und soziale Stellung der Magistratus municipales und der Decuriones. Wiesbaden.

Lantier, R. 1953. "L'Andalousie préhistorique, ibérique, et romaine," JS. 106-115, 158-166.

Larsen, J. A. O. 1934. "The Position of Provincial Assemblies in the Government and Society of the Late Roman Empire," CP 19. 209-220.

León, M. P. 1973. "Sobre Séneca el Viejo." Ph.D. diss. University of Seville.

Levick, B. 1967. Roman Colonies in Southern Asia Minor. Oxford.

Liebenam, W. 1900. Städteverwaltung im römischen Kaiserreich. Leipzig.

López Ontiveros, A. 1973. Evolución urbana de Córdoba y de los pueblos campiñeses. Estudios Cordubenses. Publicaciones de la Excm. Diputación Provincial. Córdoba. (Not seen)

---. 1974. "Parcelarios geométricos en la campiña de Córdoba," Estudios sobre centuraciones romanas en España (Madrid) 36-60.

Luzón, J. M., D. Ruiz Mata. 1973. Las raíces de Córdoba. Madrid.

MacKendrick, P. 1972. Roman France. New York.

Madoz, P. 1847. "Córdoba," Diccionario geográfico-estadístico-histórico de España vol. 6. 646-648.

Magoffin, R. 1913. The Quinquennales. An Historical Study. Baltimore.

Mangas, J. 1971.1. "Un capítulo de los gastos en el municipio romano de Hispania a través de las informaciones de la epigrafía latina," Hispania Antiqua 1. 105-146.

---. 1971.2. Esclavos y libertos en la España romana. Salamanca.

---. 1977. "Servidumbre comunitaria en la Bética prerromana," Memorias de Historia Antigua 1. 151-161.

Mann, J. C. 1963. "City Names in the Western Empire," Latomus 22. 777-782.

Manni, E. 1950. "Quattuorviri e duoviri," RIL 83. 383-396.

Mapelli López, L. 1971. "Las monedas emitidas en Córdoba romana," BRAC 42. 7-32.

Maraver, L. 1863. Historia de Córdoba. Córdoba.

Marchetti, M. 1976. "Hispania," DE 3. 745-941.

Marcos Pous, A. 1976. "Aportación al estudio de las inscripciones funerarias gladiatorias de Córdoba," Corduba 1. 15-53.

---. 1977.1. "Excavaciones arqueológicas en el solar de la Avenida del Gran Capitán (Córdoba), 1973-74," NAH 5. 217-219.

---. 1977.2. "Trabajos arqueológicos en el solar de la calle de San Pablo (Córdoba)," NAH 5. 205-207.

---. 1977.3. "Trabajos arqueológicos en el solar de la calle Osario (Córdoba)," NAH 5. 211-213.

---. 1977.4. "Trabajos arqueológicos en la ciudad de Córdoba, 1973," NAH 5. 223-226.

Marcos Pous, A., A. M. Vicent, J. Costa Ramos. 1977. "Trabajos arqueológicos en un solar de la Plaza de San Pedro (Córdoba), 1973," NAH 5. 197-201.

Marcovich, M. 1973. "The Epigram of Proconsul Arrian from Córdoba," ZPE 12. 207-209.

---. 1976. "Nochmals Córdoba, wiederum Arrian," ZPE 20. 41-43.

Mariner Bigorra, S. 1952. Inscripciones hispanas en verso. Madrid.

---. 1974. "Procedimientos indirectos de datación epigráfica," Miscelánea Arqueológica 2 (Barcelona) 7-12.

Masdeu, J. F. 1784. Historia crítica y de España. Madrid.

Matz, F. 1968. "Das Problem der Orans und ein Sarkophag in Córdoba," MM 9. 300-310.

Maurenbrecher, B., ed. 1891. C. Sallusti Crispi Historiarum Reliquiae. Leipzig (reprinted 1966).

Mellado, J., J. M. Vila. 1972. "Una inscripción romana hallado en Córdoba," Habis 3. 321-324.

Menéndez Pidal, R., ed., P. Bosch Gimpera, et al. 1935. Historia de España. España Romana. Madrid (reprinted 1962).

Milik, J. T. 1967. "Inscription araméenne et une dédicace grecque de Cordue," Syria 44. 300.

Miller, K. 1916. Itineraria romana. Stuttgart (reprinted Rome 1964).

Moffre, F., R. Etienne. 1963. Les religions orientales sous l'Empire romain dans la Peninsule Ibérique. Bordeaux.

Mommsen, T. 1860. Geschichte des römischen Münzwesens. Berlin.

---. 1893. "Zum Bellum Hispaniense," Hermes 28. 607-614 = Gesammelte Schriften vol. 7 (Berlin, 1909) 61-69.

Montenegro, A. 1978. "Evolución política durante las dinastías Julio-Claudia y Flavia," in Historia de España Antigua, J. M. Blázquez, et al. Vol. 2: Hispania Romana (Madrid) 290-344.

Morales, Ambrosio de. 1577. Antigüedades de España. Alcalá de Henares.

Moretti, L. 1959-60. "Statistica demografica ed epigrafica. Durata media della vita in Roma imperiale," Epigraphica 21. 60-78.

Mouterde, Padre. 1 May 1924. Machriq. On Syrian goddesses. Cited by García y Bellido 1963.2 p. 73 n. 48. (Not seen)

Münzer, F. 1899. "M. Claudius Marcellus Aeserninus," Claudius no. 232, RE 3. 2770-2771.

Muñoz, A. M. 1969. "La civilización pretartésica andaluza durante la edad del bronce," V Symposium international de prehistoria peninsular (Jerez de la Frontera, 1968) (Barcelona) 33-45.

Muñoz Coello, J. 1976. "Un flamen de la provincia Baetica," Habis 7. 387-390.

Muñoz Vázquez, M. 1962. "Casas solariegas de Córdoba. Palacio de los Páez de Castillejo," BRAC 33. 31-63.

Muro Meléndez-Valdes, M. P. 1977. "Inscripciones romanas de Córdoba recogidas por Fernández Franco." Tesis de Licenciatura, University of Seville.

Navascués, J. M. de. 1952. "En torno a las series hispánicas i imperiales," Num. Hisp. 33 ff.

Nierhaus, R. 1964. "Baedro. Topographische Studien zum Territorium des Conventus Cordubensis in des mittleren Sierra Morena," MM 5. 185-212.

---. 1966. "Die wirtschaftlichen Voraussetzungen der Villenstadt von Italica," MM 7. 189-205.

Ogilvie, R. M. 1965. A Commentary on Livy Books 1-5. Oxford.

Orlandis, J. 1977. Historia de España: La España visigótica. Madrid.

Ortí Belmonte, M. A. 1924-28. "Córdoba durante la Guerra de la Independencia," BRAC 3-7. Separatum published in 1930.

---. 1958. "Corduba romana," BRAC 29. 33-58.

Ortiz Juárez, D. 1959. "Las bellas artes en la Bética contemporaneo de Osio," BRAC 30. 239-279.

Otto, W. 1918. "Ianus," RE Suppl. 3. 1175-1191.

Palol, P. de. 1967. Arqueología de la España romana (Siglos IV-VI). Madrid-Valladolid.

Palop Fuentes, P. 1978. "Córdoba en la encrucijada de la batalla de Munda," Actas I Congreso Historia de Andalucía (Córdoba, 1976) (Cordoba) 159-163.

Peek, W. 1976. "Zum Arrian-Epigramm von Córdoba," ZPE 22. 87-88.

Pellicer Catalán, M. 1967. "Las civilizaciones neolíticas hispanas," in Las raíces de España, ed. J. M. Gómez Tabanera. (Madrid) 27-46.

Pflaum, H.-G. 1960-61. Les carrières procuratoriennes équestres sous le haut-empire romain. Paris.

Piernavieja Rozitis, P. 1980. Corpus de inscripciones deportivas de la España romana. Madrid.

---. 1968. "Epitáfios deportivos de la Hispania romana," Citius, Altius, Fortius 10. 293-360.

---. 1975. "Una reinvindicación deportiva," AEA 48. 157-158.

Ponsich, M. 1974. Implantation rurale antique sur le Bas-Guadalquivir. Vol. 1. Paris.

---. 1979. Implantation rurale antique sur le Bas-Guadalquivir. Vol. 2. Paris.

Poulsen, E. 1933. Sculptures antiques des musées de province espagnols. Copenhagen.

Prato, C. 1964. Gli Epigrammi attributi a L. Anneo Seneca. Rome.

Prieto, A. 1973. Estructura social del "conventus Cordubensis" durante el alto imperio romano. Granada.

---. 1972. "Sobre los límites del 'conventus Cordubensis'," Hispania Antiqua 2. 125-133.

Ramírez de Arellano, R. 1916. Historia de Córdoba. Ciudad Real.

Recio, A. 1959. "Novedades arqueológicas: el mosaico de Polifemo y Galatea en Córdoba," Oretania 4.

Reinhold, M. 1970. History of Purple as a Status Symbol in Antiquity. Coll. Latomus 116. Brussels.

Renfrew, C. 1973. Before Civilization. Cambridge.

---. 1967. "Colonialism and Megalithismus," Antiquity 41. 276-288.

---. 1979. Problems in European Prehistory. Cambridge.

Río Oliete, M. J. del, J. Santos Yanguas. 1978. "Griegos en la Bética a través de la epigrafía latina," Actas I Congreso Historia de Andalucía (Córdoba, 1976) (Córdoba) 239-246.

Ritterling, E. 1924-25. "Legio," RE 12. 1186-1829.

Robert, J., and L. Robert. 1973. Bull. Epig. no. 539 (Arrian inscription).

Rodríguez Neila, J. F. 1976. "La administración municipal en la Hispania romana (Siglos I a.d.J.C.-I y II d.d.J.C.)" Ph.D. diss. University of Seville.

---. 1978. "Las elecciones municipales en la Bética romana," Actas I Congreso Historia de Andalucía (Córdoba, 1976) (Córdoba) 165-175.

---. 1981. "Introducción a la 'Corduba' romana en época republicana," Córdoba, Apuntes para su Historia (Córdoba) 107-134.

---. 1977.1. "'Medicus colonorum' (los médicos oficial de las ciudades en época romana)," Trabajos científicos de la Univ. de Córdoba. No. 14.

---. 1977.2. "Notas sobre la 'Contributio' en la administración municipal de Bética romana," Archivo Hispalense no. 185 55-61.

---. 1975. "Notas sobre las 'annonae' municipales de Hispania," Hispania Antiqua 5. 315-326.

---. 1978.2 "Observaciones en torno a las magistraturas municipales de la Bética romana," Actas I Congreso Historia Andalucía (Córdoba, 1976) (Córdoba) 203-210.

---. 1976.2. "Los 'vici' de Hispania y Corduba," Corduba 1. 101-118.

---, ed. 1978.3. Fuentes y metodología. Andalucía en la antigüedad. Actas I Congreso Historia de Andalucía (Córdoba, 1976). Cordoba.

Roldán Hervas, J. M. 1972. "El elemento indígena en las guerras civiles en Hispania: Aspectos sociales," Hispania Antiqua 2. 77-123.

---. 1974. "Legio Vernacula, ¿Iusta Legio?," Zephyrus 25. 457-471.

Romagosa, J. 1970. "Las monedas con leyenda 'Corduba'," Gaceta Numismática 17. 8-14.

---. 1970. "Simbolismo augural en las monedas hispano-romanas," Gaceta Numismática 16. 17-20.

Romero de Torres, E. 1909. "Córdoba. Nuevas antigüedades romanas y visigóticas," BRAH 56. 492-496.

---. 1913. "Inscripciones romanas de Bujalance y Córdoba," BRAH 60. 75-76.

---. 1914. "Nuevas inscripciones romanas de Córdoba, Porcuna, y Torre-donjimeno," BRAH 65. 130-138.

---. 1910. "Nuevas inscripciones romanas halladas en Córdoba," BRAH 56. 451-455.

Rostbach, O. 1894. "Annaeus," no. 16, RE 1. 2237-2240.

Rozelaar, M. 1976. Seneca. Amsterdam.

Ruano, F. :1760. Historia general de Córdoba. Córdoba.

Ruggiero, E. de. 1895. "Aerarius," DE 1. 311-313.

---. 1900. "Corduba," DE 3.1. 1208.

Sabbatucci, D. 1905. L'edilitá romana: magistratura e sacerdozio. Rome.

Sachers, E. 1954. "Praefectus iure dicundo," RE 22.2. 2378-2381.

Sáinz y Gutiérrez, L. 1894. "Datos históricos acerca de la construcción del puente llamado de Córdoba," Revista de Obras Públicas-Anales. Cited by Romero de Torres 1922 p. 95 n. 11. (Not seen)

Salcedo Hierro, M. 1974. Córdoba ... . León. Cited by Chaves 1978 p. 15 n. 1 as Córdoba, Colonia Romana, Corte de los Califas, Luz de Occidente (León, 1975)?

Salmon, E. T. 1969. Roman Colonization under the Republic. London.

Sánchez de Feria y Morales, B. 1772. Palestra sagrada. Córdoba.

Sánchez León, M. P. 1971. Economía de la Andalucía romana durante la dinastía de los Antoninos. Salamanca.

Sandars, H. W. 1905. "The Linares Bas-Relief and Roman Mining Operations in Baetica," Archaeologia 59. 311-332.

Santero Santurino, J. M. 1978. Asociaciones Populares en Hispania Romana. Seville.

Santos Jener, S. de los. 1958.1 "Las artes en Córdoba durante la dominación de los pueblos germánicos," BRAC 29. 5-50.

---. 1950. "Corduba Marcelli aedificium," BRAC 21. 135-162.

---. 1952. "El culto de Mitras en Cabra (Córdoba)," Rev. Arch. Bibl. Mus. 58. 465-477.

---. 1927.1. "De arqueología romana," BRAC 6. 521-532.

---. 1958.2. "Ensayo de ordenación prehistórica de la provincia de Córdoba," BRAC 29. 77-96.

---. 1927.2. "Hallazgos arqueológicos en 1927," Anales ... Córdoba 13-17.

---. 1927.3. "Hallazgos arqueológicos en 1928," Anales ... Córdoba 19-23.

---. 1955. "Historia de Córdoba." Unpublished. Cited by Muro 1977. (Not seen)

---. 1955. Memoria de las excavaciones del plan nacional realizadas en Córdoba (1948-50). Informes y Memorias no. 31. Madrid. Ministerio de Educación Nacional, Dirección General de Bellas Artes, Comisaría General de Excavaciones Arqueológicas.

---. 1942. MMAP 3. 115.

---. 1926. "El Museo Arqueológico," Anales ... Córdoba 30-41.

---. 1927.4. "El Museo Arqueológico," Anales ... Córdoba 101-122.

---. 1946. "Museo Arqueológico de Córdoba," MMAP 7. 78-85.

---. 1947. "Museo Arqueológico de Córdoba," MMAP 8. 90-220.

---. 1948. "Museo Arqueológico de Córdoba," MMAP 9-10. 209-220.

---. 1954.1. "Museo Arqueológico de Córdoba, 1950," BRAC 25. 159-163.

---. 1954.2. "Museo Arqueológico de Córdoba, 1951," BRAC 25. 111-123.

---. 1955. "Notas sobre hallazgos romanos en Córdoba," III Cong. Nac. Arq. (1953) (Zaragoza) 174-176.

---. 1940-41. "Sarcófagos romanos de plomo hallados en Córdoba," AEA 14. 438-440.

Santos Yanguas, N. 1978. "Los Judíos en la Bética en época romana," Actas I Congreso Historia de Andalucía (Córdoba, 1976) (Córdoba) 247-254.

Savory, H. N. 1949. "The Atlantic Bronze Age in southwest Europe," Proceedings of the Prehistoric Society 128-155.

---. 1968. Spain and Portugal: The Prehistory of the Iberian Peninsula. London.

Scarborough, J. 1969. Roman Medicine. London.

Schanz, M., C. Hosius. 1935. <u>Geschichte</u> <u>der</u> <u>römischen</u> <u>Literature</u>. 4th ed.,
  vol. 2. Munich.

Schönbauer, E. 1954. "Municipia und Coloniae in der prinzipatszeit," <u>SBB</u>.
  der Österr. <u>Akad</u>. der <u>Wiss</u>., <u>Phil</u>., <u>Hist</u>. Bd. 2. 13-48.

Schulten, A. 1940. <u>Fontes</u> <u>Hispania</u> <u>Antiquae</u>. Fasc. 5: <u>Las</u> <u>guerras</u> <u>de</u>
  <u>72-19</u> a.d.J.C. Barcelona.

---. 1959. <u>Geografía</u> <u>y</u> <u>etnografía</u> <u>antiguas</u> <u>de</u> <u>la</u> <u>península</u> <u>ibérica</u>. Madrid.

---. 1923. "Sertorius," <u>RE</u> 2A.2. 1748-1751.

Schultze, W. 1904. <u>Zur</u> <u>Geschichte</u> <u>der</u> <u>lateinischen</u> <u>Eigennamen</u>. Berlin.

Sentenach, N. "1918?" Las murallas de Córdoba," <u>BRAH</u>. Cited with no date
  by Castejón 1962 p. 373 n. 12. Same as Sentenach 1918? (Not seen)

---. 1918. "El puente de Córdoba y las campañas de Julio César," <u>BRAH</u>
  73. 206-211.

Serrano Ramos, E., R. Atencia Páez. 1981. <u>Inscripciones</u> <u>latinas</u> <u>del</u>
  Museo de Málaga. Madrid(?).

Sherwin-White, A. N. 1973. <u>The</u> <u>Roman</u> <u>Citizenship</u>. 2nd ed. Oxford.

Simon, H. 1962. <u>Roms</u> <u>Kriege</u> <u>in</u> <u>Spanien</u>. Frankfurt.

Sotomayor, M. 1964. "Fragmentos pequeños romano-christianos en Córdoba
  y Tarragona, " <u>AEA</u> 37. 183-189.

---. 1964. "El sarcófago paleocristiano de la Ermita de los Mártires de
  Córdoba," <u>AEA</u> 37. 88-105.

---. 1975. <u>Sarcófagos</u> <u>romano-cristianos</u> <u>de</u> <u>España</u>. Granada.

Stauber, G. 1920. "De L. Anneo Seneca Philosopho Epigrammatum auctore."
  Ph.D. diss. University of Munich.

Stroheker, K. F. 1939. "Leowigild," <u>Die</u> <u>Welt</u> <u>als</u> <u>Geschichte</u> 5. 446-485.
  = <u>Germanentum</u> <u>und</u> <u>Spätantike</u> (Zurich, 1965) 134-191.

---. 1972-74. "Spanien im spätrömischen Reich (284-475)," <u>AEA</u> 45-47.
  587-606.

---. 1963. "Das spanische Westgotenreich und Byzanz," <u>Bonner</u> <u>Jahrbücher</u>
  252-74 = <u>Germanentum</u> <u>und</u> <u>Spätantike</u> (Zurich, 1975) 207-245.

Sutherland, C. H. V. 1934. "Aspects of Imperialism in Roman Spain," <u>JRS</u>
  24. 31-42.

---. 1939. <u>The</u> <u>Romans</u> <u>in</u> <u>Spain</u>, <u>218</u> <u>B.C.-117</u> <u>A.D.</u> London.

Syme, R. 1969. "A governor of Tarraconensis," <u>Epig</u>. <u>Stud</u>. 8. 125-133.

---. 1958. <u>Tacitus</u>. Oxford.

Taracena, B. 1937. "El mosaico romano de Baco descubierto en la bodega
  cordobesa de Cruz Conde," <u>Cuadernos</u> <u>de</u> <u>Arte</u> (Granada) 2. (Not seen)

Thompson, E. A. 1976. "The End of Roman Spain," <u>Nott</u>. <u>Med</u>. <u>Stud</u>. 20. 3-28.

---. 1977. "The End of Roman Spain, continued," <u>Nott</u>. <u>Med</u>. <u>Stud</u>. 21. 3-31.

---. 1978. "The End of Roman Spain, continued," <u>Nott</u>. <u>Med</u>. <u>Stud</u>. 22. 3-22.

---. 1979. "The End of Roman Spain, concluded," <u>Nott</u>. <u>Med</u>. <u>Stud</u>. 23. 1-21.

---. 1969. <u>The</u> <u>Goths</u> <u>in</u> <u>Spain</u>. Oxford.

Thouvenot, R. 1973. Essai sur la province romaine de Bétique. 2nd ed., reprint of 1940 edition with additional notes and bibliography, Paris.

---. 1939. "Les incursions des Maures en Bétique sous le règne de Marc-Aurèle," REA 41. 20-28.

Torre, José de la. 1955. "Aras o altares taurobólicos," Obras de D. Juan de la Torre y de Cerro (Córdoba).

---. 1921. "Hallazgos arqueológicos junto a Córdoba," BRAH 79. 419.

---. 1922. "El puente romano de Córdoba," BRAC 1. 87-96.

Tovar, A. 1961. The Ancient Languages of Spain and Portugal. New York.

---. 1963. "Les Celtes en Bétique," Etudes Celtiques 10. 354-373.

---. 1974. Iberische Landeskunde. Part 2, vol. 1: Baetica. Baden-Baden.

---. 1952. "Las monedas de Obulco y los Celtas en Andalucía," Zephyrus 3. 219-221.

---. 1975. "Un nuevo epígrama griego: Arriano de Nicomedia, ¿proconsul de Bética?," AEA 48. 167-173.

---. 1971. "Un nuevo epígrama griego de Córdoba: Arriano de Nicomedia, ¿proconsul de Bética?," Estudios sobre la obra de Américo Castro (Madrid) 401-412.

---. 1948-49. "Sobre la estirpe de Séneca. Estudio sobre las primitivas lenguas hispánicas," Humanitas 2. 249-253.

Trías de Arribas, G. 1967-68. Cerámicas griegas de la península ibérica I: Texto; II: Indices y Láminas. Valencia.

Turner, C. H. 1911. "Ossius of Cordova," Journal of Theological Studies 12. 275 ff.

Untermann, J. 1975. Monumenta Linguarum Hispanicarum. Vol. 1: Die Münz-legenden. 1. Text; 2. Plates. Wiesbaden.

---. 1961. Sprachräume und Sprachbewegungen im vorrömischen Hispanien. Wiesbaden.

Van Nostrand, J. J. 1916. "The Reorganization of Spain by Augustus," University of California Pub. in History 4.2. 83-154.

---. 1937. "Roman Spain," in An Economic Survey of Ancient Rome, ed. T. Frank. Vol. 3 (Baltimore) 119-224.

Vázquez de Parga, L. 1958-61. "Museo Arqueológico Nacional. Adquisiciones de 1958-61. Inscripciones romanas de Córdoba," MMAP 19-21. 27-29.

---. 1957. Tabellae Defixionum cordobesas. Madrid.

Vermaseren, M. J. 1956-60. Corpus inscriptionum et monumentorum religionis Mithriacae. 2 vols. The Hague.

Vicent, A. M. 1964-66. "Informe sobre el hallazgo de mosaicos romanos en el llamado cortijo del Alcaide (Córdoba)," NAH 8-9. 220-222.

---. 1962. "Inventorio de hallazgos: Córdoba," NAH 6. 423-425.

---. 1963. "Memoria de las excavaciones realizadas en la necrópolis romana de Córdoba, 1963," NAH 7. 209-210.

---. "Mosaicos del tipo Opus Sectile que figuran en el Museo Arqueológico de Córdoba," AEA 44.171-175.

---. 1972-74. "Nuevo hallazgo en una necrópolis romana de Córdoba," AEA 45-47. 113-124.

---. 1961. "Un sarcófago cristiano en el Museo Arqueológico de Córdoba," BSAA 27. 1-5.

---. 1973. "Situación de los últimos hallazgos romanos en Córdoba," XII CAN (Jaén, 1971) (Zaragoza) 673-680.

Villaronga, L. 1981. "Análisis estadístico de una muestra de monedas. Aplicación a las monedas de Corduba," Quaderni ticinesi di numismatica e antichità classiche (Lugano) 10. 273-283.

Ville de Mirmont, H. 1910-1913. "Les déclamateurs espagnols au temps d'Auguste et de Tibère," BH 12 (1910). 1-22; 14 (1912). 11-29, 229-243, 341-352; 15 (1913). 237-267, 384-410.

Vittinghoff, F. 1952. Römische Kolonisation und Bürgerrechtspolitik unter Caesar und Augustus. Wiesbaden.

---. 1973. "Städewesen unter römischer Herrschaft," VI Int. Kong. f. Gr. u. Lat.Epigraphik (Munich, 1972) (Munich) 85-91.

Vives, J. 1942. Inscripciones cristianas de la España romana y visigoda. Barcelona.

---. 1971. Inscripciones latinas de la España romana. Barcelona.

Vives y Escudero, A. 1924. La moneda hispánica. Madrid.

Wachtel, K. 1966. Freigelassene und Sklaven in der staatlichen Finanz- verwaltung der römischen Kaiserzeit von Augustus bis Diokletian. Berlin.

Waltzing, J. P. 1895-1900. Etude historique sur les corporations profes- sionelles chez les Romains depuis les origines jusqu'à la chute de l'Empire d'Occident. 4 vols. Brussels.

Ward-Perkins, J. B. 1970. "From Republic to Empire: Reflections on the Early Provincial Architecture of the Roman West," JRS 60. 1-19.

Weaver, P. R. C. 1965. "Irregular Nomina of Imperial Freedmen," CQ 15. 323-326.

Wegner, M. 1953. "Römische Herrscherbildnisse des zweiten Jahrhunderts in Spanien," AEA 26. 67-90.

West, L. C. 1929. Imperial Roman Spain: the Objects of Trade. Oxford.

Wiegels, R. 1978.1. "Das Datum der Verleihung des ius Latii an die Hispanier: zum Personal-und Municipalpolitik in den ersten Regierungs- jahren Vespasians," Hermes 106. 196-223.

---. 1974. "Liv. Per. 55 und die Grundung von Valentia," Chiron 4. 153-176.

---. 1973. Review of Galsterer 1971 (above), BJ 173. 560-568.

---. 1978.2. Review of Tovar 1974 (above), Gnomon 50. 654-658.

---. 1972. "Die römischen Senatoren und Ritter aus den Hispanischen Provinzen." Ph.D. diss. University of Freiburg.

---. 1976. "Zum Territorium der augusteischen Kolonie Emerita," MM 17. 258-284.

Wilkes, J. J. 1969. Dalmatia. London.

Wilson, A. J. N. 1966. Emigration from Italy in the Republican Age of Rome. Manchester.

Wiseman, F. J. 1956. Roman Spain. London.

Woods, D. E. 1969. "Carteia and Tartessos," V Symposium international de prehistoria penisular (Jerez de la Frontera, 1968), (Barcelona) 251-256.

Yoshimura, T. 1963-64. "Über die Legio Vernacula des Pompeius," Annuario Istituto Giap. di Cultura in Roma 1. 105.

Index

Plates

Fig. 1. "Roman" bridge at Córdoba. Only the foundations are ancient.

Fig. 2. Milestone in
Plaza de los
Naranjos.

Fig. 3. Inscription honoring
T. Mercello, aedile and duovir.
Corner of streets Rey Heredia and
Encarnación.

Fig. 4. Supposed location of plane tree (Martial Epig. 9.61) planted by
Caesar.

Fig. 5. Column <u>in situ</u>. Wall between Alcázar and its gardens.

Fig. 6. Reconstruction of the Roman temple (according to García y Bellido).

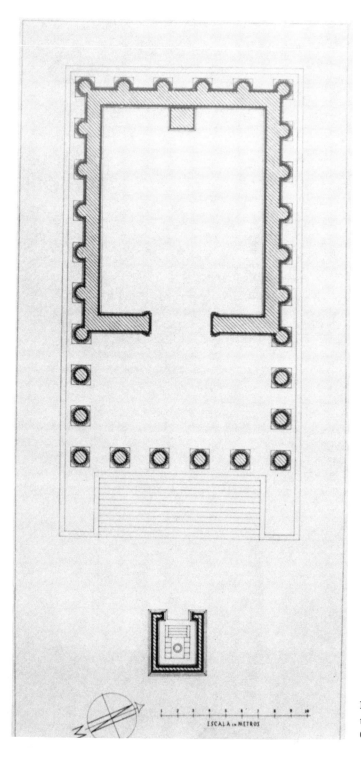

Fig. 7. Plan of Roman
temple (according to
García y Bellido).

Fig. 8. Reconstructed portion of Roman temple.

Fig. 9. Ancient remains next to temple.

Fig. 10. Roman foundations in temple area.

Fig. 11. Remains of Roman
foundations in temple area.

Fig. 12. Tomb in necropolis along old road to Almodóvar.

Fig. 13. Tomb in necropolis along old road to Almodóvar.

Fig. 14. Dedicatory inscription to
L. Axius Naso, set up by the <u>vicus
Hispanus</u>.

Fig. 15. Dedicatory inscription to
L. Axius Naso, set up by the <u>vicus
forensis</u>.